Humanity and the Cosmos

Proceedings of the Brock Philosophical Society Conference on Humanity and the Cosmos

Daniel McArthur and Corey Mulvihill

Global Academic Publishing
State University of New York at Binghamton
2003

Acknowledgements

The Editors are indebted to the many people and organisations whose hard work and financial support has made this volume possible. In particular we would like to thank the Brock Philosophical Society who, over a period of years, has organised the Humanity and the Cosmos conference series where almost all the papers in this volume were originally presented. Each year its members including Keith Sudds, Sylvia Baago, John Black and many others work tirelessly to make the event a success. We would also like to thank Brock University and the Brock University Philosophy Department who, every year, support and host the conference.

The 2000 conference, from which the bulk of this volume was drawn, was supported through the generous financial support of the Templeton Foundation. The Templeton Foundation continued its financial support in 2001. We are very grateful to them for without their generosity this publication would not have been possible. We are also very grateful to Prof. David Goicoechea for his generous support, to Lori Anne Parker and Michelle Jones for their editorial and formatting help, and to Lori Vandermark of Global Academic Publishing for her help and patience during the editing process.

We are also grateful to Mark Spooner of The University of Ottawa Graduate Student Association who provided travel funding to the editors to attend both the 2000 and 2001 conferences.

Academic projects like this book are always the result of the efforts of a large number of people and we are indebted to them all. It is to them that we dedicate this volume.

Library of Congress Cataloging-in-Publication Data

Brock Philosophical Society Conference on Humanity and the Cosmos.
Humanity and the cosmos: proceedings of the Brock Philosophical Society Conference on Humanity and the Cosmos / edited by Daniel McArthur, Corey Mulvihill.
p. cm.
Chiefly based on the 2000 conference but also includes papers from the 2001 conference.
Includes bibliographical references.
ISBN 1-58684-241-2 (pbk. : alk. paper)
1. Religion and science—Congresses. I. McArthur, Daniel. II. Mulvihill, Corey.
BL240.3.B73 2003
215—dc21

2002018973

Published by: Global Academic Publishing
Binghamton, University, LNG 99
Binghamton, New York, USA 13902-6000
Phone: (607) 777-4495; Fax: (607) 777-6132
E-mail: gap@binghamton.edu

Contents

Introduction

Humanity and the Cosmos: An Introduction

Daniel McArthur and Corey Mulvihill

Each winter the Brock University Philosophical Society, and various co-sponsors, host a conference on the interaction between science and spiritual values which characterise so much of our modern life. While a very broad spectrum of essays have been presented at the conferences and the debate has often been freewheeling and fierce, much of the discussion has focused again and again on strikingly similar themes. This is in spite of the fact that many of the papers not only expressed widely different conclusions but did so from a wide band of disciplines and schools of thought. This holds true in this work even though it contains papers fro everyone from astrophysicists and analytic philosophers to liberation theologians to "postmodernists." This book is an attempt to present some of that wide ranging discussion and to try to distill from the mash some of the central themes that vex attempts to forge a unified view of modern intellectual life. Hopefully the papers collected also point toward some new directions for solutions to the crises that face civilisation, that at the same time do not ignore broad and important aspects of the human experience.

This book is comprised of eighteen papers that have been adapted from lectures presented at the annual conferences. Each year the conference has focused on a topic within that broad field: Cosmology, Spirituality and The Environment, and Ethics. Although each conference has focussed on a specific theme there have always been a variety of papers that tackled in a the overall relationship between scientific and spiritual world-views and the first section of this volume has been set aside for essays dealing with this. We have chosen to do this for two reasons. On the one hand, many of these papers generated interest and discussion at the conferences and we wanted some of these to be presented here. On the other hand, since each of the papers deals in some way with the collision of human and religious values with the world of modern science, a section devoted to the relation between science and spirituality seemed an excellent way to set the stage for discussion of the more specific themes.

It is likely that book like this will raise more questions than it provides answers, most of the papers do point towards fairly specific turns that discussion is likely to take in the coming years. This is especially apparent in the first section. It has to be noted that many of the eminent philosophers and scientists of the past century have tended to view the acceptance of the views of modern science as something that tends to rule out religious belief. Stephen Hawking, Carl Sagan and Bertrand Russell for example all fall into this category. None of the authors in this book suggests that science does (or ever could) prove the validity of religion and they are not at all univocal about the mutual implications that science and religion have for each other. Nevertheless, a very general consensus among them is apparent that these two ways of seeing the world and humanity's place in it are not so immutably hostile or mutually exclusive after all.

The first paper presented at the first Brock conference was by Keith Sudds and it is the first paper in this book for it directly addresses the role of the spiritual in the scientific. Sudds does not deny the difficulty of finding a place and a role for religion in the sweeping explanations provided modern science. But he does argue that the appreciation of nature itself, astronomy in particular, almost inevitably leads to spiritual questions in part because of the grandeur of the night sky alone, "the cathedral of night" as he describes it. This, he argues is especially true for amateur astronomers, many of whom do possess a sophisticated appreciation of the professional scientific view, but for whom the night sky holds more mystery and primeval fascination that leads almost inevitably to the questions, "Why am I here?," "Is there any larger significance to all of this?"

George Ellis on the other hand argues that some religious perspectives are clearly ruled out by modern science: specifically, fundamentalist views that rely on simple-minded and literal readings of religious texts. However, Ellis urges that in fact science and religion have both achieved a parallel progress in so far as advances in theology would rule out exactly the same religious perspectives. That is to say no religious person who has given her beliefs any serious thought would want to be associated with the sort of dogmatic fundamentalism that science rules out. In this sense, science, for Ellis can hardly be seen as the enemy of religious belief, although by no means does it provide direct support for current religious thinking.

From an explicitly secularist perspective, Idil Boran sees the relation between religion and science in rather a different light. Drawing from the views of Wittgenstien and similar thinkers within the tradition of analytic philosophy, Boran argues that religion and science have different "depth grammars." That is to say that the two provide quite different contexts wherein sentences acquire meaning. A religious or metaphysical picture (like the idea of a last judgement) for Boran does not offer itself as an empirical hypothesis to rival those of the sciences, it serves a role in helping a person guide their ethical life. To take an idea of the last judgement as something like an hypothesis is to simply be confused about the way the concept is meaningfully used in religious discourse. Boran, argues that a fair number of eminent scientists like Paul Davies and Fred Hoyle have engaged in exactly this sort of confusion when touching on spiritual and metaphysical questions. For Boran the question of the conflict between religion and science is something to be dissolved rather than resolved, since the whole notion of mutual conflict rests upon conceptual confusion. For Boran, science and religion have nothing whatever to do with one another. Moreover, Boran leaves open the question as to whether or not a religious "grammar" can continue to be of use in a modern secular world.

Robert Logan, in the last paper in this section, does not deal directly with the question of the relation between religious and scientific worldviews. Instead his paper is a subtle meditation on the role and ability of science to describe and predict affairs that relate to humans, their beliefs and societies. Logan's reflections draw on the latest developments in the sciences of complex systems and argue that when the implications of these and other of the twentieth century's sciences (e.g., quantum theory) are considered, some striking conclusions follow. The new sciences of complexity, according to Logan, imply the more complex the system in question, the less able science will be able to either predict its specific small scale changes or provide detailed causal descriptions based on reduction to its constituent parts. From these considerations it follows that much of the human world must fall outside the traditional view of science in its role of providing deterministic accounts and complete reductionistic causal descriptions.

We have included Logan's paper in this section because if he is correct than it follows that developments in twentieth-century science do imply that a new stance must be taken to the human experience that stands outside the all encompassing mechanistic views that nineteenth-century science seemed to imply. Religion must then be seen in this light, as a human activity and product, and not as a just an archaic superstition in conflict with the comprehensive mechanistic world-view of a Laplace or a Newton. It must be taken as part of the complex phenomenon that is human civilisation.

The authors in section two tackle the interaction of science and religion in the field of cosmology. Cosmology taken in either its scientific sense or its theological is a rich field for the purposes of this book. This is so because both ask questions that relate to the ultimate origin and structure of the world or universe taken as a whole. Questions like "Where does everything come from?" and "Was the universe created?" are common to both. Moreover, in recent years the fields of scientific cosmology and astronomy have been revolutionised by the spectacular findings that a new generation of instruments has delivered. With the new discoveries, fresh interest in cosmological questions has arisen on the part of philosophers, theologians and scientists alike.

Theologian Paul Allen has taken up this question in an interesting manner arguing that scientific cosmology does have a role to play in modern theological debates. For Allen the natural sciences are to be distinguished from the humanities and social sciences through their general unity of method (foundational debates and historisist upheavals in the philosophy of science notwithstanding). Theology has been particularly plagued by both its difficulties in coming to grips with the scientific revolution and the methodological divisions that characterise debates in the field today. Cosmology, for Allen, *via* the realist type philosophy of science of thinkers like Ernan McMullen has a role in inspiring a new unity both in method and vision for current theology.

Cosmology is particularly suited for this role in that questions like "Why is there anything?" give rise to philosophical and ultimately theological queries. In addition cosmology's transcendental subject matter (the origin of anything at all) and unity of method (its realist descriptions of creation on its largest scale) invites a new unified approach to theology, wherein theological understanding of the significance of the universe described by scientific cosmology can flower. Allen, like McMullen is cautious about proclaiming scientific justification for particular religious perspectives, the anthropic principle for example, for Allen, does not necessarily provide evidence for a specifically Christian world-view. The relation between cosmology and theology is indirect, mediated by common philosophy and relates to the intersection of their transcendental subject matter. "Why is there anything?" addresses a question that eventually leads to the still more transcendental consideration of specifically theological questions about the personal relation of humanity with a providential creator. For Allen, scientific cosmology does not support this theology or that but its questions and answers lead to a theology that can be inspired by its unity and philosophy.

McArthur too takes on the question of "creation" as it relates to physical cosmology, philosophy and metaphysics. McArthur takes issue with philosophers like Adolf Grünbaum who attack scientists who seek an explanation for the creation of the universe (usually taken in the form of the "big bang"). For Grünbaum the question of "creation" is a scientific "pseudo question" to be distinguished from meaningful empirical questions about what can be deduced about the universe in its very early stages. McArthur argues that Grünbaum can only make his case if he can provide a clear definition of what counts as a pseudo question. McArthur draws on the long debate in the philosophy of science over the issue of the demarcation of science and argues that no such clear distinction can be drawn. While all of this will be fairly familiar ground for anyone familiar with contemporary literature in the philosophy of science, McArthur tries to draw some morals from the failure of projects like Grünbaum's. McArthur argues that as the line between the scientific and the metaphysical is a blurry one, questions that once seemed metaphysical can someday admit empirical treatment. Recent inflationary cosmology, for example, does indeed postulate reasons for the sudden expansion of the universe. He thus argues that taking Grünbaum's arguments as methodological advice can stifle scientific progress as they would render exactly this sort of theory as addressing "non-questions." Furthermore, McArthur points out that metaphysical considerations can sometimes inspire scientific research programmes (as in the case of inflationary cosmology) and even vice versa. McArthur, although arguing from an explicitly secularist perspective, concludes by drawing a very loose analogy from Carnap, urging a "tolerance" of the metaphysical on the part both scientists and philosophers of science.

George C. Coyne examines the evidence for extra-solar planets and derives some very penetrating questions for theology. As Coyne points out one of the more interesting astronomical discoveries in recent years has been the unambiguous evidence for planets that exist in other solar systems. It is now clear that the possibility for life outside our solar system is a very real one indeed, even though a surprisingly small percentage of the newly discovered solar systems are likely to have life-capable planets like ours. For Coyne these discoveries present some extremely difficult questions to the Christian understanding of the relationship between God and humanity. Does the concept of original sin apply to life on other planets? Did Christ redeem the dwellers on faraway worlds as he did here? Need God choose the same way to redeem life elsewhere? While Coyne offers few answers to the questions he poses, he does present a clear case to the effect that the theologian cannot ignore the developments in astronomy and the cosmological sciences.

A slightly different sense of the term cosmology is employed by Yvon Provençal in his paper. Provençal uses the term in its more traditional sense rather than as specifically referring to the modern study of the universe taken on its largest scale using the means and theories of physics and astronomy. We have chosen to include it in this section since Provençal is referring to the role of science and religion in forging a way of seeing and discussing the structure of "the world" i.e., "creation" or the "cosmos" on its largest scale.

Provençal, in a manner not unlike Logan, draws on the set of metaphors provided by the new sciences of complexity to sketch the outline of a new way of conceptualising the place of humanity within the context of a larger world-view. Provençal argues that when the features that are common to many human activities, e.g., science, are considered the outline of a "language" which emerges conceptualises humanity's contact with its world. For Provençal this conceptualisation is characterised by the metaphors of maternal love, i.e., humanity and its civilisation grows and learns about the universe in a manner similar to the way a child learns. The universe itself, for Provençal, plays the maternal role in this relationship, and this he argues encompasses both the scientific view as well as the religious metaphors of divine love.

The third section takes on the roles of religious and scientific world-views in dealing with the many environmental crises that face humanity today. The role of science in finding technical solutions to various problems (new, cleaner fuels and so on) and in outlining the scope and nature of the difficulties of course is obvious. But science itself is very much a part of the industrial civilisation with its rapacious values that has created the crisis science must solve. Can religion offer moral, spiritual or even political guidance in this situation? If so, how can the often uneasy relations between science and spirituality be worked through in such a way as to best facilitate the approaches society will need to take? These and other questions are taken up in the selection of papers making up section three.

Christine Vanin, drawing on a variety of commentators, argues that the current ecological crisis in large part stems from the mechanistic and deterministic characterisation of the world that arose with the modern sciences. Such a view of nature left no room for human, moral and religious values, relegating them to the realm of the "subjective" and therefore the not "really" real. Vanin however draws on twentieth-century re-evaluations of scientific epistemology and argues that this view of both human values and of scientific objectivity is now quite obsolete. For Vanin, the sciences and the human "subjective" values are to be reconciled through a re-evaluation of scientific "objectivity" as "authentic subjectivity" which includes the human, moral and even religious world. Such a re-evaluated view of objectivity, for Vanin, is to form the basis of new approaches to the modern ecological crisis.

John Mitterer on the other hand is quite critical of traditional western spirituality's ability to play a role in the mitigation of the current environmental crisis and loss of biodiversity. In fact Mitterer puts much of the blame squarely on the feet of western spirituality, traditionally conceived. Religion in the west has nurtured a "psychology of domination" which regards humanity as a separate "steward" of the natural world and not as an intrinsic part of it. Seen this way, the meta-narrative of human interaction with the natural world is that nature is "there for us" to use and apparently to look after. But this approach has lead to disaster. Mitterer proposes a new meta-narrative where spirituality is conceived in terms of an immanence of nature, in other words where humanity is seen as a part of nature and not its separate ruler.

In sharp contrast to Mitterer, David Seljack does see an anthropocentric spirituality as having a clear role to play in forging humanity's response to the environmental crisis. Seljack notes the increasing interest among even secular scientists and policy makers, like David Suzuki or Al Gore, in seeing a return of the concept of the sacred to public debates about the environment. With the natural world seen as "sacred" the moral calamity of its destruction can be better appreciated, Seljack of course welcomes this turn. However, he argues that if this is to amount to more than vague idealism, a more articulated and ramified conception of the sacred is needed than the loose and undeveloped conception offered in current secular discussion. Seljack finds his candidate for this conception of the sacred in recent Catholic literature that grounds the sacred in a conception of the common good. For Seljack, this anthropocentric conception can grow from the new scientific revelations of humanity's interconnection with nature while counteracting the individualist tendencies of the vaguer notions of the "sacred" that might render collective action impossible.

Muldoon in a manner similar to Seljack also welcomes the call from secular voices like David Suzuki's that call for a return of the sacred into discussion of the environmental crisis. He too seeks a conceptualisation of the sacred that can address the current environmental crisis. Muldoon points out that the accumulation of scientific facts about the magnitude of the crisis, which he illustrates through a discussion of the degradation of the Great Lakes region, has had little effect in changing people's behaviour toward the environment. Neither have traditional views of Christian contemplation and spirituality, often derived from Aquinas. Muldoon proposes Thomas Merton's vision of Christian spirituality as leading to political action as a model for Christian life that can respond to the environmental crisis.

Darren Domski takes on the tricky issue of the proper philosophical approach to environmental ethics. In this way his paper could have been included in either this or the next section which deals specifically with the topic of ethics. We have chosen to include his paper in this section because its theme while ethical is presented as a correct approach to humanity and the environment. We have placed it last in this section in order to introduce the specific theme of ethics, humanity and science that will take up the next section.

Domski provides a critical analysis of the "subjective" environmental ethics of J. Baird Callicott. Callicott is one of the main representatives of that school of ethical thought that claims to follow Hume in categorising the human moral faculty as just "sentiment" and not the product of reason. Morality for Callicott is just "feeling" and cannot be arrived at by reason and is not moved or changed by it. However, this view is wedded to Darwinian thought by Callicott who claims that certain sentiments favouring the biotic community (i.e., the health of the environment) are adaptive and therefore selected for in the long run. Domski identifies a variety of difficulties with this approach, not least of which is the difficulty such an approach has in laying claim to any normative force.

The last section of this volume deals with the greatly contentious debates that have raged over the ethical implications of the scientific revolution. With science offering accounts of almost every aspect of the human condition, what room is there left for human concerns and valued that transcend the mechanistic world often envisioned in the sciences? Moreover, where do ethics come from? Is ethics just a survival strategy, if so, what of our notions of right and wrong? What are the ethical responsibilities of the scientist? What role if any can spiritual or metaphysical values play in guiding the course of science? These are some of the questions taken up in section four.

Anoop Gupta like Domski takes up the question of the ethical implications of Darwinianism and deals with many of the concerns that occupied Domski's paper. We have chosen to place Gupta's paper in the last section because Gupta, while addressing Darwinian approaches to ethics only touches on environmental ethics and discusses rather the possibilities of universal ethics and the social and political implications of Darwinism. Domski on the other hand has the environment directly in mind.

Gupta does hold out some hope that Darwinian thought can play a role in conceptions of universal ethics. Although he strongly urges that much caution must be exercised in such a procedure. To illustrate this point Gupta discusses some of the more chilling passages from Darwin witch openly embrace eugenics, cultural genocide and chauvinism against traditional cultures. Applying natural selection to every aspect of humanity and then taking the process to be prescriptive can indeed give rise to Nazi-like depredations where the most venal activities might be seen as a biological imperative. For Gupta this danger is to be avoided by recognising the limits of Darwinian explanations of human cultural traits. In other words, while the general Darwinian imperative of facilitating survival might well explain many traits, it can never be the full explanation and cannot therefore justify or explain all human activity and can not therefore have bearing on a great deal of things. Suitably limited, Darwinism might thus be seen to be compatible with a universal ethics, but is neither necessary nor sufficient to have one. Similarly if the goal of ethics is seen in a Darwinian light, i.e., human survival, then this is a naturalistic explanation for ethics but it cannot supply anything other than this general goal and cannot supply the substantive content of our ethics.

Kalvin Hayes uses the venerable format of the philosophical dialogue to rehearse some of the perennial problems that vex the debates on ethics (religious and secular) as much today as they did twenty five hundred years ago. In this often humorous dialogue philosophers as diverse a St. Thomas, Socrates and David Hume discuss the dilemmas that face ethics when religion (among other things) is taken into account with various characters like the popular (and often controversial) secular Canadian politician Svend Robinson. Hayes's dialogue also raises more questions than answers, but it successfully identifies many traditional problems that are still important and places them squarely as they present themselves in their modern context To touch on just a few points in Hayes's freewheeling discussion, the problem of grounding ethics on religion is identified by recalling the well known "Euthiphro problem" (i.e., is something right because God says it is or does God say it is right because it is?). Hayes also points out the dilemmas that face a purely secular conception of the good through an amusing encounter between Neitzsche and Svend Robinson.

This part of Hayes dialogue may for many be the most controversial. Nietzsche, for Hayes, represents an almost fascistic inegalitarianism where the good and raw-power are conflated. Svend Robinson plays the role of a callow and insincere publicity hound who appropriates social causes and left wing politics for his own gain. Admirers of either might well be appalled by these characterisations (and we for one must confess an intermittent fondness for both). But it must be noted that Hayes has taken the literary licence that the dialogue format allows in order to illustrate a philosophical point. Christian style ethics (represented by "Svend") without some transcendental ground can degenerate into a watered down, self-serving judgmentalism, while the complete rejection of these values (Hayes's Nietzsche) can just as easily lead to fascism.

David Goicoechea provides a subtle argument that trades on the distinction between the genuinely moral and the self-serving as a means of identifying the nature of morality as it is revealed in the sciences, ethics and religion. Goicoechea, following Kierkegaard, points out that morality and apparently moral actions can be ultimately self serving or vainglorious. A more profound sense of morality can be seen in those actions like Christ's death, or the long suffering servant which are decidedly not self serving. In such action the genuinely moral and indeed the glorious (and even the divine) as opposed to the vainglorious can be appreciated. There are then, in a sense, two moralities.

In a related way there are two sciences (or rather two ways of thinking about the accumulation of scientific knowledge). Traditionally taken by Aristotle the scientific is taken as describing the world in terms of a natural necessity, where only the potential can be actualised (e.g., nothing in the oak is not found in the acorn) and all events fall within a rigid deterministic causal framework. For Goicoechea this idea of metaphysical necessity began to break with Hume, deterministic necessity was for Hume never experienced. Science ever since has embraced contingency, custom and belief. Goicoechea argues that thinking about science this way reveals the germ of genuine creation and new possibility (i.e., the glorious and even the divine) latent in the scientific. An interesting parallel exists for Goicoechea between the glorious in ethics and in science. To abandon self-love and to suffer is to make a leap of faith and to affirm the possibility of the glorious. Similarly, to embrace science bereft of its metaphysical trappings of necessity and determinism, to see it in terms of contingency and custom is to affirm the reality of belief and to make a similar leap. It is in making such leaps, argues Goicoechea that the reality of the transcendent becomes apparent.

We have included a second paper from Robert Logan in this last section more for what follows from his reflections than for what the paper directly says about the relation between ethics, science and religion. Logan has provided in "Understanding Language and Thought in terms of Complexity and Chaos Theory" what he playfully calls a "grand unified theory of the mind." In this model Logan uses the new sciences of complex systems to explain the emergence of human consciousness and all of its products, scientific and mathematical abstraction, language, artistic conceptualisation and so on. Essentially Logan argues, following the metaphors of the chaos theory, that ordered systems are the result of chaos. In the case of language and conceptual thought, these can be seen as complex concomitants of the chaotic "information overload" that resulted from early hominid adoption of tool using and cooperative hunting. From this early language of practical activity emerged still more abstraction and complexity and eventually the vastly ramified mental and social life of modern humanity. Of course, included in this list of human capacities for abstraction lies the origin of ethical and even metaphysical thought. If Logan's model is correct then it clearly follows that ethics, science and religion are all results of what Logan describes as the bifurcation of concrete perceptions into abstract thought and social language. Equally, all these will play a role in whatever emerges from the sum total of these human social products.

It might seem to some that this paper might be better included in the first section which deals with general approaches to religion and science. However, we included it here because it speaks to the origin of human cultural production such as science and, of course, ethics. For while Gupta touched on some of these themes from a Darwinian point of view, with Logan we see an explanation of quite similar human capacities from a point of view quite different from Darwin's own view. Logan does reflect on how his view fills in some gaps in evolutionary thought by filling in some of the "missing links." However, evolution for Logan is punctuated by periods of very rapid change when new complex structures emerge according to his model.

Here we have an evolutionary view of ethics closer to Gupta's than it is to those of Darwin himself. While evolution might well form part (and only part) of the explanation for the emergence of moral concepts, it cannot perhaps explain the nature of the emerging complex systems. This line of inquiry while naturally highly speculative and provisional struck me as being significant enough to at least draw attention to by including Gupta's paper and Logan's in the same section.

The last paper of this section, and the book, is a meditation on the ethical implications of what it means to be a scientist by Edmund Bertschinger, an astrophysicist. Bertschinger approaches this question by reflecting on the nature of "vocation" or "calling." Originally associated with the religious professions, the term has now become secularised and has lost some of its original meaning. However, its initial stronger sense of serving both humanity as well as some larger (even religious) purpose might well describe the attitude of many of the early modern scientists like Robert Boyle. Bertschinger highlights these reflections through an interesting historical exploration of the connection between the Calvinist work ethic and enlightenment science. For early scientists like Boyle, this Christian ethic of hard work for God and humanity was central. However as time has gone on as science (and society) has become secularised, much of this notion of the scientific "vocation" has become obscured.

Bertschinger points out that while the more extreme forms of postmodern relativism have little to offer to the understanding of science, it must be admitted that science ought not to be seen as completely value free. Science cannot simply be seen, he observes, as providing simply one leg of the classical triad of truth, beauty and justice. Science and the scientific endeavour cannot be separated human values or social goals. Science for example can foster a sense of value of the natural world. Speaking from a personal perspective and generalising from these reflections, Bertschinger argues that a place still exists in the modern world for a sense of scientific vocation not unlike Boyle's.

Section A

The Relation Between Science and Religion

Chapters 1 to 4

Chapter 1

Amateur Astronomy: A Renewal of the Cosmic Perspective

Keith Sudds, Brock University

"The Cosmos is all that is or ever was or ever will be" (Carl Sagan, 1980, 1). Here's William Blake:

> Now I a fourfold vision see
> And a fourfold vision is given to me;
> 'Tis fourfold in my supreme delight
> And threefold in soft Beulah's night
> and twofold always. May God us keep
> From single vision and Newton's sleep (Blake, 1802)!

Two views, the scientist and the poet, expressing two visions of the world: Sagan, the populariser of post-Newtonian cosmology, the proponent of a universe that is materialist, without meaning and reducible to "billions and billions" of pieces, connected only by causal laws; and William Blake, the mystical poet, to whom the material universe was confined to a fourth place, beneath layers of numinous vision. In our day of ongoing scientific discovery and technological advance we stand between these polar opposites, the "Two Cultures" as C. P. Snow described them more than forty years ago (Snow, 1959).

I would like to discuss the development of our current perception of the cosmos from pre-scientific times, and how the rise of modern science has radically dislocated all of the human scale perspectives. And I will suggest that in science oriented pursuits, at a public level, such as the activity of amateur astronomy, there can be seen an understanding, often an advanced understanding, of the science involved and the accompanying materialist perspective, and simultaneously the appearance of a distinctly visionary perspective, pointing to the numinous; that even in the presence of an understanding of all that is revealed by scientific knowledge, the spiritual imperative asserts itself anew.

Before the era of modern science, humanity's knowledge of the world was confined to what was directly perceived by the senses. The earth where people stood was the most tangible: ground, water, trees, animals, were available to all the senses. The things of the sky, however, were somewhat more elusive and open to conjecture. Because the heavens were available only to sight, pre-scientific cultures were able to interpret them in ways that conferred meaning upon the world below, a cosmic order. Cosmologies reflected the perspectives of the cultures that held them; they saw the universe as centered upon themselves, with the Earth, usually a flat plain, and the sky a solid roof with the stars set into it. A natural hierarchy, reflecting the everyday order and vicissitudes of life helped people take sustenance from a natural order, a *telos*, built around them and presided over by spirits of Earth and sky.

Some four hundred years ago the Copernican revolution began its worldwide displacement of the mythological. The movement became entrenched in the 17th century with the publication of Isaac Newton's *Philosophiae Naturalis Principia Mathematica*, which delineated the methodology of modern science. By the mid 18th century science had become the dominant explanatory form, its analytic and descriptive powers facilitated new, powerful technologies, which promised to emancipate humanity from its bondage to nature, and inaugurated the horn-of-plenty that is our present-day consumer society. The powers of myths and priests were usurped, the common person was liberated, expectations rose and to some it seemed that even the inevitability of death would be challenged. But it was a Faustian bargain. During the time of the Copernican revolution, unsettling discoveries were made about the structure of the cosmos. While Copernicus moved the Earth from the center of the universe and Kepler described the orbits of the planets, it was Galileo's telescope that unequivocally disrupted the ancient cosmologies. Telescopic views of the cratered moon, the phases of Venus, the orbits of Jupiter's Galilean satellites, and the resolution of the Milky Way into individual stars led inevitably to a concept of infinite space and worlds without end. There was no place for heaven or God, and humanity itself was consigned to a status of insignificance in a purposeless, amoral, indifferent universe. By the mid 19th century this notion had become the predominant model (or paradigm, as it is now fashionably termed), although it did not invade the general culture of western society until the 20th century. The notion of the sacred had been usurped, society and the individual stood alone, unaccountable and unaccounted. This is where things stood at the culmination of the era of classical physics.

But even as this paradigm has completed its seeming conquest in the 20th century, challenges emerged to its bland vision of certainty. Einstein's theory of relativity and the development of quantum mechanics theory early in this century replaced the classical "Newtonian" science with a paradigm of uncertainty and counter-intuitive events at both the sub-atomic and macro-cosmic levels, intimating that there are boundaries to the universe and to the human ability to investigate or understand all that there is.

In recent decades a concerted attack upon the hegemony of science came from the direction of philosophy in the form of epistemological relativism. The movement was spearheaded in the early 1960s with the publication of Thomas Kuhn's *The Structure of Scientific Revolutions* (1970). In this work Kuhn draws the conclusion that scientific theories are axiomatic and supported by convention, and not by objectively solid bodies of empirical data. Science progresses, he suggests, not by way of objectively true facts, but by *a priori* interpretive structures—scientific paradigms—which serve to select and interpret empirical evidence. In this way, claims Kuhn, scientific theories can retain the status of official dogma even in the face of considerable contrary evidence. Kuhn himself has resisted the conclusion that his work points to a thoroughgoing relativism, but relativism is most certainly the opinion of the many philosophers who followed him, and also provides much of the sceptical underpinning of post-modernism. In the wake of Kuhn, philosophers such as Paul Feyerabend have espoused a relativism in which any and all theoretical structures can have equal validity, requiring only explanatory frameworks to support them (Feyerabend, 1978).

Despite this tumult modern science continues to be the most successful means of revealing the world. Technological successes are brought to us continually, via the media and the local shopping mall; consumer goods, new medical breakthroughs, computers, photographs from space telescopes and the surface of Mars, all serve to convince us of the invincibility of our scientific culture. The musings of post-modern relativists and quantum theorists, in truth, hold no currency in the present culture, and Newton's "sleep" holds sway. The scientist proceeds by gathering empirical data and using it to test theoretical structures, regardless of the question begging and logically circular claims of epistemological relativists. Relativism is counter-intuitive, impossible to demonstrate and leads only to empty solipsism. Claims that essential characteristics (haecceity, univocity, etc.,) define underlying reality are seen as nothing more than medieval curios, as Aristotelian and Platonic myths, which in the past stultified scientific progress and served to perpetuate superstition. Although scientists work without the constrictions of a *geist*, and in fact certainty *is* undermined by their non-essentialist, non-realist, nominalist outlook, nevertheless the proponent of science is confident that the world itself *does* conform to objective forms, and not to the capriciousness of paradigmatic shifting, as some relativists have claimed. To the scientist the world is not changed by scientific paradigms, just better understood.

So it seems that astronomy was the instrument by which modern science gained ascendancy, and in so doing, disenchanted the world and displaced the soul from its integrated place in the scheme of things. Human beings no longer saw themselves as part of the natural order, but rather as something over and above that order, a kind of *deus ex machina* that can aspire only to greater control, but is incapable of finding meaning. I want to suggest that this dismal outlook is not necessarily the case, and that in the cultural assimilation of scientific knowledge can be seen a kind of re-emergence of the divine, by way of an aesthetic wonder in the face of the vastly greater cosmos revealed by science.

There is no doubt that science, in demolishing all previous cosmologies, has enlarged the cosmic domain enormously. From simple pre-scientific, anthropocentric cosmologies to the vast expanse of intergalactic space is an equally vast distance for the human psyche. Displaced from the center, humans look with awe at the ever-greater complexities of the world uncovered by science. And it is within this vastness and complexity that the individual finds a new source of mystical experience; the disclosure of order in vastness and complexity calls forth a new sense of higher organizing principles that are beyond the descriptive, reductive sciences that uncover them. This can be glimpsed in popular treatments of biological science by interpreters, such as Steven Jay Gould and Lewis Thomas, where perceptive readers can glean impressions of the miraculousness of life, even though these authors pointedly eschew all supernatural or other teleological notions. Amateur naturalists, uninhibited by the protocols of professional science, gain from their studies an aesthetic appreciation of nature that borders on the mystical.

Likewise the amateur astronomer pursues, not the study of astronomical science itself, but rather a deeper experience that derives from the actual viewing of the universe. The scientifically educated amateur perceives at the telescope eyepiece a universe that, in its massive splendor, points to a transcendent reality far beyond anything envisioned in prescientific cosmologies. These earlier systems served mainly to place mankind at the focus of all things, inside an enclosed universe not much bigger than the land they inhabited, and small enough to assuage terrors of the contingent unknown. Although the cosmos of modern science has forever cast us adrift from such anthropocentric comforts, and it seems as though our significance has been reduced to cosmic dust, there are signs, not only among the informed public, but also within the ranks of scientists, of a re-emergence of teleology.

In the last two decades some scientists, specifically in the field of astrophysics, going a little further than scientific dogma allows, have proposed a new theory known as the Anthropic Cosmological Principle. In brief, this theory notes that the boundary conditions, allowing the universe to exist in the way that it does (its current form, which allows life to exist), are so finely balanced that even the most minuscule deviations in the underlying laws of physics—atomic forces, etc.,—would result in a universe radically different from this one. For instance, even minuscule differences in the values of either the strong or weak nuclear forces would make it impossible for heavy elements to form, or would radically change the laws of chemistry, leading to a universe with a much different appearance than ours, and without the possibility of the bio-chemistry of life. In effect the Principle suggests, that of all the uncountable ways it is possible for the universe to be, it just happens to be organized in the way that permits life to exist. Further, although our universe is structured in such a way that life may exist, it is clearly not a benign abode for life, even in the short term. Our Earth maintains its habitability through a large number of coincidental factors: the Earth's intense magnetic field, a result of tidal effects in the planet's core caused by the orbit of the moon, protects the biosphere from the destructive effects of solar and galactic radiation; though the sun's luminosity has increased over the last four billion years, and in addition it is a short term, though slight, variable, nevertheless, its variability and tumescence has not been sufficient to overwhelm the biosphere's ability to compensate and maintain optimum conditions for life. These, and a volume of other factors, first discussed by astrophysicists John D. Barrow and Frank tippler in their book *The Anthropic Cosmological Principle* have been widely dismissed in the scientific community as little more than question-begging curios (Barrow and Teppler, 1988). But there is a groundswell of opinion, particularly among interdisciplinary scholars, that there is substance to the idea; that indeed the juxtaposition of so many factors leads to the conclusion of either a very incomplete scientific knowledge of the true natural order, or to the concept of a higher—even a supernatural—organizing principle.

Similarly, in the biological sciences, Rupert Sheldrake, has drawn attention to dogmatic shortcomings in his own discipline. Sheldrake's semi-popular book *A New Science of Life* (1985) proposed that the existing explanation of the basis of biological systems, genetics, is not sufficient to explain morphology—the forms of plants and animals. The accepted mechanistic explanation he claimed, is not supported by any experimental data—other than at a very rudimentary level—by experiments on fruit flies, etc. In place of the mechanistic genetic paradigm, Sheldrake proposed a hypothesis that he called formative causation. This concept suggests that organisms and species can learn and adapt by means of a kind of field effect that he calls morphic resonance. Sheldrake points to the abilities of plants and animals to regenerate after damage; to ants and termites who can quickly rebuild a damaged nest structure, recreating the precise features of the old nest; to puzzling phenomena, such as the ability of rats to learn tricks more quickly in one place, than rats who had previously learned that trick in another place; also, to the case of new chemical compounds, which initially may be difficult to crystallize, but subsequently may be crystallized with increasing ease anywhere else in the world. Sheldrake devised experiments to test his hypothesis, some of which involved millions of people in different parts of the world, using national television networks. The results of these experiments—performed in the early 1980s—though somewhat preliminary, have encouraged a number of researchers to consider more detailed experiments, although it must be noted that many mainstream biologists reject the validity of these experimental designs.

Sheldrake, Barrow and Tippler have drawn the wrath and disdain of their disciplinary establishments. In an unprecedented editorial published in the prestigious journal Nature, Sheldrake's book was described as "This infuriating tract ... is the best candidate for burning there has been for many years." Abuse like this is seen by some as an endorsement; vitriol is often a way of dealing with a perceived threat. A scientist who has simply gone-off-the-rails, lost his touch, or is otherwise considered a crank, is more likely to be ignored; morphic resonance, the Anthropic Cosmological Principle and other less prominent challenges to orthodoxy, are not likely to overthrow modern science—at least, not overnight. The threat they represent is as much to the hegemony of prominent reputations and areas of funding as to the integrity of hard-won reason and order against the encroachments of irrationalism and atavistic, pre-scientific quackery.

These novel, and perhaps far-fetched, hypotheses do not re-enchant our modern cosmology, nor imbue it with theological meaning. What they do achieve is to bring to the fore the tentativeness of scientific knowledge. While the epistemological relativists may stretch too far with their critiques, and the indubitably of what science has revealed about the structure of the world and its workings is not in question, nevertheless, to hold that what is known at any particular time as almost the total picture is completely unjustified. At this juncture, nobody can say whether Sheldrake's or Barrow's and Tippler's hypotheses are indications of the divine, or of further layers of complexity in an already difficult to understand cosmos. But what can be said is that at every level of scientific revelation there can be seen an extraordinary interconnectedness, an order that defies the arrogance of assuming that all is simple and close to being encompassed by current knowledge. As we look into the world with our instrument of science, it is humility that brings us closer to truth; herein lies a sense of the numinous.

In medieval times the great cathedrals of Europe served to inculcate in their congregations a sense of divine order and purpose. These buildings still today invoke the sense of awe that was originally intended.

The medieval congregations would see, in the architecture, and in the pageantry of services, the order of God's cosmos brought directly to them in a single building. Their short, and by today's standards, deprived lives were transported, and they were assured that God was in His heaven; it was all there, right in front of them.

As I emphasized before, such consolations are no longer possible for modern humanity, we disabused inheritors of modern science. However, I have also suggested that this sense of the numinous reasserts itself in the world as experience by the participant in scientific revelation. "Starfest" is a annual congregation of amateur astronomers, held in rural Ontario. For about five days every August as many as fifteen hundred astronomers and their telescopes and assorted equipment, meet in a large field in rolling countryside. During the daytime, among the city of tents, R.V.s and telescopes, it is a hive of activity: things being traded and sold, lectures given, old acquaintances renewed, quantities of beer being consumed. But as the sun goes down activity ceases, covers are removed from telescopes (the skies are usually clear in August), and as the sky darkens and the stars come out, there is almost a sense of the sacred that descends on the congregation. I do not know who it was who coined the poetic phrase "The Cathedral of the night" but this is the impression one receives when witnessing this event. The splendor of the universe unfolds in a night sky much darker than any in the vicinity of towns and cities; all involved, both astronomers and visitors, seem to experience an uncommon sense of divine mystery.

One cannot justifiably argue, on the basis of this and similar examples that the religious is re-emerging, that God will leap into the scientific textbooks of the future. The miraculous seems to have little part in the running of the cosmos. But in the hearts of people, as we experience the world and its marvels, the numinous presents itself to us. This is how we engage the existential dilemma of our being; by the very act of knowing, we understand ourselves to be a part of a transcendent realm. The order of the cosmos around us, its size and majesty, resonate within our being as our purpose. Whether this purpose is supernatural, or the effect of some other teleological principle is not within the conceptual grasp of modern science.

References

Barrow J. D. and F. Teppler. 1988. *The Anthropic Cosmological Principle*. London: Oxford University Press.

Feyerabend P. 1978. *Against Method*. London: Verso Editions.

Kuhn, T. 1970. *The Structure of Scientific Revolutions*. Chicago: The University of Chicago Press.

Sagan, C. 1980. *Cosmos*. NY: Random House.

Sheldrake, R. 1988. *A New Science of Life*. Toronto: Paladin Grafton Books.

Snow C. P. 1959. *The Two Cultures*. Cambridge, MA: Cambridge University Press.

Chapter 2

Intimations of Transcendence: The Cosmos and the Underlying Order

George F. R. Ellis, University of Cape Town

Prologue

I approach this topic as a scientist who has already devoted some time and energy to thinking broadly about issues in this area. My underlying position is that while individual commitment and practice are fundamentally important to a spiritual life, they need to be underpinned by, or at least related to a viable world-view, otherwise they will in the end whither away (and may indeed ultimately turn out to be based on self-deception or delusion). Thus developing a viable intellectual position in this area is important to me, not as a substitute for personal commitment or action but as a necessary concomitant.

Comparing Science and the Spiritual Quest, a viable view is that these explore different aspects of the same underlying reality, together enabling a reasonably comprehensive understanding that is both consistent and theoretically and practically viable. Either is incomplete without the other, in terms of providing an adequate overall world-view. They in turn must be supplemented by experience and understanding in practical arts and methods in order to allow a satisfactory overall approach to life.

Both science and the spiritual search (properly understood) rely on the same broad methods of intellectual understanding, but applied in somewhat different ways to different data. Science attains near-certainty by limiting itself to very specific quantifiable issues, but consequently cannot look at many issues of vital importance to human beings. Theology uses broader classes of data which deal with much wider issues, of major significance to everyday life, and so where much less certainty is attainable.

Both rely on judgment and discernment in their practice, and in essence use authorities and scriptures to proclaim the current canon; both test their views in relation to data, but theology relies much more on personal data while science relies more on public data (in principle science relies solely on public data; however in practice it is not possible to describe everything about even the simplest experiment. The language of description is a shorthand that may or may not give a complete description of all significant aspects of the actions and experience of the experimenter; a myriad of minor details, decisions and judgments are omitted from the publicly available description). However, if properly pursued, both allow a very similar attitude of questioning and process of testing, which in the long term leads to a continually improving representation of and understanding of reality. In both cases this needs to inform and be informed by experiential methods of learning and understanding which ensure that theory and practice are closely related and properly integrated.

Curiously, each touches deeply on some fundamentals of the other and on important underlying attitudes, yet neither deeply touches the practice of the other, provided one has already in both cases adopted a mature open and enquiring attitude appropriate to that domain which is in any case fundamental to pursuing either enterprise with integrity. Given that the practice of science per se has long been independent of overt religious influence and has developed a mature open approach—by and large—the point here then is that most of the religious viewpoints and practices that are excluded by science are in fact immature religious practices, being also excluded on purely religious grounds if one adopts a "right" attitude.

Clearly this needs justification: what religious attitudes am I rejecting here, and on what grounds? The claim is that many, perhaps most, of those religious attitudes that are rejected by scientists as immature or objectionable can also be rejected from the religious side if one adopts a coherent approach to religion of a particular kind that is not only in tune with the present age but also with millennia-old spiritual traditions that have always been aware of the major pitfalls in religious attitudes and practice. This approach is in essence epitomized in the attitudes of my own present spiritual home, the Quaker tradition—which claim means my approach to religious viewpoints as set out above would be simply self-serving and empty were it not that I have consciously chosen this tradition rather than being born into it or having drifted into it unthinkingly. Indeed, historically this tradition has been sympathetic to and had strong links with science—as for example in the life of Arthur Stanley Eddington, one of the foremost astrophysicists and relativists of this century. Furthermore there is evidence that this broad approach occurs in almost all major religious traditions, albeit it emerging in a variety of ways with very different surface structure.

This paper develops these themes by looking in turn at the following issues. First, given the power of science and indeed the omnicompetence that is claimed for it by some, it is important to consider:

1. The limits of science. This locates the religious themes discussed here as not being related to a "God of the gaps" but rather as being essential in consideration of boundary issues that science by its very nature will never be able to answer. Next, if the spiritual quest is to have any meaning other than being a human invention, it must relate to something real; so one needs to consider—from a viewpoint that is compatible with modern science.
2. The possible basis for a comprehensive world-view that, as well as taking science seriously, consistently includes in some way a spiritual element that relates to the Transcendent.
3. The Nature of Transcendence (which of the many possibilities is proposed as true?). Here is where a particular subset of religious traditions is accepted and others excluded. Further if such a viewpoint is to be held in a way that is compatible with modern scientific understanding, there must be some kind of evidence for such a view.
4. Intimations of Transcendence. With this basis set up, the main science-religion relation is already defined in broad terms.

5. Physical Cosmology and Spiritual Issues: what are the relations between them?

Overall, the suggestion is that a traditional (strong) religious view is viable and indeed appropriate, provided one avoids some of the monarchical trends in religious approach, rather adopting a kenotic world-view. Substantial support for such a view comes from consideration of the broad sweep of evidence.

It should be noted that much of what is stated here has been known by many others, perhaps for thousands of years. However the particular integration of these ideas given here is specially useful at the present time.

1. Limits of Science

The fundamental issue here is that as the achievements of science accumulate and our understanding of what it is able to achieve increases, we are also in a position to start delimiting what science cannot do. Thus we can identify some of the boundaries beyond which science will never be able to go because of its very nature. Specifically, I mention three areas:

- Science cannot deal with *aesthetic issues*, because there can be no scientific criteria for "beautiful" or "ugly"; no experimental apparatus can scientifically prove a greater aesthetic value in one painting as against another. Thus art lies outside the domain of science.
- Science cannot tackle *moral issues*, because there can be no scientific criteria for "good" or "bad"; no experimental test can prove that some action ought not to have been taken, because "ought" is not a scientific category. Thus ethics lies outside the domain of science.
- Science cannot deal with *metaphysical issues*, including those that underlie science; specifically, it cannot answer any of the fundamental cosmological questions:
- Why are there any regularities in nature that can be described by physical laws?
- Why do these regular behaviours have the form they do? i.e., why do the laws of physics have the specific form we determine by scientific investigation?

- Why is there a universe? Why does anything exist?

There are various philosophical possibilities here but science cannot choose between them, for there is no experimental way to investigate these questions. We can investigate the implications of various options, but ambiguity will remain: a variety of consistent possibilities are available. Thus making a choice between metaphysical options lies outside the domain of science.

There are from time to time various writings that explicitly or implicitly claim that science can resolve some or all of these issues; but whether this is admitted or not, these all of necessity proceed on the basis of some a priori philosophical assumption that is untestable, that is chosen on the basis of individual experience and prejudice. Thus the challenge to scientists who wish to extend beyond the limits of science proper into issues regarding the deeper meaning of our lives is to be open to all the possibilities, and to pay proper attention to metaphysical/philosophical issues which underlie science and in particular underlie physical cosmology (*cf.*, Brockman, 1995). These are seldom dealt with adequately; indeed a simplistic technocratic approach ("there are only technical issues involved here") is often taken as a substitute for thinking the issues properly through.

This becomes acute in relation to the very existence and nature of the laws of physics, for example when authors either assume that various fundamental physical principles are in some sense valid and hold sway when the universe did not exist, even before the beginning of space and time (and hence can causally give rise to the universe), or claim that they can arise out of pure chaos. The first is difficult to make sense of unless one adopts a more or less theological position—it is an implicit recognition of a transcendent reality; and the second is very problematic; can one really create order out of total chaos or pure chance? In fact in the end this is an incoherent idea (as has been explicated by Paul Davies); order (laws of physics, the nature of matter) can only emerge out of a substratum of previous order of some kind, for otherwise there is no foundation from which it can develop. Again, "chance" is not a cause, as is often assumed in scientific discourse—it is rather a statement that we do not know the cause (as has been explained by Keith Ward). Furthermore, the fundamental problem of initial conditions for the universe cannot be resolved by science, despite valiant efforts, because science cannot conclusively treat unique events; it is designed to handle classes of similar events.

In all these cases, the point is that these are not "gaps" in present day science that will some day be filled; they are boundaries beyond which science cannot go. They define some of the limits of science. Anyone who claims that science by itself can deal adequately with these issues (in the sense of providing a properly testable theory that can reach scientifically based valid conclusions) is in fact knowingly or unknowingly transgressing the bounds of science. This may occur through wishful thinking, or perhaps through trying to use the prestige of science to claim certainty in buttressing some form of personal prejudice or strongly held philosophical opinion; neither is legitimate. However this happens not infrequently.

While much attention has been given recently to the problem of postmodern interpretations of science and the denial that science says anything about reality—a denial that no working scientist with experimental experience will assent to—much less attention has been given to this tendency to claim for science more that it can in fact achieve, which is also a real problem.

In particular, this applies to religious issues: it is important to realize that

- science can neither prove nor disprove the correctness of a sensible religious stance towards metaphysical issues;
- neither science nor philosophy can give a conclusive answer as to the existence of God.

Any claims to the contrary—either way—should be resisted as illegitimate and unacceptable.

The problem lies in claims of certainty about ultimate reality, which is unattainable. The fact is that neither science nor religion can attain intellectual certainty about ultimate issues—which does not prevent one from having deep convictions about it which may amount to personal certainty, but this is not the same as scientific or philosophic proof.

Most of the errors on both sides come from trying to claim certainty where it is not achievable. The illusion of certainty is usually achieved by excluding yourself from the same criticism that you apply to other people's analysis. The necessity is acknowledging the cultural and intellectual limitations of each approach to knowledge, including the "scientific" approaches, and the way they restrict the nature of the conclusions attained (Paden, 1992).

2. The Possible Basis for a Comprehensive world-view

In relating science to spirituality, there is a need for a coherent approach to Cosmology in the broad sense (*cf.* Swimme, 1963), relating daily life, the world, and the universe. This requires an integration of scientific and everyday views of life: it enables the scientist as a coherent believer, and can arrive at a position in which a traditional spiritual approach is essentially vindicated—provided one takes a strong view of religion as well as of science, and adopts a pre-power play (kenotic rather than monarchic) view of religious reality. This standpoint will be explained further in the next section; it can form the basis of a consistent transcendent world-view. The first issue to be addressed here is,

1. *How broad/narrow is the focus of cosmology?* When a decision is made on that, the second issue is,
2. *What is the appropriate range of data* to take into account to address such a viewpoint?

Finally there is an issue of congruence of approaches:

3. *How can the full range of issues be developed in a broadly compatible way*, without obvious areas of disagreement?

The first question, (1), is a choice we have to make. Assuming we agree to pursue a broad-ranging (human-related) Cosmology, then the answer to (2) follows: as well as cosmological data such as that from the HST, COBE, etc, the broad range of human experience is also important data. The issue is how to take this properly into account. This is actually a continuation of one long-standing stream of cosmological enquiry. Indeed there have been two trains of thought in scientific cosmology:

A: Microphysics => cosmology

We understand here the origin of the universe in a hot big bang, then its expansion, decoupling of matter from radiation, and then creation of structure through gravitational attraction (resisted to some degree by radiation pressure). Evidence is trying, from galaxy redshifts and from the existence and isotropy of the Cosmic Blackbody radiation (*cf.*, Ellis, 1993).

B: Cosmology => microphysics (*cf.*, Olbers, Mach, Bondi, Wheeler and Feynman, Penrose):

Writers such as H. Bondi and D. W. Sciama emphasize the unity/interconnectedness of the universe (Bondi, 1960). So if you study any one detail enough you should be able to tell about it all (e.g., a train ticket implies the expansion of the universe). Thus the nature of the universe can affect the nature of physics in the universe.

The former approach now dominates, but thoughtful books still consider the latter. The usual anthropic principle arguments (Barrow and Tipler) are examples, but they are too narrowly focused—they don't relate to humanity specifically, despite the name. We need to take into account truly human issues to take the argument seriously e.g., ethics/morality (Ellis, 1993; 1996). So the essential claim here is we also need to take these kinds of issues seriously if we want to talk about Cosmology in the broad sense (the relation of the universe to humanity) rather than simply cosmology (the physical evolution of the universe but not its philosophical implications). It follows that when we approach the cosmology/spirituality interface we must take the relevant data into account too.

We can legitimately study cosmology (small "c") without this data, then this is a complete study at its own level of the hierarchy of the sciences, disconnected from the more fundamental issues; but then we must not start to make pronouncements on such issues. If we want to do so legitimately, we must take into account the relevant (higher-level) data, and insist that our world-view/theory accommodate this.

There is still a major problem to be faced here: namely the issue of discernment:

- What is reliable and what is unreliable data?
- What is the essential ("guiding") data as opposed to the misleading (secondary) data?

This is already a problem in science, but is much more acute in the broad area of claimed religious or spiritual experience. Hence a key element is developing tests of discernment of what is valid and what is not valid data. However this has indeed been a long-standing concern in the area of spirituality, there is much experience to go on in developing such tests. The approach of scientism is to assume none of this data has any validity. However, that stance—which is conceivably correct—cannot be developed adequately without indeed looking at the data seriously. If that stance is held without serious consideration of the full range of data, open-mindedly considering if it can reflect reality or not, then the conclusions arrived at will be determined by this choice of a subset of data, and will simply reflect whatever prejudice was used in selecting that data.

As to the third question the congruence of approaches: this is firstly based in using a suitable epistemological approach. This is well developed (Murphy, 1990). A key part of the approach is an awareness of the nature of knowledge representation by use of models of whatever kind, and the limitations of their use. In particular, we must avoid approaches that confuse models with reality. We need an awareness of the partial nature of representation of reality by models, and the limits of use of each one we employ. This is particularly relevant when we consider models of the transcendent, which by its very definition cannot be fully captured by any description or analysis based on our experience.

Secondly, it is based in ensuring no specific unacceptable anomalies between the different approaches to the different areas when one tries to integrate them. Clearly one needs to take this very seriously if trying to form a coherent overall approach. The issue here is that paradox is often a central feature of spirituality (Chesterton, Palmer and Elliot, 1987), particularly because our partial view of the transcendent whole may be misleading. Thus one must be very careful not to reject a theory by mistaking a genuine paradox in an acceptable approach for an anomaly that should lead to the rejection of the approach. They may be hard to distinguish. Finally it is based on a general consonance of approach that is partly a matter of taste. While science can raise metaphysical questions but not determine a philosophical view, it can perhaps support some philosophical positions as being more in consonance with the scientific method than others, for example in terms of openness and readiness to explore alternatives; and in particular in terms of looking for testable causal reasons for what happens rather than explanations in terms of undetectable demons and spirits (*cf.*, Sagan, 1997). But when any such claim is used to reject a world-view, this has to be treated with the greatest care: it can easily turn out to be just a way of supporting previously adopted prejudice. The vital question here is whether all philosophic positions consonant with a scientific view have been considered, or whether some have been refused consideration on emotional or political grounds, or simply because of personal prejudice.

The specific need is to distinguish between well-considered religious positions that may be consonant with science, and superstition. The problem of course is that some religious positions are indeed superstitious. However a trained intellect should be able to distinguish these from those that are not—just as we are able to distinguish pseudo-science from science. We do not claim that astronomy does not make sense because some people believe in astrology; similarly it is not sensible to claim no religious positions are compatible with science because there are some that are not.

Thus an openness of approach is required that will take all the alternatives seriously. This is indeed in principle the scientific way; however this courtesy is not always extended to approaches used in looking at the broader area considered here. However it remains an essential ingredient in an open approach to knowledge.

3. Nature of Transcendence

This is to a weak extent captured by the religious traditions; it is deeply encountered in some religious experience and practice. However the point now is that properly interpreted it profoundly underlies all everyday experience—it is not to be specifically found in way-out esoteric phenomena but rather in the properly understood nature of the ordinary (see e.g., Hanh, 1987)—which, in fact, is remarkable but we have come to take it for granted. If seen properly it becomes extraordinary for it is all sacramental. The transcendent is immanent in every time and place. Thus the view I support is that, based on a broad variety of data discussed below,

- we can indeed consistently and logically propose a view of God as creator and transcendent (metaphysics) and also active in the universe in a immanent kenotic way (truly human data).
- this view can be evidenced by a mass of data, not of "way out" experiences, but of experiences from ordinary everyday life (*cf.*, e.g., Lewis, 1960).

- However this position is not consistent with all views of the nature of God. Rather it is specific to a Kenotic-theological-ethical view as consistent world picture that validates all levels in the hierarchy of sciences in coherent way in overall world-view and that accepts evolving universe and evolution of life. Hence I see a Kenotic understanding and love as the overall key to understanding the deep nature of creation:

> *Kenosis* (or *letting go*): a joyous, kind, loving attitude that is generous and creative, and—if needed—willing to give up selfish desires and to sacrifice on behalf of others, but in a humble way, avoiding the pitfall of pride, doing this all in the light of the love of god and gift of grace.

Thus kenosis is seen as the key to understanding morality, God, and thence the created universe (see Murphy and Ellis, 1996).

The evidence for this comes from a great variety of experience. The basis for why this should be so is theological: this is an essential part of the nature of God. It is here that I reject the many religious traditions that are militant, monarchical, or tyrannical, and accept at least provisionally those that are genuinely loving, freedom-based, and with a strong element of self-sacrifice as an essential ingredient. This includes, but is not restricted to, a major strand of the Christian tradition. It informs the nature of ethical behaviour, which should be along these lines in order to be consonant with the nature of reality.

The implication is that moral commitment is a real way of interacting with spiritual reality. Consequently this is the focus of my book with Nancey Murphy, and is seen as a way to complete the overall structure of a coherent epistemological view of the universe. However it is not the only way: it happens to be the one that is most real to many people at the present time.

What is the evidence for this higher level vision? It is based on discernment: the gift of seeing what is truly there, which may be obvious yet hidden, or may not be obvious (this is an essential part of the hidden nature of the universe).

4. Evidence: Intimations of Transcendence

To make a strong case, we need the full range of data: we can see as channels of transcendence, daily life as well as scientific data. We now consider the different channels of such evidence. The basic common theme I will use is not merely that the evidence exists, at least to some degree, in each case: the essential point will be that in each case, there is more there than is needed. There is a superfluity of abundance in what is achieved by the physical universe. This is the sign of grace.

4.1 Scientific => Metaphysical Issues

The scientifically based support comes from contemplation of the existence of a universe leading to the origin of intelligent life (the anthropic issues, as so often discussed): the required fine-tuning has a metaphysical base, and the creator-designer hypothesis is as persuasive as any (indeed it is fascinating how non-religious cosmologists so often feel compelled to use the image of the creator-God in their discussions). While this has an intellectual base and can be comprehended and argued that way, it also has a strong intuitive and experiential component.

It is common that the natural world leads to wonder in the spectator (in the face of mountain views, sunsets, flowers, animals, the heavens, etc.). In particular this wonder and awe may surface in the face of the miracle of life (contemplating babies for example). What it is that touches each person will be individual and different: it may be birds and butterflies, blue disas, sunset at Noordhoek. This wonder is a legitimate reaction to the self-creative nature of creation. It suggests a beneficent creator God. This is not a logically necessary conclusion: but it is a credible reaction to what we see around us.

Given that any physical universe existed, it was not necessary that it lead to this kind of complex structure and function. This is much more than is needed if one simply contemplates the requirements for the existence of a physically realized universe. So the point here is the extraordinary order in nature: it is at a fundamental level expressible as mathematical laws, allowing self-organization properties and emergent order to arise, and results in an intelligible universe giving rise to self-conscious beings who can contemplate that order. The question is what underlies this form of nature, however creation is construed: what is the metaphysical underpinning of cosmology. Some choice has been made somehow amongst all contingent possibilities; that which has occurred allows this extraordinary capacity for structure and life. Thus this—essentially the age-old design issue—can be seen as an intimation of transcendence: an expression of the creativity of God .

4.2 Moral => Ethical Issues

Given the existence of intelligent life, the question of meaning in the individual's life arises. This relates to ethics which embodies the idea of Telos or purpose. Now to some degree one can put together explanations of generous behaviour on the basis of socio-biology arguments. However that is not in any way an adequate explanation of morality: rather it is an exercise in explaining morality away (Murphy, 1995). My view is firstly that morality is real, and secondly that this is based on the nature of God. This gives a basis for the reality and meaning of concepts such as justice and sympathy, generosity and giving.

The point to be made here is that true morality goes way beyond anything that socio-biology can accomplish: it entails sacrifice and self-giving love that is incomprehensible simply in terms of evolutionary mechanisms, but makes solid sense when seen as a consequence of the existence of "that of God" in everyone. It entails the sacrificial reaction based on the potential for change and for good even in the enemy, the attempt to change the hardened heart instead of annihilating the enemy, thus imitating the kenotic and willing suffering of God on behalf of His creation (as specifically revealed to us in the life of Christ). Its reality is made clear in many examples: Mother Theresa, Gandhi and Martin Luther King, Christ and the disciples.

What we see is more than is needed for the biological functioning of life. It is an intimation of and response to the transcendent nature of God. It is the foundation of an ethics of persuasion and sacrifice instead of coercion and punishment, and hence serves as a criterion of authenticity: any truly valid religion must mirror this quality.

4.3 Creativity

One of the characteristics of God is creativity: and one of our possibilities is to mirror that creativity in our own lives, to become "co-creators with God" (Phil Hefner). We see this creativity in daily life, in economic achievements, in artistic endeavours, in sport, in education; we see it in scientific discovery, and in technical achievement. Again the point is that the time and effort put into this, and the joy that is got out of it, is more than the necessary minimum. Our creation of technology and beauty is much more than is needed to sustain life. It can be regarded as a reflection of the creative nature of God, another intimation of transcendence.

One of the hallmarks of real creativity is the giving up of the creator's power in the face of the reality of the created object (Vanstone, 1977): a truly creative act requires the creator to acknowledge and respond to the nature and integrity of that which is created, which develops its own inner logic and autonomy. This can be seen in great art and literature.

A specific aspect that has been developed by Peter Berger is the way that the creativity of humour is a sign of transcendence. A confusion of inside and outside views of human life leads to exposure of the pathos of the human condition (as in Peanuts). The incongruence at the centre of humour hints at something beyond, at the greater reality lying behind the appearances of this world, of a larger framework of meaning and life when the limits of this one are stripped away.

4.4 Aesthetic => Beauty as Revelation

While a created artifact or theory may have functional or technical excellence, it may also have beauty: and again here we see much more than is necessary in the dedication people put into the creation of beauty, and into its appreciation. This is of quite a different character than is simply required to live one's life at a materially satisfactory level. Furthermore the beauty of natural creation is far in excess of what is required by the fact of material existence, or even by the possibility of life; and the human response to this beauty mirrors that fact. Neither in any way demands beauty of the order we see in the world around us, or that we see created lovingly with enormous dedication by men and women. This may again be seen as an indication of transcendence: as intimations of the beauty of the underlying nature of God, calling forth a corresponding response in men and women.

This theme can be developed in depth by referring to the variety of art, its depth and the devotion given to it: in painting (Rembrandt), sculpture, music (Bach, de Bussy, Ravel), ballet, plays (Shakespeare, *Les Miserables*), novels (Dostoyevsky, Saint Exupery), architecture (Gaudi, the Mendel church), photography (Walker Evans), films, handicraft (pottery, weaving, baskets, clothes, etc) to mention just a few. They all provide astonishing evidence of creative capacity and dedication of the kind alluded to above (as well as in other cases providing evidence of self-indulgence and lack of ability; but that is precisely where the issue of discernment arises).

This leads to a further theme: the distinction between art that points beyond itself, as opposed to that which points to itself or to the artist. It leads again to the issue of Artists and kenosis: the requirement of giving in to the vision. Pursuing this would take us too far off course; the point at present is that again we see much more than the necessary minimum: we see a kind of achievement that can indeed evoke awareness of and response to transcendence, in those whose minds are open to it.

4.5 Love and Joy

Next, as emphasized by Peter Berger and C. S. Lewis, is all the evidence from love and joy: the evidence of the value of the individual seen in both the unreserved love of the mother and baby, and of the lover and loved. While a socio-biological explanation will be valid as far as it goes, on the present view that will be a very partial explanation: what we see evidenced around us is more than is needed for survival of the human race. The deeper meaning is seeing this as an intimation of transcendence, indeed of the nature of God, as made explicit in the *Les Miserables* line: "To love another person is to see the face of God." This fits in strongly with the Quaker concept that there is "that of God" in everyone—we each are both images of and realisations of divine love—which then becomes a guiding feature in how we treat each other. It affirms the value and mysteriousness of the individual (e.g., St Exupery's *Flight to Arras*).

4.6 Specifically Spiritual => Interpretational Keys

Finally, there are the specifically spiritual visions and intimations of various kinds, which may sometimes be delusion, but sometimes may be what they claim to be: Visions of transcendence, intimations of the presence and nature of God. This may take many forms: preconceptual experience of God (Edwards, 1983), an awareness of the immanent presence or of a gathered meeting, leading to prayer and contemplation, and the practice of the presence of God; or a sense of transcendence, sometimes a gradual hardening of perception until a definite intimation of what should be done is present as something given to one, rather than representing one's own will.

This sense of divine presence, often within the community of the Church, can be a vehicle for and make a reality of a kenotic Christian vision in accord with centuries old traditions and patterns of revelation. Many issues arise: how to withdraw one's own will and centre down so as to be accessible to this inner-voice; how to test for self-delusion and self-interest; how to decide what action to take, however painful or difficult, in response to a felt calling from God; above all, the fundamental issue of pride and humility—remembering the contrast between the Creator and the Created, the finite and the infinite, and so avoiding the temptation to seek to be God (as opposed to being like God).

However many centuries of experience with such issues is available, for example in the writings of the saints and mystics of old, that deal with such issues (these writings must be sharply contrasted with much of what is called "spirituality" today, which does not have the hallmarks of true spirituality, namely a relation to the transcendent that seriously deals with the above issues; without those concerns being properly met, this is simply self-indulgence or superstition).

In summary, the avenues for intimations of transcendence mentioned above can be represented as the following diagram shows:

FIGURE 1.

Intimations of Transcendence:
Patterns of understanding
More than the necessary minimum

Aesthetics:
The beauty of
Transcendence

Love and Joy:
The Father/Mother
Companion/Friend

Spiritual Awareness:
Awe, Wonder at Creation,
Transcendent Reality/Immanence
Faith and Hope

Creativity:
Co-creators,
Inspiration,
Humour, Ability

Ethics:
Right and Wrong,
Justice and
Forgiveness

As mentioned above, the point is not just the existence of these features, it is the unreasonable joy and illumination they provide, and correspondingly the unreasonable amount of effort that people are prepared to put into them, e.g., devoting their whole lives to art or music. This is an illustration of the importance of what Peter Berger calls "ecstasy": visions that illuminate and transcend our daily lives, giving us an understanding of a much greater reality that is present but hidden in our daily lives.

Note that none of the above gives a logical proof of the reality of what is experienced: rather it gives a pattern that you either recognize or you do not recognize.

5. Cosmology and Spiritual Issues: What Are the Relations?

Given this understanding of the nature of transcendence, what are the implications for the science-religion issue?

5.1 Scientific Method as Broad Method of Understanding

The broad method of determining the nature of reality should be based as far as is reasonable on the very successful method used in science: use the available data to test hypotheses and modify them in response to the observations. This method is verified by its success; so should be extended as far as possible. This approach

- supports the idea of transcendental reality (in terms of the existence of reliable laws of physics, or some other underlying way that matter is constrained to behave in a reliable manner that is well-described by physical laws)
- challenges authority (in principle)
- insists on openness to data and seriously responding to it
- insists on dealing with counter evidence successfully
- insists that any argument used against opposing views is also deployed and tested out against the speaker's position: it is untenable to implicitly claim exemption from the argument you use to dismiss opposing positions (but this frequently happens—for example when the argument from evolutionary origins is used against religion but not against science).

It can be taken to underlie a skeptical but positive approach to larger issues which is well developed and can handle theological issues in an appropriate way, provided the needed realm of data is taken fully into account (Murphy and Ellis, 1996).

5.2 Scientific Discoveries as Background for Viable Theology

The nature of the world as determined by science and particularly cosmology is the background in which we live and make our moral decisions. It excludes certain visions of the universe, for example an unchanging universe or one where we are at the centre. It also requires an overall assent to a causally based universe where physical laws underlie what happens, so superstition is replaced by laws of nature. Viable theology cannot ignore this; it excludes simplistic conceptions of God acting in the world, e.g., it undermines special creation, and calls into doubt the idea of God causing rain to fall in answer to prayer (although curiously this is not impossible in terms of physical law: quantum uncertainty combined with chaos theory makes this technically feasible!). However most of these simplistic models were not theologically viable anyhow.

The key issues that arise are not the nature of creation of the universe or the mechanism of evolution, both of which are largely theologically neutral, nor the alleged ability of genes and/or culture to control completely what we are (which ignores the integrity and freedom of the individual, see Bowker, 1995); rather they are

- whether *free will* is real or not,
- whether there is a possibility of some *channel of revelation* to the human mind, allowing the spiritual experiences claimed in the great religious traditions to be authentic.

Thus there is an important relation between neurology, consciousness, and the transcendental. We do not understand these issues. My view will be that we have sufficient data here that we can require of a viable theory that it accept this data as real and needing to be explained; we will reject a theory of the mind that cannot explain them (just as we will reject a theory of the mind that cannot explain or at least accommodate consciousness, in contrast to those theorists who in essence explain away consciousness rather than accepting its reality).

Apart from these specific issues, one would like a broad consonance between the world seen by science and the theological stance that one wishes to incorporate into a larger coherent world-viewworld-view. This is true to a considerable degree if one takes a kenotic view of the nature of the universe (Murphy and Ellis, 1996). This consonance is one reason why the two areas do not significantly influence the practice of the other.

5.3 Science as Illuminating One Side of the Mind of God

The implication is that one can see something of the way God thinks by the way he/she has chosen to create by self-organizing principles enabling existence of moral beings. Thus one can pursue a Natural Theology along these lines, firstly by finding overall agreement in spirit:

- nature of divine action as non-coercive and self-creative

- supernovae, sun giving off energy, animals giving of life as models of kenosis (Murphy and Ellis, 1996; Swimme, 1996)

There is a broad consonance, and lack of definite disjunction; hence Science provides models of aspects of theology. This is also true of the epistemology of religion:

- relativity theory and many viewpoints on religion both illustrate how a variety of different views can be had of some invariant reality (but with these different views strictly constrained and related)
- selecting data to construct a model and then later deal with the counter data (broken symmetries) as a way of approaching the issue of good and evil, and particularly the counter-evidence provided by the behaviour of some churches and self-proclaimed believers.

But perhaps most fascinating is the contemplation of God as the supreme technologist: decoding the way nature works is indeed a way of seeing the Mind of God (as it was for Einstein and Davies). This used to be the spirit in which scientists such as Newton undertook their work.

Most religions do not emphasize thinking of God as a technologist, super-expert in mathematics, physics, chemistry, biochemistry, astronomy, and so on: but this is a viable and fascinating thing to do!

5.4 Metaphysics Provided by Theology as Ground for Science

I have emphasized that theology can answer metaphysical questions science cannot tackle, linking them in to larger picture, e.g., as in the case of creation of the universe and the anthropic issue (Ellis 1993, 1996). Theology can provide a *consilience*, in E. O. Wilson's terms, linking these metaphyical issues in cosmology to the issue of the foundation of ethics, for example.

Thus this provides a metaphysical base for science that is otherwise missing or thin by conceiving of an ultimate transcendent reality who creates (some of the quantum creation ideas presently current come close to this concept of a creative transcendent reality that precedes the universe: indeed as has been pointed out by Davies, the way some scientists refer to the Laws of Physics confers on them many of the properties normally associated with God!). This metaphysical base:

- does not affect the way science is carried out in practice, except perhaps when it tries to touch issues such as the creation of the universe,
- insists on recognising the uncertainties and limitations of science and the ultimate mystery that remains after science has determined all it can,
- must be consonant with both the proposed theology and established science serving as a unified base for both.

5.5 Ethics and Life Experience Provides Data for Science

As has been emphasized above, data from life is valid as a source of understanding of cosmology: e.g., existence of consciousness, free will (agency), the range of data discussed above: science must be compatible with this (see section 5.2).

5.6 Ethics Provides the Context for the Practice of Science

Finally the scientist, even as a scientist, has to make personal choices of an ethical nature—how to spend ones time as well as how to use science. The view put forward here insists on identifying humans as moral agents and denies the possibility of doing science in a moral vacuum: thus one must to some degree consider why is it worth doing, spending resources on, devoting one's life to it?

Ethics is based on theology: so this is the real basis (*Telos*) for all activity including science. Man being created in the image of God is the ultimate rationale for doing science (we are "created co-creators"). We have a possibility of understanding reality and the mind of God by being creative ourselves—which involves kenosis in terms of giving up preconceptions in order to see what is there. In the end this activity is part of the worship of God and enables a deeper relationship with God. It also can be viewed simply as giving fulfillment to ourselves as human beings, and as opening up access to technology which has the possibility of greatly improving human life (and also of destroying life and the environment).

So wherever it relates to practical applications it brings with it an obligation to consider its uses and the benefits and dangers of those uses. This is one of the areas where science has been weakest in the past: by insisting on a divorce from issues such as ethics, science has been unable to tackle the ethical issues that inevitably arise in its practice. This is one of the reasons it has been able to be used for mass destruction. A holistic view will insist that scientists get some education in ethics—and hence become fuller human beings as they practice their craft, as well as being more responsible in relation to the rest of humanity.

5.7 Parts of a Whole

Both science and theology illuminate an ultimate transcendental reality that cannot be captured by any of the words or models we attempt to use to understand it—they each provide only a very partial illumination: each models part of the whole. Each needs the other for a broad understanding that starts to capture the full dimensions of the reality of the universe.

We can allow a reality to its moral and ethical nature as also to its physical nature, and try to see how they relate to each other; this will inevitably end up considering spiritual and theological aspects. That in turn will allow consideration of a whole range of data on these matters that convey real information on the nature of the universe. The whole will be much more complete and satisfying than the parts, and help us become whole human beings. In the end science cannot dispel the ultimate mystery of creation, nor should it be allowed to diminish our sense of awe at the universe and life. Rather science should help us to understand better the remarkable nature of creation and its mechanisms; spiritual experience and practice can help us understand why it is the way it is. Consonance is possible.

References

Barbara, I. and B. Butler. 1996. *Just Spirituality in a World of Faiths*. U.S.A.: Mowbray, 1996.

Barbour, J. 1997. *Religion and Science: Historical and Contemporary Issues*. New York: Harper.

Barrow J. and F. Tipler. 1990. *The Cosmological Anthropic Principle.* Oxford: Oxford University Press.

Berger, P. 1990. *A Rumour of Angels*. U.S.A.: Anchor Books.

———1993. *A Far Glory*. U.S.A.: Anchor Books.

Bondi, H. 1960. *Cosmology*. London: Cambridge University Press.

Bowker, J. 1995. "Is God a Virus? Genes, Culture and Religion." *SPCK* 25.

Brockman, J. 1995. *The Third Culture*. U.S.A.: Touchstone.

Cronin, K. M. 1996. *Kenosis*. New York: Continuum.

Edwards, D. 1983. *Human Experience of God*. U.S.A.: Paulist Press.

Elliott, C. 1987. *Praying Through Paradox*. New York: Collins.

Ellis, G. F. R. 1993. "The Theology of the Anthropic Principle." In *Quantum Cosmology and the Laws of Nature*. ed. R. J. Russell, N. Murphy and C. J. Isham. U.S.A.: Vatican Observatory.

———1993. *Before the Beginning*. London: Bowerdean Press/Marion Boyers.

———1994. "God and the Universe: Kenosis as the Foundation of Being." *Bulletin of the CTNS* 14: 1–14.

———1995. "Ordinary and Extraordinary Divine Action: The Nexus of Intervention." in *Chaos and Complexity: Scientific Perspectives on Divine Action*. Ed. R. J. Russell, N. Murphy and A. Peacocke. U.S.A.: Vatican Observatory/Center for Theology and The Natural Sciences.

———1996. *The Thinking Underlying the New 'Scientific' World-Views*. Paper for Vatican Observatory/CTNS Conference, Castel Gandolfo.

Gorman G. 1990. *The Amazing fact of Quaker Worship*. U.S.A.: Quaker Home Service.

Hanh, T. N. 1987. *The Miracle of Mindfulness*. U.S.A.: Rider.

Hubbard, G. 1976. *Quaker by Convincement*. New York: Penguin.

Lewis, C. S. 1960. *Mere Christianity*. London: Collier Books.

Murphy, N. 1990. *Theology in an Age of Scientific Reasoning*. Ithaca: Cornell University Press.

Murphy N. and G. F. R. Ellis. 1996. *On The Moral Nature of the Universe: Cosmology, Theology, and Ethics*. Minneapolis: Fortress Press.

Paden, W. 1992. *Interpreting the Sacred*. Boston: Beacon Press.

Palmer, P. 1990. *The Promise of Paradox. A Celebration of the Contradictions in the Christian life*. Indiana: Ave Maria Press.

Priest, G. 1995. *Beyond the Limits of Thought*. London: Cambridge.

Sagan, C. 1997. *The Demon Haunted World: Science as a Candle in the Dark*. New York: Headline Books.

Soskice, J. 1992. *Metaphor and Religious Language*. Oxford: Oxford University Press.

Swimme, B. 1996. *The Hidden Heart of the Cosmos*. U.S.A.: Orbis.

Vanstone, W. H. 1977. *Love's Endeavour, Love's Expense.* U.S.A.: Darton, Longman and Todd.

Chapter 3

An Ordinary Language Approach to Theology and Cosmology

Idil Boran, Queen's University

This paper is neither about God nor the cosmos but an analysis of the nature and purpose of the language that talks about these two things. It is my intention to explore the nature and limits of these two domains of discourse in order to elucidate fully the relationship, if any, that exists between the two. I will take Gilbert Ryle's observation, "if the seeming feuds between science and theology are to be dissolved at all, their dissolution can come not from making polite compromises but only from drawing uncompromising contrasts between their positions" (Ryle, 1954, 81) as its guiding motto.

The argument I will develop will draw on ideas indebted to the later philosophy of Wittgenstein. Essentially I will contend that many attempts to reconcile religious or theological conceptions with current cosmological hypotheses will misrepresent either the nature of religious language or the language of cosmology or both. In other words, I will demonstrate that theological and scientific discourse take on their meaning in terms of very different activities with very different aims and objects. This will be accomplished with the question in mind of whether or not the statements made in these two domains have implications for one another. It will become clear that to a large extent a great deal of conceptual confusion arises when the two domains are carelessly conflated or are seen as having direct implication for one another. To illustrate this point several conceptually confused examples drawn from recent writing on cosmology will be considered in the "philosophically therapeutic" manner derived from the "ordinary language" strand of the analytic tradition.

If these arguments prove to be sound, several conclusions follow. For starters, current conceptions of the origin and fate of the universe can neither imply the validity nor the invalidity of religious conceptions. The converse is also the case—religious views neither imply nor contradict scientific hypotheses. The main reason why I will argue for this conclusion derives from Wittgenstein's observation that religious conceptions simply do not provide hypotheses about the nature of the physical reality in the way that cosmological conceptions do. Thus the two activities simply do not offer competing conceptions of the ultimate nature of reality that require reconciliation or adjudication.

In order to present this argument, I will first of all make a very brief overview of salient aspects of Wittgenstein's later view of language, focusing in particular on his notion of "depth grammar." In the second part I will argue that the very different depth grammars attending the two disciplines can often lead to conceptual confusion when the two sorts of activities are carelessly conflated as amounting to the same thing. If my arguments are correct then there are serious implications for research programmes and ideas that are current in both theological and scientific circles. Research programs, for example, like "creationism" that seek scientific proof for fundamentalist dogma not only produce questionable science but also bankrupt theology.

Wittgenstein did give a series of lectures on the topic of religion and the nature of religious language, but those arguments are based on his reflections on the nature of language that eventually became the *Philosophical Investigations*. Thus while some mention will be made of his specific comments on religion and the nature of religious pictures, it will first be necessary to briefly review the important concepts from Wittgenstein's latter thought.

Language, for Wittgenstein, is a social phenomenon shared by a community of speakers. The community of speakers provides a context where a shared "form of life" and a shared language overlap. The meaning of a proposition in language or one of its terms is, in this view, a function of the use of language in the context of the shared "form of life" (customs, habits, cultural practices) of a given community. Propositions make sense in that they are undetachable from the context of other propositions with which they relate and their connections to the cultural and social environment in which they are used. The use of language in this view then is a purely social activity. Generally speaking, the context in which particular propositions are uttered establishes the parameters of what can be discussed, and acted upon. These parameters, a social "institution" (*Investigations* I, 337), are what Wittgenstein refers to as a given "language game."

The later Wittgenstein's view of language can be contrasted with the idea that words always function as proper names for specific objects, and that propositions refer to states of affairs in the world in a mirror-like fashion. This view of language assigns truth-value to propositions, based on their correspondence with these states of affairs. To Wittgenstein of the *Investigations* this view of language as "words as proper names" is a fallacy that has influenced much of the philosophy of language since St. Augustine (*Investigations* I, 1). For Wittgenstein, sentences are meaningful in terms of the shared context and rules of usage established by the linguistic community—the rules of the relevant language game. For Wittgenstein, the ability to ascertain if a participant in a particular "game" has followed the rules correctly implies knowing how to follow the rules yourself. A "language game" then is the set of parameters a given activity (like swimming) that establish the guidelines for the meaningful use of language. Different activities establish different parameters for the correct use of words.

For example, a film critic uses the word "shallow" in a different way than a lifeguard. "Shallow" in the former case connotes "not very insightful" or "conceptually immature," but a lifeguard would be talking nonsense (literally) if he announced that the water past the pier "displays no real insight." One comes to understand the critic's use of the word "shallow" by watching a lot of films and reading a lot of film criticism and generally acquiring the critical vocabulary through participation in the critical appreciation of that sort of art. One comes to understand the lifeguard by learning to swim and learning to differentiate various descriptions of water depth.

An understanding of the context, or rules of the language game, then, is vital in order to use and understand words and sentences correctly. If you walked into a dinner party and over-heard a guest at the next table announce, "well I found it a bit shallow" to you would not be able tell if a beach or a film was being described until you were able to familiarise yourself with the context in which the sentence was uttered. An understanding of such a sentence requires participation in the social context in order to establish which language game is in play.

For Wittgenstein, this contextual account of meaning explains the source of philosophical problems. Philosophical problems arise when words are used outside of their proper context. Using his terminology, philosophical problems arise when "surface grammar" is confused with "depth grammar." Depth grammar, for Wittgenstein represents the rules of a language game (*cf. Investigations* I, 664). By this he means the function and use of terms in their context within a language game. The surface grammar simply represents an the superficial structure of sentences. The form "subject-copula-predicate" familiar to any grammar school student represents an example of surface grammar.

For example, the sentences "This is good." and "This is silver." have the same surface grammar, however the depth grammar (the correct use in context) of a term such as "good" is very different from a term such as "silver." Silver, of course, is ductile, melts at a given temperature, and has many attributes. It is used (non-metaphorically) as an adjective to describe certain physical situations and as a noun to name the substance the adjective "silver" describes. It is used in this fashion only in a descriptive way, no value judgement or statement of taste is at all implied. Good on the other hand is not a thing like silver at all and is used in different sorts of contexts, contexts when classifications of taste or value are called for. Good can be used as an adjective or a noun of course, as the case may be (this is a matter of surface grammar), but it can never be used without conceptual muddle as a descriptor of some physical situation without considerable clarification or a specially defined sense. No clear list of things like ductile can ever unambiguously correspond with the term "good." Nevertheless, much philosophical energy and ink has been wasted trying to determine what sort of thing "good" is and to discover its attributes as if it were a "thing" or "stuff" like silver. From a Wittgenstinian point of view the entire debate surrounding the attributes of "good" and whether or not they "really exist" stems from the detachment of the word from its proper use in context. There is, of course, much to be said about "good" and how it is to be used, but questions about the good do not bear any relation to discussions about the physical properties of things and talking about "good" in the same way can only lead to confusion.

Another significant example of this sort of conceptual confusion can be found in the debate over the notion of free will. The debate is a familiar one—if all events have a cause then the casual chain behind any human action must lead back to before the birth of that individual, thus nobody has any real choice in their actions. The debate over whether or not free will exists, then presupposes that free action is uncaused. But is this what we usually mean by freedom of action in everyday language?

In point of fact, "uncaused" is not what we usually mean by free in ordinary language. "Uncaused" implies "for no reason" and the term "free action" does not imply "events that happen for no reason." If my arm were to suddenly and for absolutely no reason jump up in the air, this would not be what is usually considered free action. However, such random occurrences do qualify as free action in the traditional terms of the debate. But what "free action" typically means is doing something in a way that *could have* been done otherwise. This requires the agent to take a rational decision.

If a police officer pulls my car over and then tells me that I am "free to go," she does not mean that my next action can occur without influence from any past causation. She means that I can leave if I want to and the decision is left to me. Freedom, then, is the ability to perform an action upon a decision that I take or a choice I make among various options. Indeed, an indeterminate universe is as antithetical or hospitable to freedom as a fully determined one.

It is interesting to note that the well-known physicist Roger Penrose seems to be making precisely this error when he argues that human freedom is based on undetermined quantum events that influence the overall condition of the brain. If human desire or action were to really spring from uncaused quantum states, then freedom implies "uncaused." This as we have seen has the odd result of implying that if someone's arm were suddenly to rise up in the air without warning or cause then this would be a case of free action. In fact such an action would still be "free" even if the sudden event is unwelcome from the point of view of the owner of the arm. But this sort of event is hardly what people have in mind when they talk of "free action." Free action does not mean "uncaused," it means desired action that is unhindered. To suppose that the former is the "real" meaning of "free" is simply a mistake, from the point of view of Wittgenstein's contextual account of meaning, about what the term means and how it functions.

P. F. Strawson refers to this account of the source of philosophical problems as the "therapy analogy." For Wittgenstein, someone comes to a philosopher with a conceptual problem in a manner similar to the way someone might go to an analyst. The business of the philosopher, then, is to diagnose the root of the philosophical problem by showing the "patient" where language has been detached from its use in ordinary language, leading to conceptual confusion.

Wittgenstein notes in the *Philosophical investigations*, "Philosophy may in no way interfere with the actual use of language and may only describe it" (*Investigations* I, 124). As was noted in the introduction, the aim of this paper is to describe the use of language in the domains of cosmology and theology and inquire into the extent (if any) of their mutual implication. To address this question it will be helpful to begin with a description of the language of cosmology, in so far as it is an empirical science.

The language of the practitioners and publications in the natural sciences is framed in terms of the confirmation and or the falsification of theories. Taking the definition of "theory" in its most general possible sense; a scientific theory is generally understood to be a statement (or set of statements) that makes truth claims about the world or universe (with the possible exception of some theories like quantum mechanics, although these theories still make truth claims about the readings of instruments). In order to confirm or refute a theory, experiments are conducted to test predictions deduced from the theory. If the results do not contradict the predictions the theory is tentatively held to be true. However, if the experiments unequivocally contradict the predictions (and do so over and over again and cannot at the end of the day be otherwise explained away) then at the very least the theory (by modus tollens) is cast into serious doubt. It is true of course that this simple description of the workings of confirmation has been cast into doubt in recent philosophy of science (there are, for instance, many socio/psychological motivations for theory choice as Kuhn and others have noted). The points here, however, are not to be taken as a psychological account of the actual rational of working scientists but as a description of how working scientists would generally agree that the nature of scientific discourse *about* confirmation is structured.

The important point that needs to be made about experimental testing (whether it focuses on falsification of false theories or verification of true ones) is that a theory as a statement has a truth value, i.e., it is to be taken that it is an empirical statement (or set thereof) that is informative about the world (or universe). In this sense they can be generally contrasted from non-empirical statements that are not even indirectly empirically corrigible. For example, the statement "water boils at 100 degrees Celsius" is an empirical statement that can be tested by measuring the temperature of boiling water. However, "a bachelor is an unmarried male" cannot be tested in this way. It is true by virtue of the definitions of the words in the sentence and tells us nothing about the world other than to draw attention to a defined identity. Now it is true that a rigid distinction between empirically corrigible and non-corrigible statements cannot be made. This is so because (as we saw above) terms in an empirical sentence will take on their meaning through their relation to other terms and propositions at play in the same context. Nevertheless there are terms and propositions in some contexts that are clearly not meant to be to descriptions of physical situations. There are also those that clearly are, however inscrutable and contextually embedded the reference of their terms might be, the rules for their use imply their deployment in a physically descriptive role. All of this, at the end of the day, then, amounts to the following general rule for theoretical statements in scientific discourse, theories are to be taken as sets of empirical statements and are to be understood as to be verified empirically through experimental tests.

It has, of course, been clear for many decades that this description is an oversimplification of the way science actually works. Clear accounts of what verification and falsification always amount to have proved untenable as have accounts of the distinction between empirical and non-empirical statements. However, this is not directly relevant to the issue here. While philosophers and scientists agree that a general account of what counts as empirical content or a verification will never apply to all science for all times and places; the individual sciences themselves do employ localised criteria for the correct use of these terms. In other words they each operate with a readily identifiable "depth grammar."

That is, the particular needs and activities of a scientific discipline form the basis for scientists to determine what counts as an empirical theory or a confirmation. The localised criteria serve as the basis for a *grammar of empiricism* that functions in a way more or less like the account of scientific language given above. This grammar of empiricism, then, functions as the depth grammar (in the Wittgenstinian sense outlined earlier) that establishes the context and practice of the language of the empirical sciences. Cosmology, for example, is the scientific activity that asks and answers questions about the large-scale structure of the universe. Its conclusions are comprised of empirical statements. This amounts to saying that the community of cosmologists employs the general grammar of empiricism to address theories that are either true or false about the large-scale structure of the universe.

How does the grammar of cosmology differ from the grammar of theology? The questions raised by theology are not framed in terms of the grammar of empiricism. Theological statements are not generally taken by theologians to be subjected to verificational scrutiny in the same way empirical statements are. Instead, according to Wittgenstein's lectures on religion, religion provides a "picture" that helps members of religious communities regulate their lives; theology provides the rules with which it employs and clarifies that picture (*cf.* Wittgenstein, 1967, 67–71).

A picture, as opposed to a scientific theory, is a way of looking at the world. It is a world-view, it is *not* a description of the world. It is not taken to be subjected or even claimed that it is subjectable to empirical tests, it is to be taken as basic and accepted as certain. There are non-religious examples of orienting pictures that can help illustrate Wittgenstein's point. G. E. Moore once noted that the world existed many years before he was born. This claim cannot be tested like a theory about the boiling point of water (because we cannot go back in time or recall events before our birth), yet it is a picture we all accept as certain.

The belief in a Christian "last judgement" is just this sort of context-establishing picture. Various moral opinions and recommendations for life choices take on their meaning with reference to a last judgement. For example, Thomas Carlyle, appalled by the moral vacuity of his acquaintances wrote, "How will this look in the universe before the creator of man?" (Hudson, 52). Carlyle's idea and the corresponding moral attitude take on their sense in terms of a depth grammar structured by the axiological presence of the last judgement. Likewise, Wittgenstein noted that if a gifted person could see into the future and the scientific community accepted her visions as facts, her vision of a last judgment would not amount to the same thing as a picture like Carlyle's. Her vision would be a fact to be accommodated by theory, and held to be falsifiable on the basis of further visions, it would not necessarily serve as the basis of a moral/theological grammar for either the visionary or the scientists (Wittgenstein, 1967, 55–57).

Theology relates to religion then as a depth grammar does to a "language game" in the Wittgensteinian sense. For example the theologian Donald Hudson notes, "grammar has to show what would and would not make sense in a language ... theology has to show what it would and would not make sense, accordingly **to say** in a religion" (Hudson, 68). Theology is fundamentally different from the depth grammar of science because the nature of the claims made in the respective domains are fundamentally different. The delineation between the two domains is important. This is what Hudson (following Wittgenstein) calls "mapping the frontiers of religious belief" (Hudson, 62). Therefore, taking theological questions to be the same as scientific hypotheses would amount to a conceptual confusion. One of the philosopher's tasks then is to indicate whether or not there is a conceptual confusion over the frontiers of religious or scientific belief resulting from a careless use of a concept outside of any meaningful context.

Having delineated the logical frontiers of theology and cosmology, it is worthwhile to provide some examples of the sort of confusion that can arise when the two domains are conflated. In one such case Carl Sagan in his introduction to Hawking's *A Brief History of Time* takes Hawking's arguments to the effect that the universe's lack of a beginning in time and edge in space implies the redundance of any recourse to a creator. By talking this way Sagan seems to be implying that the belief in a creator is an hypothesis that predicts (and requires) a beginning in time, and that this prediction fails if Hawking is correct. I hope I have made it clear by now that Sagan is simply confused about how theological grammar functions.

The steady state cosmologist Fred Hoyle entered into a similar confusion. He sometimes indicated that his latter formulations of the steady state theory might imply that the observed universe was created by a super being rather like Plato's demiurge. Paul Davies summarises this view in his popular work *The Last Three Minutes*: the infinite age of a steady state universe implies that a huge (perhaps infinite) amount of the universe would have been colonised and technologised by super intelligent civilisation. This is so because given an infinite amount of time for things to happen in, everything possible must have happened at least once, including alien construction of vast tracts of the universe (Davies, 153). As infinite age implies that anything that could have happened will have happened, the universe we observe must result from this super-intelligent technologising activity. This picture of the universe around us having been formed by super-intelligent aliens is, for Hoyle, supposed to be consistent with Plato's idea of a deity bound by the universe's physical laws (Davies, 153).

This is a ridiculous reading of Plato, and neither Davies nor Hoyle of course ought to be read as propounding any such thesis as a credible interpretation of what Plato had in mind. However it does follow from their conclusions that the demiurge (in the form of an advanced civilisation of some kind) is implied by the acceptance of Steady State cosmology and that this is not necessarily consistent with other cosmologies. It also follows that it would be a dubious proposition in the absence of steady state cosmology. But it is in this use where conceptual confusion arises. The demiurge as part of the moral/metaphysics of Plato amounts to an ethical picture and world-view. In this sense it bears some resemblance to a theological picture, Plato would never regard any set of scientific speculations to have any bearing on the validity of his moral metaphysics. In other words Plato's demiurge has moral and not empirical significance. The validity of Plato's moral metaphysics stands or falls on moral and metaphysical considerations, not on the empirical plausibility of any given physical cosmology. The case for Hoyle's reading becomes worse when one considers the fact that he seems to have become confused about the nature of cosmology as well as Greek philosophy. While the thesis can be largely ruled out in the situation where steady state cosmology is not accepted and some other cosmology is, how could it be tested if the steady state view had turned out to be true? Because the super beings' existences imply no testable predictions and indeed seem to entirely lack any form of empirical corrigibility, its value as an empirical thesis is dubious. No doubt both Hoyle and Davies would defend the idea as a speculative one and not as a scientific one. If so then it is entirely empty speculation, neither does it shed light on our scientific view nor does it shed light on our religious, moral or philosophical view. Indeed it sheds no light on anything at all.

The steady state theory (minus the diemiurge) was a perfectly sound hypothesis that explained the observed cosmological "red shift" well. Most of its adherents never entertained the slightest belief in Hoyle's superbeing. It was, however, unable to account for the background microwave radiation predicted by the big bang theory and was therefore (after some debate) abandoned. Nevertheless, Paul Davies reflects that the superbeing idea may be salvageable if Andrie Linde's "inflationary bubble" theory proves viable (which can, as Davies points out, be seen as a sort of return to some of the tenets of the Steady State Cosmology, especially in the sense that it cleaves to an infinite universe). But because this notion of superbeing is empty, no purpose is served through this speculation. Cosmologists, theologians and philosophers alike, then, need to avoid these sorts of muddles.

None of this is to argue that religious pictures are unquestionable. There are, of course, perfectly good reasons not to believe in God and many people do not. For example, the argument from evil questions whether or not the picture of a good God is coherent in a world full of suffering. This argument tackles theological conceptions on their own ground, it questions the internal coherence and rationality of the theological picture. But this is all part and parcel of theological discussion and, naturally, forms the subject matter of Christian apologetics. The objection to God's existence on the basis of the "argument from evil" is exactly the sort of thing any credible theologian can conceptualise in his own context and respond to. The ongoing debate takes place within the parameters delineated by the theological "depth grammar."

To sum up, theology and cosmology are different domains of discourse characterised by different language games. The grammar of one domain of discourse cannot be straightforwardly brought to another without considerable conceptual violence. The two domains are made up of discourses that are not informative of one another, and the attempt to speak for one domain from the point of view of another will lead to conceptual confusions and theoretical muddles. Therefore, the arguments of cosmology and the arguments of theology can neither be mutually supportive or mutually conflicting, they are simply different. The conclusions of this argument, then, are neither about God nor about the universe. They amount to an argument for an appreciation of the frontiers that exist between the two disciplines. These frontiers, naturally, are not to be mapped out and fixed rigidly from the point of view of some ultimate meta-language. Indeed this would be impossible. The task can, however, be done equally well from either a theological or scientific point of view both of which can in their own context identify terms that serve no function, are empty or are removed from any sensible context. The role of philosophers in this task, many of whom have familiarised themselves with the context of both religious and scientific usage, is simply that of an assistant, helping either scientists or theologians identify conceptual confusion from their own points of view.

References

Davies, P. 1994. *The Last Three Minutes*. New York: Basic Books.

Hawking, S. 1988. *A Brief History of Time*. Toronto: Bantam Books.

Hudson, D. 1968. *Ludwig Wittgenstein*. London: Lutterworth Press.

Ryle, G. 1954. *Dilemmas*. Cambridge: Cambridge University Press.

Wittgenstein, L. 1967. *Lectures and Conversations*. Ed. Cyril Barrett. Berkeley: University of California Press.

———1953. *Philosophical Investigations*. Trans. E. Anscombe. Oxford: Blackwell.

Chapter 4

Science as a Language: The Non-Probativity Theorem and the Complementarity of Complexity and Predictability

Robert K. Logan, University of Toronto

Science as a Language

In a study dating back to 1995, language was shown to be not merely a medium of communication but an information processing tool or system that changes the way we think (Logan, 1995). Building on this idea it was shown that speech, writing, mathematics, science and computing represent an evolutionary chain of languages. This hypothesis was justified by first showing that each of these languages has its own unique semantics and syntax. Next it was demonstrated that each new language arose as a bifurcation from the set of older languages each time a new level of information processing was required. Writing and math, the second and third language, arose from the need to keep records of agricultural commodities given as tributes to Sumerian priests for redistribution to irrigation workers (Schmandt-Besserat, 1986). Writing and math gave rise to formal education and schools. The scholarship of the teachers who taught in these schools produced a new information overload. The need to organize the new knowledge created by the scholars resulted in the new language of science, the fourth language. The information overload generated by science gave rise to need for the development of automated information processing and resulted in the advent of computing, the fifth language.

Within the framework of this model of the evolution of language, mathematics and science are distinct languages each with their own unique informatic objectives. Mathematics strives to solve equations and to prove the equivalence of sets of statements involving the semantical elements of its language, abstract numbers (such as integers, irrational numbers, imaginary numbers), geometrical objects (such as points, lines, planes, triangles, pyramids, vectors, tensors), sets, operators, etc. A theorem or a proof is a unique syntactical element of the language of mathematics which we will show cannot be an element of the language of science. Using logic, a theorem or a proof establishes the equivalence of one set of statements, which includes axioms, whose truths are assumed to be self-evident, and at times other theorems, which have already been proven with the proposition whose truth is to be established by the theorem.

Science, on the other hand, establishes the veracity of a proposition using the technique of the scientific method of observation, generalization, hypothesis formulation, and empirical verification. The scientific method is a unique syntactical element of the language of science. In addition to trying to provide an accurate description of nature, science also attempts to describe nature in a systematic manner using the least number of elements possible. The description of one phenomenon in terms of another is often claimed to be an explanation. This is one way to interpret this reduction of the number of basic elements needed to describe nature which is a basic goal of science. Science also endeavors to make predictions that can be tested to establish the accuracy of its models. No matter how refined this process becomes and no matter how many reductions and simplifications are made there always remain some irreducible elements that resist explanation or description in terms of simpler phenomena. The process of reduction has to end somewhere. The basic elements in terms of which other phenomena can be thought of as the basic atoms or elements of scientific description (*cf.* McArthur, this volume).

Scientists often make use of mathematical language to construct their models of nature, especially in the physical sciences. They often employ mathematical proofs to establish the equivalence of mathematical statements within the context of their models. This has led to the popular belief that science can actually prove things about nature. This is a misconception, however. No scientific hypothesis can be proven; it can only be tested and shown to be valid for the conditions under which it was tested. Each proposition must be continually verified for each new domain of observation.

The purpose of this paper is to make use of mathematical reasoning to show and actually prove that science can never prove the truth of any of its propositions or hypotheses. To establish our theorem, the Science Non-Probativity Theorem, we will make use of a basic axiom of the scientific method, namely, that for a statement or an assertion to be considered as a scientific statement it must be tested and testable and, hence, it must be falsifiable. If a proposition must be falsifiable or refutable to be considered by science then one can never prove it is true for if one did then the proposition would no longer be falsifiable, having been proven true, and, hence, could no longer be considered within the domain of science. We have therefore proven that science can not prove the truth of anything. Let us repeat this argument using as a formal theorem making use of two axioms.

The Science Non-Probativity Theorem

Axiom: A proposition must be falsifiable to be a scientific proposition or part of a scientific theory.

Axiom: A proposition can not be proven true and be falsifiable at the same time. (Once proven true, a proposition can not be falsified and, hence, is not falsifiable.)

Theorem: A proposition can not be proven to be true by use of science or the scientific method.

Proof: If a proposition were to be proven to be true by the methods of science it would no longer be falsifiable. If it is no longer falsifiable because it has been proven true it can not be considered as a scientific proposition and hence could not have been proven true by science, Q.E.D.

In the spirit of the Science Non-Probativity Theorem, we cannot be certain that this line of reasoning is absolutely valid or true. After all we have just used the theorem, a syntactical element of the language of mathematics, to establish a proposition about the language of science. Our theorem is not scientifically valid but, as a result of mathematical reasoning, we have created a useful probe—one that can lead to some interesting reflections and insights into the nature and limitation of science. If it helps scientists and the public—who tend to accept the authority of science more or less uncritically—to adopt a more humble and modest understanding of science, it will have served its purpose.

All that science can do is to follow its tried and true method of observing, experimenting, generalizing, hypothesizing and then testing its hypotheses. The most a scientist can do is to claim that for every experiment or test performed so far, the hypothesis that has been formulated explains all the observations made to date. Scientific truth is always equivocal and dependent on the outcome of future observations, discoveries and experiments. It is never absolute.

A scientist who claims to have proven anything is being dogmatic. Every human being, even a scientist, has a right to their beliefs and dogmas. But it does not behoove a person who claims to be a rational scientist and who claims that science is objective and universal to be so absolute in their beliefs and in the value of their belief system, science. Scientists are not immune to dogmatic and intolerant views as Dr. George Coyne has pointed out in some of his discussions.

I believe, it is altogether fitting and appropriate, that scientists should display greater humility and tolerance in the practice of their vocation and calling (*cf.* Bertschinger, this volume) in view of the lessons to be learned from the following historical vignettes where well-established scientific theories and dogmas had to give way to newer ones.

Newton's theory of motion gave way to Einstein's theory of relativity when one considers velocities that approach the speed of light. The Newtonian picture also underwent major revisions with the introduction of quantum mechanics needed to describe atomic systems. Neither the contribution of Newton to science nor the validity of his model of dynamics for non-relativistic and non-quantum events were in any way diminished by these 20th century discoveries. In fact, many elements of Newton's theory survived in both relativity and quantum mechanics and one can not imagine how these theories could have been formulated without the pioneering work of Newton. Even today's current version of quantum mechanics requires the use of the classical Newtonian Hamiltonian to formulate the energy operator.

Einstein helped to launch quantum mechanics with his explanation of the photo-electric effect in 1905. Despite this pioneering work he turned on the child of his own creation, quantum mechanics, claiming that it is an incomplete theory. Einstein's objections have given way to the acceptance by the main stream of the physics community of probability as being an intrinsic part of our observation of nature due to the Heisenberg uncertainty principle. Einstein's hypothesis that quantum mechanics is an incomplete science can never be disputed or disproved according the Non-Probativity Theorem formulated above. The usefulness of his hypothesis, however, dwindles in the absence of any concrete progress towards a complete non-probabilistic theory of quantum mechanics and atomic systems. And this despite the valiant efforts of David Bohm, Roger Penrose, and others to find the hidden variables or structures that they claim would make quantum mechanics a complete theory. One cannot but help to conjecture that perhaps the reason that these variables are so well hidden is that they do not exist, but this is only my conjecture and belief and not anything I could prove.

Einstein, *Time Magazine*'s man of the 20th century and whose name is now a metaphor for genius, had no problem rejecting one of the elements of his theory of general relativity. He introduced a cosmological constant into his theory in 1914 to describe what he thought at the time was a steady state universe. When Hubbell showed in 1929 that we lived in an expanding universe Einstein immediately dropped this element of his theory. It has since been resurrected by some contemporary cosmologists because they find it might serve a useful purpose in their attempts to explain or describe specific observations of the cosmos.

Another interesting shift in attitudes within the physics community is illustrated by the recent emergence (pun intended) of chaos theory, complexity, simplicity, plectics, emergence, and self-organizing criticality all of which concern themselves with non-linear dynamic systems. It was once claimed, not very long ago, that the complications that non-linear equations presented were mere details not worthy of attention since the basic equations of motion, while not soluble, in closed form are at least amenable to numerical if one needed to solve these equations.

With the availability of computers, especially microcomputers because they provided researchers with low cost computing power that allowed them to play, scientists were able to explore and examine the complexity of non-linear dynamical systems and their sensitivity to initial conditions.

As a consequence many interesting results were arrived at and it is now widely recognized that non-linear physics is not a special case or the anomaly of nature but rather the norm that requires detailed attention. The shoe is now on the other foot and it is realized that it is the dynamical systems that can be described by linear equations that are the anomalies.

In light of the Non-Probativity Theorem it is clear that the role of science is to probe and not to prove. It is interesting that the two English words, prove and probe, both derive from the same Latin root, *proba*, which means prove. The words probability, problem and probable all have the same root. This makes Einstein's rejection of probability in quantum mechanics all the more ironic.

Science, The Language of Metaphor

Science involves the process of representing empirical observations in terms of models many of which are mathematical models. These models whether or not they are mathematical are metaphors and abstractions from nature. The spirit in which the elements of scientific models are described as metaphors is the same as that of the proposition that all words of a spoken language are metaphors. The idea that all communication is metaphor is an idea that "has ancient origins in oral cultures and has been repeated and debated through history" (Gozzi, 2000) by Plato, Vico, Keats, Shelley and many modern linguists. McLuhan quotes Quintillian, "Nearly everything we say is metaphor" (McLuhan, 127).

Once a model is formulated then the scientists find mathematical and/or logical relationships between the metaphors of their models. They then find and prove that certain relationships exist between these metaphors which serve as predictions of their models. The scientists then test the validity of these relationships that they have discovered in their toy or model world of metaphors and mathematics. By testing we mean that the scientists try to match their new metaphors transformed or calculated by their logical or mathematical operations with observables in nature. The most one can say, *à la* Hume, is that the new metaphors transformed by mathematics from the original metaphors of the starting model make a good match to the observed phenomena of nature. This agreement supports the scientist's model but does not prove that the model is correct because one must leave open the possibility that the model can be falsified or refuted. If, as noted above, all words are metaphors and all scientific models are also metaphors there is no need to prove scientific statements are true.

One can not prove a metaphor is true—one can only test whether or not it provides a useful description of nature which leads to greater insights and, in the case of science, to more predictions. It is the natural process of a language to evolve; the same is true of the meaning of words and metaphors. Words are continually bifurcating, keeping their old meaning and taking on new meanings. The new meanings, however, carry with them vestigially some of the structure or meaning of their ancestors, just as animals and plants vestigially retain structures from their ancestors.

Scientific theories, models, which are made up of metaphors, also evolve and bifurcate into new models which vestigially retain remnants or earlier theories. Relativity and quantum physics still retain much of classical Newtonian physics. *Plus ça change, plus c'est la même chose.*

All models are abstractions from nature and hence represent a reduced reality. Mathematical transformations of the abstractions or metaphors of a model may further degrade their accuracy and reduce their match with empirical reality.

The role of science is not to prove or even to explain the phenomena of nature but rather to uncover patterns that relate one set of phenomena to another. The mathematizing of scientific models and metaphors and the process of subjecting them to mathematical operations has proven to be a successful technique in uncovering these patterns especially when predictions that can be observed or measured are made.

The Complementarity of Complexity and Predictability

The assumption that the metaphors contained in mathematical models used to describe nature can then be operated upon using linear mathematical operators to obtain new relationships among the elements of the model which will then correspond to what is observed in nature is premised on the notion that the relationship between the elements of the model and the elements of reality are linear. This is an assumption or basic presupposition which cannot be proven mathematically but must be tested empirically and cannot be presumed to be necessarily true.

The effect of a non-linearity between the model and reality can become magnified if the mathematical equations relating the elements of the model are themselves non-linear. A small difference or non-linearity between the mathematical model and the reality being modeled can lead to vastly different outcomes *à la* the butterfly effect of Lorenz.

Quantum mechanics and the uncertainty principle have taught us that the process of measuring nature at the atomic scale changes the phenomena we are observing and scrutinizing. The modeling of nature using metaphors introduces a new level of uncertainty in matching one's model with nature especially when one attempts to represent the nonliner phenomena using classical pre-chaotic physics. Paradoxically the introduction of chaos has led to the discovery of new patterns and insights into the nature of non-linear dynamic systems ranging from ecosystems to the origins of the universe.

Within the new physics of chaos or complexity theory, chaos or the uncertainty associated with not being able to make predictions of the behavior of non-linear systems leads, as Prigogene first suggested, to new levels of order. The Heisenberg uncertainty principle in quantum mechanics leads to an understanding of the wave nature of particles and the particle behavior of light and by association to the wave behavior of the probability amplitudes needed to describe atomic and sub-atomic particles and make predictions about their behavior. Just as momentum and position (or energy and time) play complementary roles in the Heisenberg uncertainty principle, complexity and complementarity seem to play a similar role. When dealing with non-linear phenomena like the weather, the greater the scope of a model the more complexity it can embrace, but the less predictability it incorporates and the greater is its chaos. This parallels the Heisenberg uncertainty principle where the more one knows about the momentum the less one knows about the position and vice versa. A similar situation holds in dynamic modeling as well. The greater the predictability of a model the less complex it is and the smaller the number of elements that can be successfully modeled. Consider gravitational systems like the solar system. The two body problem yields total predictability as the equations describing motion can be solved in a closed form. With three or more bodies as the number of bodies increases, the complexity increases and the predictability decreases. Complexity and predictability are complementary in the same sense as momentum and position within the context of the Heisenberg uncertainty principle.

The decrease in the predictability of a model of a non-linear dynamics system resulting from the increase in chaos does not represent a shortcoming of the model, but rather an attempt to be complete by including the full complexity of the phenomenon being represented. In the spirit of the Non-Probativity Theorem there is no reason to believe *a priori* that a model representing nature should be both complete and totally predictable.

Goedel's Theorem can serve as a possible model to better understand the complementarity of complexity and predictability. Goedel's Theorem states that a mathematical system can not be both complete and logically consistent at the same time. If we think of predictability of phenomena as a form of logical consistency with the basic laws of nature and consider complexity as a form of completeness then Goedel's Theorem also supports the notion that total complexity or completeness of a model precludes complete predictability.

The rejection of chaotics and complexity theory by adherents of the older paradigms of Newtonian physics, relativity and quantum mechanics is due to the fact that the new physics places limitations on the predictability of nature. Einstein critiqued quantum mechanics because he proclaimed, "God does not play dice." The new physics is even more disturbing to this new generation of skeptics who have to contend with the notion that not only does God play dice at the atomic and subatomic level but he also plays it at the macro level. As a consequence of this, one must give up on the notion of prediction of certain phenomena at the macro level, something that not even quantum mechanics required despite the fact that it made use of probability at the micro level. Equally disturbing to some is the fact that the very existence of human life might also be the result of a random roll of the dice.

The new physics places limitations on the ultimate ability of science to predict certain phenomena critical to human survival such as the weather and large scale climatic change no matter how sophisticated our computational skills become. Buying into the new physics requires accepting the fact that some problems are intractable. This requires a new level of humility on the part of science which has enjoyed a period of unprecedented success for over 500 years in which it has been able to describe and explain almost every phenomenon it has encountered. Are we willing to sacrifice the sacred cow of predictability and accept a more modest role for ourselves in our quest for understanding our universe?

Will we accept a world view in which chaos and non-predictability are regarded as natural outcomes of the complexity and diversity of our universe, a richness which makes it possible for us to formulate this dilemma. I believe that the next generation of physicists will happily sacrifice this sacred cow and move on to a higher and deeper understanding of nature in much the same way that the Hebrews gave up the golden calf at Sinai and embraced ethical monotheism, but not without becoming stiff-necked, however. The only solace that can be offered to those who are disturbed by the lack of predictability of the new physics is that events are still causally connected but that at the edge of chaos where self-organizing criticality takes place science will not be able to determine which new form of equilibrium will emerge.

Conclusion

In this paper we have attempted to show the strengths and limitations of science when regarded as a language with its dual role of communication (description) and information processing (predictability). The Non-Probativity Theorem underscores a long held belief that scientific truth is not absolute but always subject to further testing. We have tried to link the limitations on predictability within the framework of the new physics of non-linear dynamics with the Heisenberg Uncertainty Principle and Goedel's Theorem. We have suggested that the chaos and non-predictability of complexity theory allows a more complete and full description of nature.

Acknowledgments

I wish to thank the organizers and particpants of the Humanity and the Cosmos Symposium, January 20-22, 2000 sponsored by Brock University and the Brock Philosophical Society where the ideas for this paper were incubated. I would also like to thank George Coyne personally for his powerful key note address which inspired the ethical dimensions of this paper. For their insightful presentations and lively discussions I would like to individually thank, Hugo Fjelstad Alroe, David Atkinson,

Richard Berg, Edmund Bertschinger, Leah Bradshaw, Bruce Buchanan, David Crocock, G.E. Dann, Darren Domski, George Ellis, David Goicoechea, Anoop Gupta, Calvin Hayes, Daniel McArthur, K. McKay, M. J. Sinding. I would also like to acknowledge my colleagues on the Media Ecology listserve for a recent stimulating discussion of metaphors with Jim Curtis, Raymond Gozzi, Randolph Lummp, John Maguire, Eric McLuhan, Lori Ramos and Lance Strate.

I also wish to thank my colleague in the Physics Dept. at the U. of Toronto, Prof. Ken McNeill and Marek Swinder, my former graduate student, for their comments which improved this paper.

References

Bertschinger, E. "The Call of Science: Theological Reflections on the Ethics of Vocation," *This Volume.*

Coyne, G. "When the Sacred Cows of Science and Religion Meet," *Symposium Paper.*

Gozzi, R. 2000. Private Communication by E-Mail.

Logan, R. K. 1986. *The Fifth Language*. Toronto: Stoddart Publishing.

———2000. *The Sixth Language*. Toronto: Stoddart Publishing.

McArthur, D. "Cosmology, Creation, and Psuedo Questions," *This Volume.*

McLuhan, M. 1964. *Understanding Media*. New York: McGraw Hill Signet Edition.

Schmandt-Besserat, D. 1986. "The Origins of Writing," *Written Communication* 19: 13–22.

Section B

Cosmology: Scientific and Religious

Chapters 5 to 8

Chapter 5

Science and Spirituality: The Meaning of Cosmology for Theology

Paul Allen, St. Paul's University

Introduction

The January 1999 issue of *Scientific American* contains a fascinating set of articles, each of which speculates on recent developments in cosmology. These developments, apparently, throw fresh doubt on the standard version of the Big Bang theory of universal origins. On the opposite side of the physical scale, in the domain of the microworld, there is a fascinating recent report about a physicist at Purdue University who has postulated that the electron may contain a fundamental structure. If verified this hypothesis re-establishes the unlikely possibility of a return to understanding micro-entities as *aether*-like (*National Post*, Jan. 6, 1999).

Such reports inspire a sense of marvel about the ongoing revolutionary character of scientific inquiry. Yet, the scale and rate of changes in scientific understanding do not, I contend, cast doubt on the basic practice of science. Rather, such changes raise questions of a philosophical and even theological significance about the universe and its basic character. In spite of the rise of the historicist turn in the philosophy of science this century, there is still good reason to be confident in the structure of inquiry that methodologically identifies a general fit between observation, fertile theories and resultant new questions. This is even the case in cosmology, an inherently theoretical discipline, in which there is a realization that recent spectroscopically-aided empirical discoveries have greatly assisted the verification of certain cosmological theories.

Regardless of such abundant confidence, thinkers in the human and social sciences are bound to share a more pessimistic sense of *déjà vu* concerning these latest reports which *Scientific American* terms a "revolution in cosmology." Revolutions, crises, paradigm shifts: all of these eruptions are merely more reminders of enormous shifts in consciousness in the human and the natural sciences to which we have grown accustomed since the advent of modernity. But in the natural sciences, a commonly acceptable method of seeking answers to questions persists. The human and social sciences have yet to return to this state of affairs. In science, despite vexing disputes concerning core issues, broad agreement exists that insights into empirical data fulfil the conditions by which nature is explained through a process of cumulatively interconnected scientific theories and hypotheses. The scientific method is widely accepted as providing valid knowledge in the traditional, more historical sciences such as geology and chemistry, even by "anti-realist" philosophers.

Such is not the case, however, in theology, to take the most glaring example from the humanities. Insofar as Christian reflection on religious experience is concerned, contemporary theologians exhibit little indication of pursuing a common method to explain what it is they do, and the disclosing nature of the object that they are talking about—God. Many religious adherents, on whose behalf most theologians reflect, would be shocked to discover the degree to which diverse methodologies have been both accepted and embraced in theology. This is above and beyond the widely understood divisions between Catholics, Orthodox and Protestant traditions. Indeed, many theologians would judge that their situation lies in keeping with credible "postmodern" instincts to foster virtue through diversity, whatever the costs of fostering methodological diversity might entail. Consensus does exist in the fact that, for a variety of reasons, a dramatic transformation in theological discourse has occurred, due to the multiple and interconnected shifts in meaning, language and culture, since the Scientific Revolution.

In what follows, I outline why the act of wondering about the universe and the structure of questioning itself is instigated by contemporary cosmology. While the conclusions to this inquiry appear to be primarily philosophical, it obliges theologians to survey this situation with a critical eye on its own sources. How *does* theology mediate the spiritual quest with diverse cultural audiences in mind, given the state of contemporary cosmology? I argue that cosmology's existential *telos* enforces upon theology an indirect yet profound resolution of opposing methodologies by opening up new questions for analysis concerning persons, as the distinctively intelligent level of the universe. Virtually by accident, philosophical reflections on contemporary large-scale cosmology have come to suggest certain questions about the *nature* of human inquiry and human existence that imply a common theological object over which diverse theological methodologies can freely converge without casting aside their own locus of concern. I will clarify what I mean by first summarizing the contemporary setting in Christian theology, then selectively referring to the work of philosopher Milton Munitz, astrophysicist William Stoeger and philosopher of science Ernan McMullin, whose work collectively indicates why contemporary cosmology's impact on theology via philosophy is so powerful.

Christian Theology

I want to stress that my interest and diagnosis are directed towards contemporary Christian theology in its ongoing mediation of religious experience and culture. I would not want this focus to upstage any similar potential that may exist for other religious traditions. Scientific cosmology has blossomed at a peculiar moment in the history of Christian theology. A split, which opened up in the nineteenth century between theological styles that were either receptive or hostile to the modern world has widened. Two theological styles that were originally European have replicated themselves in increasing varieties. On the one hand, there are the *public* theologies: the liberal, contextual, hermeneutical, liberationist, feminist, ecological and other forms of theological expression that are, at their core, *correlationist*. This general style of theology seeks to correlate different patterns of human experience and history with generalized religious patterns of living and expression. The names chiefly associated with this style are Schleiermacher, Tillich, Bultmann, Küng and lately, Sallie McFague and David Tracy to name several. For the correlationists, culture is normative yet historically dynamic (Ormerod, 1996, 707–19).

The second style of Christian theology, which continues to thrive, is a more strictly spiritual theology. It tends to be a doctrinal or systematic style of theology. Frequently, it is ecclesial, liturgical, hermeneutical, iconic, mystical and inwardly directed. In this style, culture plays a supporting role in reflecting and representing particular spiritual and theological identities. These identities provide privileged symbolic, affectively construed access to the spiritual life, which is a distinct form of drama. The names associated with this style of theology include Barth, von Balthasar, Niebuhr and more recently, the non-foundationalists such as Hans Frei, George Lindbeck and John Milbank.

While public theology stresses culture and its spiritual component, spiritual theology focusses on the spiritual life with its culturally-formed extensions. Increasingly these two styles of theology employ different methods that cut across other traditional theological demarcations, such as denominational tradition. A glance at many recent theological journals, I think, would confirm this broad theological division.

So, how might cosmology concern itself with this situation of theological dialectic? At first glance, it might appear to fit with correlationist theology in the act of determining patterns of meaning. But, there seems to be more to it than this. First, I believe the findings of cosmology over the last 50 years raise philosophical issues so fundamental that they put the basic post-Enlightenment assumptions and self-styled opposition of these two theological styles into serious doubt. The result might be that a cosmological contemplation of our "friendly universe," a reflective discourse that suggests God-content, will impel theologians to think more seriously about the adoption of a common method.

In summary, my argument is that contemporary cosmology functions in a dialogue with Christian theology as a discipline from which theologians learn new language and new dimensions of a spiritually coherent worldview. Cosmology illumines the God question by working in and explicitly acknowledging the transcending structure of human inquiry and the ultimate meaning of that inquiry (in a way that other sciences partially do). In so doing, it asks philosophical questions that in turn give rise to theological questions. It demands that theologians pay attention to how interdisciplinary correlation and spiritually oriented reflection fit together. A political kind of polarization in Christian theology need not be unending. A major clue to how dissatisfying this polarization has been is the debate initiated by John Milbank over his theological proposal of "radical orthodoxy." Conspicuously absent from both his work and the rebuttals of his detractors are references to the natural world. These debates have begun to resemble a competition for select historical and hermeneutical retrievals, without a perspective on an originating horizon of creation. What this dispute shows is that, *inter alia*, correlationalist and spiritual theology are two different and often competing methodical inquiries within a single discipline and religious tradition. Yet, the basic character of the discipline is meant to orient us to the mystery of God however this task is conceived. Cosmology, with its wondrous attention to the latest understandings of the universe, re-situates theology in terms of the human subject's quest for purpose and destiny, but not in the way that liberal theology once presumed.

The Cosmological Trajectory (Toward Theology)

By way of establishing the cosmology-theology connection, I will quote from the philosopher Milton Munitz's *Cosmic Understanding: Philosophy and Science of the Universe*. Here, Munitz succinctly lays out a careful reading of the way in which cosmology relates to philosophy with a distinction that goes to the heart of the theme of this symposium:

> The need to have a cosmology, an acceptable picture of the universe, generally derives from two principal motives. One is curiosity, a purely intellectual craving and sense of wonder that prompts the asking of certain questions [...] These are questions about the temporal, spatial, compositional, teleologic properties of the universe [...] A second motive underlying the search for a satisfying cosmology derives from the human need to "situate" the life of human beings in the universe [...] The combination of these two motives has been the principal sustaining incentive in the pursuit of cosmology (Munitz, 1986, 5–6).

Restating what Munitz believes are two cosmological motives, I would say that the first is in terms of the cognitively attentive search for truth, a truth that is indicated but not totally accounted for, in scientific forms of inquiry. The second motive is in terms of existential meaning, a wholly distinct search for patterns of (as Munitz says) "goals, purposes and values." Note how, as Munitz says, a unity of these two basic motives within cosmology is accepted without entailing a methodological crisis in the discipline. Indeed, entire civilizations and their common cultural stories are built, in part, on the practice of scientific cosmology in partnership with an interpretive or existentially-directed cosmology.

Commonly, the relationship between cosmology and theology is conjectured on the basis of a direct implication that blurs this key distinction that Munitz introduces early in this authoritative text. Commonly, there is an assumed philosophical warrant, where science somehow *implies* spirit, where scientific cosmology implies a religious or moral cosmology. Often, this takes the form of a design argument for the existence of God, but I am hesitant to embrace this kind of implication for a number of reasons. One of these is based on a reading of what happened to theology as the scientific revolution materialized. Michael Buckley masterfully details this dramatic turn of events (see Buckley, 1986). Citing the influence of early figures such as Leonard Lessius and Marin Mersenne, Buckley analyses how the turn away from christology toward the nature of proportionate space and time in natural theology set stage for the onset of atheism. He shows how theologians gave up on religion and religious experience at a key moment in the intellectual history of the West. Theology has still yet to recover from this.

But, my hesitation for seeing direct implications from the universe to spirituality is also based on the legitimacy of the distinction in cosmology that Munitz draws. Relating cosmology and theology indirectly regards the God question as operating in contemporary culture, but not through an implication to theology from any particular cosmological data or theory. Rather, the relationship lies in paying attention to what cosmologists do when they do cosmology and to see what a study of the structure or method of their discipline does to unfold a broader structure of inquiry in human consciousness itself. Since it is cosmology that is the implicated discipline, my argument is not a Kantian or Cartesian reduction. This focus on methodology and inquiry does not depend on particular findings, as tempting as they may seem in welcoming "God-talk." Rather, it stresses the character of the intention of seeking answers to questions, and the successful results that transpire from this intention.

William Stoeger

In a number of stimulating articles written over the past 15 years, astrophysicist and Jesuit William Stoeger has reflected on the key features of science and cosmology that pertain to understanding the place of theological discourse as it affirms the universe as a created reality. In his article "Contemprary Cosmology and its Implications for the Science-Religion Dialogue," he draws a distinction between different cosmological questions that serve to extend Munitz's dual motives with greater precision (Stoeger, 1988, 219–47). For Stoeger, there is an important additional distinction not immediately addressed by the one I have cited from Munitz. First, there are questions that address "the very early features of the observable universe" such as a) the quality of the four force interaction as the foundation on which atomic particles and properties unfolded, b) the determining source of the arrow of time, c) the status of entropy and so on (Stoeger, 1988, 220).

Second, there are a set of what Stoeger calls bolder questions—not yet the existential questions of meaning that Munitz posits in relation to cosmology, but bold questions nonetheless. These questions transcend the concerns around early universe structure by turning to more basic problems that arise in the very act of questioning about early universe structure in the first place. These questions are, for example, "How do the fundamental constants come to possess the values they have?" or "Can the initial conditions of the universe be given or determined *within* a cosmological model or theory or will they instead always be outside any adequate scientific explanation or account?" (Stoeger 1988, 221).

These bolder questions, as Stoeger calls them, justify cosmology's reputation as a "boundary discipline." As a discipline, it is both a science and not a science at the same time. Questions about the strictly scientific character of the universe are scientific because they arise in the effort to understand physical process in a single object—the universe. Yet, they are non-scientific, since the features of the universe which a scientific cosmology is trying to uncover are so pervasive of knowledge and the acts of knowing, that they appear pre-scientific and therefore philosophical.

Does cosmology need philosophy? What warrants the requirement for a philosophical interpretation of cosmology? Stoeger, I think, pinpoints the issue, in light of the fact that the sciences themselves are "cumulative, not just analytic." Cosmology, of all the scientific disciplines is the most inherently cumulative of all:

> [...] the subject of cosmology is pervasive—but pervasive, so to speak, in its object, not in our experience or knowledge of the object. In philosophy, both the object and our experience of it are pervasive or general. Thus, philosophy attends to the intelligible wholes and structures, and to their interrelations, which must be assumed or presupposed by the sciences, including cosmology. Cosmology and philosophy deal with the same realities—but each with a different focus, and relying on different evidential grounds. Philosophy may attend to the details, when invited to do so by the sciences, but only as instances of the general; the details are not its focus. Cosmology may attend to what is pervasive or general in our experience—in order to orient itself—but this is not its focus. It is on the particular (Stoeger, 1988, 226).

Leaving aside the critiques of the postmodernists, it would be fair to say that philosophers have indeed understood themselves to be devoted to these kind of ultimate, or what Stoeger calls "general" questions, in relation to cosmology. With regards to cosmology, philosophers are asked to focus on inquiry itself not merely in relationship to other inquiries, but on human inquiry in light of the intelligibilities of the universe as a whole. For Stoeger, the transfer from cosmology to philosophy equates to a transfer from a focus on observers and observation (which I take to mean the acts of understanding that occur in recurring sets of cognitive operations including yet incorporating much more than perception) to knowers and the acts of knowing (Stoeger, 1988, 236). Questions about the knower and knowing the conditions and limits of knowing are more fundamental.

The ultimate in science, as expressed through cosmology, raises the notion of interdisciplinary limits or horizons: at what point do scientific models and theories stop fuelling the growth of knowledge and give way to a process of philosophical speculation that arguably does the same? Is knowledge still growing in the real sense of what "growth" means? With Stoeger, I would respond "yes," not because science is justified by the pre-scientific discipline of philosophy. Rather, it is because philosophy serves to concretely assist scientists understand what they are doing as scientists, even as they become aware of the fact that their questions transcend the limits of science per se. Philosophy, as I have outlined it here with Stoeger's assistance, is the metaphysical bridge between the purely scientific questions arising out of raw data and the existential questions of meaning that matter to us personally. This bridge, therefore, consists of two spans, not one. Philosophy is a mediating mid-point between cosmology and theology. Furthermore, as my frequent mention of the reflection on particular questions shows, this metaphysical bridge is not a traditional categorical, idealistic, reductionistic metaphysics, but a metaphysics founded on the transcending character of human inquiry into the act of identifying recurrent levels of questioning through cosmology into philosophy and beyond. In a sense therefore, there is not a bridge to be built, as if what is presupposed are two separate islands of knowledge. On the contrary, the "construction project" under consideration is more like constructing one's own personhood. It is like a tower that is built on the foundation of transcending levels of knowledge, wisdom and spiritual growth.

So what does this attention to cosmology and philosophy have to do with the place of spirituality? Perhaps the most important implication of understanding the distinction between cosmology and philosophy for spirituality derives from the realization of time's internal character along the space-time continuum. According to Stoeger, the beginning of time as a point of absolute beginning is "highly unlikely" to be unveiled by cosmology as a solution to a scientific investigation, in the sense that one could affirm that absolutely nothing existed "before" that point (Stoeger, 1988, 240). The natural sciences cannot, by themselves, supply the demarcation line beyond which a divine primary causality could be inferred. Since this unlikelihood pertains to scientific cosmology and the reality that is bound by space-time, our reliance upon other disciplines to carry forward the questions about existence further indicates once again that no direct route from cosmology to God exists. It is not that scientific inquiries into the causes of the universe's existence cease. It is just that another radically different avenue must be taken in order to get a satisfying answer to this ultimate cosmological puzzle.

This puzzle, which Stoeger's bolder questions imply, has historically been posed in terms of asking "Why is there something rather than nothing?" This question, which Paul Davies highlights in his well-known work *God and the New Physics*, is more valid today than ever before. It is obviously a philosophical question, but since it arises in the face of science's exhaustion in trying to come to terms with an understanding of the universe, it might be worthwhile to pursue another line of thinking on this open-ended question. The avenue of faith seems to offer obvious possibilities because of the resources it brings to these manifolds of questioning. Faith literally opens up meaning.

Faith in God, as Creator of the universe, is traditionally expressed both through the doctrine or idea of creation, and the experience of hope as a key basis for faith. It is hope in a reality that informs our acts of understanding, judging and deciding. This theological affirmation accounts for the reality of love as well as hope by affirming the sheer giftedness of the universe. Faith begins somehow by bracketing the something vs. nothing problem by simply taking stock of the incredibility of the "something." Faith seems to account for the fact that love and hope arise out of human inquiries into the meaning of our existence from deep within this "something." Faith also presupposes a dimension of human experience that is oriented to God's "self-communication" to us, a "special action" of God that is distinct from "the creative and sustaining action of all that is not God" as Stoeger says (Stoeger, 1996, 163). In a sense, faith is anticipated by Munitz as a potential resource in developing cosmic meaning. Before describing some of the theological implications of this, I want to briefly note the contribution of Ernan McMullin to this problem.

Ernan McMullin

With the writings of Ernan McMullin, there are additional resources to support the case for an indirect relationship between cosmology and theology. This relationship is, first and foremost, respectful of the investigations in both disciplines. McMullin is a philosopher and a historian of science, whose best known contribution in the philosophy of science is his defence of scientific realism in a sustained dialectic with a number of "anti-realist" philosophers. I raise McMullin's contribution as a complementary perspective to Stoeger's on related issues concerning the status of scientific knowledge and the meaning of the fact that science progresses, while standing incomplete vis à vis the range of human concerns.

McMullin defends scientific realism through his nuanced and historically referenced theory of scientific rationality, which he calls "retroduction." This explanatory theory of scientific inquiry attends to the historical record of the varieties of explanatory inferences used in scientific method such as the more well known and understood "induction" and "deduction." Retroduction is a theory of scientific rationality that highlights the role and the significance of the act of theorizing as it occurs through the indispensable role of the human imagination, especially since the seventeenth century, when theory's status became firmly entrenched as a pivotal heuristic tool in scientific knowledge. The implications here for a philosophical understanding of cosmology, and of what it means is relevant, since the human imagination is customarily construed as an impediment to scientific precision and a position of scientific realism. But if the imagination is affirmed, as McMullin says, as the key to hypothesis making and theory verification, then we also have a key link with religion. The imaginative horizon of religion and religious experience is a given, regardless of whether that is appraised positively or negatively.

It is a fact that cosmology is intrinsically theoretical, and cosmological theorizing is highly imaginative. Cosmology's aims and disciplinary structure investigate, identify and disclose the existence of theoretical entities, such as the measurable universal constants. In going beyond the employment of induction and deduction, retroduction is a generalized term that explains a) the process of a scientific explanation, b) the verification of that explanation through certain interconnected values as criteria for successful explanation and c) the actual success that a progressive validation of certain findings brings to a wider, ontological affirmation of a value-filled, anthropically teleologic universe. As McMullin says:

> It is on ... this powerful pattern of inference that cosmology mainly relies. And indeed cosmology could now be counted on as one of the domains in which this combined mode of validation and explanation has gained its most notable successes [...] to which the most *general* theories [...] can provide coherent explanations of known cosmological data (McMullin, 1981, 180).

I would emphasize, in clarification of this claim, that cosmological understanding develops concretely by virtue of a complementary set of explaining and verifying vectors of operations by the inquirer, whose pure curiosity to know, and whose freedom to employ imaginative schemes are crucial to obtaining this knowledge.

The success of hypothetical cosmological modelling occurs as follows:

> [w]hen the spectra of distant stars, or the velocities of distant galaxies, continue to be interpretable by schemes derived from terrestrial processes [...] Confidence quite properly grows in the assumption that these schemas are not just conventions imposed for convenience's sake or because our minds cannot operate otherwise, but that all parts of the universe are united in a web of physical process which is accessible through coherent and ever-widening theoretical constructs created and continually modified *by us* (McMullin, 1981, 181 italics mine).

Furthermore, our efforts of creation and modification that successfully operate in acquiring and accumulating knowledge are testimony to what I would call a fascinating coherence. This metaphysical coherence gives evidence of being isomorphically structured between the human act of knowing and the known. The operations of human intelligence, in what seems to be a contingently-structured universe rather than a necessary one, raises the whole issue of the anthropic principle, which has intrigued a number of theologians.

I will not summarize the debates that have been carried out over the anthropic principle, since they are complicated. I will, however, refer to a judgment McMullin makes in addressing this issue of the "improbability of observed isotropy." While some philosophers and theologians have made much out of a straightforward interpretation of the anthropic principle for strictly philosophical or theological purposes, McMullin reverses the logic and establishes another way to ask about its meaning. In a reminder that is typical of his cautious approach, McMullin notes that the anthropic principle is, in fact, quite vulnerable. The anthropic principle derives:

> from the claim (1) that the most basic structures of the universe might have been different from what they are; and (2) that the development of rational life in the universe depends on their being more or less exactly what they, in fact, are (McMullin, 1981, 186).

In addressing the vulnerability of the anthropic principle, McMullin foresees two distinct solutions. One solution is where the anthropic principle becomes explanatory if the universe *is already* understood as the work of a Creator.

> Reasons can be given in the traditional Judaeo-Christian perspective, why God *would* want humans in the world. Thus, the explanation is

> not merely by the presumed fact of choice, but by some presumptive *reasons* for that choice. The anthropic principle, if fortified by the traditional doctrine of creation, does therefore give an explanation, though it is no longer, of course, a scientific explanation (McMullin, 1981, 186).

The alternate, second solution is that all possible universes do in fact exist in isolation from one another, each "created" from within the parameters set in the early universe(s') conditions. It is important to note how both of these solutions thrusts the anthropic principle, due to its inherent vulnerabilities, into the realms of theology or speculative philosophy respectively. The first raises the significance of the human to a glorified level, while the other reduces human significance to one among an infinite number of cosmic possibilities. The answer to this choice would then lie in appraising our destiny from within the anthropic range of meaning.

By referring back to the idea of creation in the first solution, McMullin places certain restrictions around the anthropic principle in its capacity to communicate meaning. Creation is a notion with completely different terms of reference, which I would summarize with reference to the ethical dimension of our experience, and to the use of the word "good" in Genesis, chapter one. Returning to the focus on the human imagination in constructing scientific theories which McMullin highlights in his theory of retroduction, I would go further by extending the emphasis on imagination and creativity through his reference to the notion of creation itself, with its conceptual dependence on the evaluation of the goodness of the universe.

I would speculate that goodness is associated with what McMullin refers to as the presumptive reasons in the doctrine of creation for explaining why we exist. Goodness itself is not "out there now real" in the universe. It stems from an intentional reflection on the performances of human action to enact meaning. This human drama is foreshadowed by both the reliance on certain values such as coherence and fertility in scientific knowing generally as well as the inherent limits of cosmological knowledge to account for the realm of meaning. It is explicated by the advertence to other sets of human desires that are able to connect value with a sense of personal meaning about the universe as a whole. This is no smooth deductive trajectory or inductive generalization of metaphysical knowledge involving the apprehension of certain explanations, concepts, principles or categories. Any metaphysical claim, no matter how modified, must take into account the trenchant critiques of Heidegger and Husserl, among others. While in full recognition of the power of these critiques, it must also take up the reconstructive philosophical contributions of such figures as Ricoeur and Lonergan.

Instead, there is the realization of limits in respective disciplines due to limits of certain questions, a realization so accutely felt by cosmologists. I interpret the existence of these limits followed by emergent, new questions through a notion of transcendence. Transcendence is empirically rooted in the recurring levels of inquiry in human consciousness. It is an explanation of what is going on when questions about intelligence and value succeed each other. No one piece of cosmological data, such as the Big Bang theory or a philosophical interpretation such as the anthropic principle therefore warrants an immediate theological appropriation without first having recourse to this elevating and recurring transcendence evident in human consciousness.

Here is where McMullin's caution concerning the well known work of theologian Wolfhart Pannenberg is perhaps germane. In his article "How Should Cosmology relate to Theology?" he cites a plausible interpretation of Pannenberg's *Theology and the Philosophy of Science* as suggesting that scientific theories themselves imply specific implications and critiques for Christian faith to draw upon. Pannenberg's intended meaning is proximate enough to numerous other cases that purport to show an epistemological link between science and spirituality as simply another level of superimposed understanding of explanation (Pambrun, 1993, 103). It is, however, deeply problematic, because it bypasses self-knowledge. The history of science contains numerous examples of the flaws of such an approach, such as the later efforts of none other than Isaac Newton:

> [...] the stubbornness of Newton in adhering on part-theological grounds to a version of the principle of inertia which represented matter as a wholly inert principle, with "active principles" affecting it only "from the outside" ought to be recalled. Despite the obvious implication of his own gravitational theory, he continued for several decades, without success, to find a locus of these "active principles" which would (from his point of view) better satisfy the theological demand that matter have no activity in its own right. All activity, he thought, must be seen to come from the conserving action of God (McMullin, 1988, 51).

Over against a strict epistemological control of the terms and relations in competing scientific and theological warrants to various data, I propose instead the spiritual relevance of the universe that is tied up in the act of noticing what happens in oneself when one moves to questions about goodness and love. The meaning of meaning emerges in understanding a transcending movement from inquiries in cosmology to philosophy and, based on the irreducible experience of goodness, value and the utter gratuitous character of the universe, to spirituality and theology. This interior reflection begins afresh from a consideration of the macro-level of the proportionate universe, and is not brought to an abrupt halt through a solution at the level of concept, category or epistemology. It continues onward in the effort to unite the metaphysical and the intentional in differentiated disciplines. This transcending movement is indirect, and recurs in multiple sets of meaningful questions, according to which questions are asked. The response of faith mirrors the other leaps in human questioning similarly undertaken, an indication that the limits faced by transcending levels of questions requires the leap that other human experiences such as love and hope impel.

One way McMullin expresses something like this indirect relationship of the scientific and the spiritual is through his specific characterization of the cosmology-theology relationship in terms of consonance (McMullin, 1988, 51). As a result, according to McMullin, the aim of establishing a relationship should "be consonance rather than direct implication" (McMullin, 1988, 51). The aim is a "coherent world view" as McMullin says, with full recourse to philosophy. In my view, this recourse involves attending to the specific levels and concerns of human consciousness, each with their own specificity of question-types. A worldview's coherence ought to refer to the more complex and multifaceted coherence that comes from being attentive to understanding what kinds of inquiries are directed to distinct objects for the purpose of expanding certain horizons of knowledge to their limits until we reach the questions pertaining to an ultimate source—God.

Conclusion

In attempting to question how it is that cosmology contains essential aspects of meaning for theology, it is worthwhile to return for a moment to the cosmological side of the dialogue to ask: "where do goodness, love and hope come from?" The answer lies not in terms of a "God-of-the-gaps" where divine action is supposedly discovered as filling a material void, but rather through some revelation at another "level" of the universe entirely (Stoeger, 1995, 252–53). They stem from an autonomous source of human reflection that runs in consonance with the transcending stages of questions directed towards knowledge of the universe, and then beyond the universe. But this source of reflection is distinct by virtue of its orientation to identifying mystery. It endeavours to understand the God who actively sustains us in a providential relationship within history. This is the god who is revealed in sacred texts and intended through moral and ethical deliberation (Stoeger, 1996, 163). This is the God spoken of in the spiritual theology of the Jewish, Muslim and Christian traditions, a God who is revealed as extremely personal. Stoeger goes so far as to identify the "personal" as a level of reality in which "divine action" is manifest, an interpretation of cosmology that is connected with the central premise of my paper: spirituality is a route of access to God through the cumulative and intentionally self-aware inquiries of human existence, which are already noticed both partially yet exactly in cosmology (Stoeger, 1995, 258).

The unity and significance of the person, apart from the specific historical meanings that this word possesses in trinitarian Christian theology, also arises from a reflection on cosmology. This is the argument I would make based on an interpretation of selected writings of William Stoeger and Ernan McMullin. My purpose, however, has *not* been to prove that the Christian use of the word "person" aligns with a particular cosmological worldview. It has been to show how a study of the transcending levels of questions that range from cosmology through philosophy reveals the foundational role played by personal inquiry, especially into the implications that arise from an inquiry into these inquiries. Attention to this philosophical strategy of relentless interiority is the "personal" alternative to simplistic solutions that intend a categorical, implicative or conceptual unity to the cosmology-theology dialogue.

This alternative succeeds on the frontier of meaning that Munitz illumines in his discussion of the purposes of cosmic understanding. This alternative, based on personal interiority is a better long-term strategy, because it is clear that no immediate clarifications exist "out there" in the universe to the distinct human experiences of love, goodness and hope. Extra-terrestrial intelligence, were it to be "discovered," would confirm what we know about the personal nature of the universe, if we are already attentive to human inquiry as a whole. I say this not to be anthropocentric but simply to point out that once we recognize and communicate with other intelligent beings, given that "intelligence" is understood, then we are not dealing with aliens. Nevertheless, attention to the irreducible role of human inquiry shows how a study of the universe is nevertheless open to God through the same human who studies cosmology, reflects philosophically and theologically.

And, this same human person is the same subject of either style of theology being practised, whether it is correlationalist or spiritual theology. Both fundamental styles are ultimately premised on the one subject in act in the one universe. Science and spirituality are not connected, by virtue of any single concept or category "out there," but rather through the foundational reality of the human person seeking truth and meaning. This is the case with cosmology, and it is, therefore, surely the case in theology.

Personal meaning and the search for truth seem to be linked in an extended and radically non-linear form of transcendence. Transcendence, in my outline of the centrality of human experience and inquiry into the universe is a theological category, it is true. But transcendence is theological when we see that no logical reason exists to restrict the parameters of questions being asked. And this is due to the fact that we always ask further questions. I think of transcendence based in a study of what we do in cosmological inquiry and theologically interpreted as a result of this inquiry, so long as a philosophical reflection that takes interiority seriously is undertaken. As a result, I agree with Stoeger who says that "God is fully and actively immanent precisely because God is fully transcendent" (1995, 257). It is not a question of one or the other. This transcendence in immanence is not a dialectic to be resolved by any particular cosmological finding, but a fully coherent reflection of what, analogously speaking, goes on within you and me. This is also the kind of analogy that was first articulated so famously within the Christian tradition by Augustine.

Science is rendered personal in some way through intelligent questions that receive answers, especially since theory became pivotal and values are given their due in a position of scientific realism. Spirituality is inherently personal as well, ultimately because of the personal love that lies beyond the limits of questions, but which we are capable of exercising in personal and corporate ways. Whatever the implications of the duality of theological styles, the attention to cosmological and philosophical interactions that I have discussed here could help resolve certain longstanding blockages that prevent Christian theology from communicating itself effectively through a single method to contemporary cultures. Theologians have an intense interest in hearing about the personal "level" of the universe from the natural sciences as a "wake-up call" to focus on the person of faith who lives in a world that is significant because of who we are.

References

Buckley, M. 1987. *At the Origins of Modern Atheism*. New Haven: Yale University Press.

McMullin, E. 1981. "Is Philosophy Relevant to Cosmology?" *American Philosophical Quarterly* 18: 180–91.

———1988. "How Should Cosmology Relate to Theology?" In.*The Sciences and Theology in the Twentieth Century*. Ed. A. Peacocke. Notre Dame, IN: University of Notre Dame Press.

Munitz, M. 1986. *Cosmic Understanding: Philosophy and Science of the Universe*. Princeton: Princeton University Press.

Ormerod, N. 1996. "Quarrels with the Method of Correlation." In *Theological Studies* 57: 707–19.

Pambrun, J. 1993. "Lonergan and Ricoeur: Emerging Complementarity. Philosophical Approaches for Theological Views of Science." In *Lonergan Workshop* 9. Boston: Boston College.

Ricoeur, P. 1978. "Explanation and Understanding: On Some Remarkable Connections Among the Theory of the Text, Theory of Action and Theory of History." In *The Philosophy of Paul Ricoeur: an Anthology of his Work*. Eds. Charles Reagan and David Stewart. Boston: Beacon Press.

Stoeger. J.W. 1988. "Contemporary Cosmology and its Implications for the Science-Religion Dialogue" In *Physics, Philosophy and Theology: A Common Quest for Understanding*. Eds. R. J. Russell, William Stoeger S.J. and George Coyne. Vatican City: Vatican Observatory Publications.

———1996. "Faith Reflects on the Evolving Universe: Divine Action, the Trinity and Time" In *Finding God in all Things: Essays in Honor of Michael J. Buckley S.J.* Eds. M. J. Himes and S. Pope. New York: Crossroad.

Chapter 6

Cosmology, Creation and Pseudo-Questions

Daniel McArthur, University of Regina

This paper will address the question of whether or not the "problem of creation" is a genuine question for scientific cosmology, or whether or not it is an illegitimate "pseudo-question" as Adolf Grünbaum would have it.[1] I argue in this paper that the distinction between scientific questions and pseudo-questions is a pseudo-distinction. I also argue that maintaining such a distinction is methodologically and philosophically ill advised in so far as it places science in a straightjacket that can potentially stifle the development of new approaches. While I agree with Grünbaum that the religious doctrine of "creation *ex nihilo*" is not entailed by current cosmology, this does not imply that questions about the cause of the universe ought to be ruled out in principle, as Grünbaum argues. Finally, I argue that the conclusions resulting from my analysis of the failure of Grünbaum's arguments bring to mind to some extent the

1. This paper was partially motivated by a lengthy correspondence on these issues with Steve Zicopoulas who also provided detailed criticism of early drafts of this paper, I am very grateful to him for this. I would also like to thank Idil Boran for her support and help in writing this paper.

now often ignored logical empiricist doctrines of tolerance to (seemingly) external questions to science. I will provide a philosophically reformulated version of this principle that takes into account recent developments in the philosophy of science and argues for an open minded and tolerant view of what sort of question should be seen as scientifically meaningful. In order to make this case I will begin my discussion with an analysis of Grünbaum's arguments about the so-called pseudo problem of creation.

Grünbaum and Pseudo-Questions:

In his article "The Pseudo-Problem of Creation in Physical Cosmology" Grünbaum argues that a distinction must be drawn between the genuine question "does the physical universe have a temporal origin, and—if so—what does physical cosmology tell us about it" from the meaningless pseudo-problem "was there a creation of the universe … and what light can science throw on it, if any" (Grünbaum, 1990, 92). Grünbaum notes that a long string of commentators writing about the cosmological debates of this century have become confused over this distinction. Arguing in favour of the steady state cosmology, Hermann Bondi complained that the big bang cosmologies leave creation unexplained while steady state cosmology includes continuous creation as a physical feature of the ordinary operations of the universe. Arguing for the opposite conclusion Herbert Dingle notes that the steady state theory taxes credulity exactly because it postulates a steady string of miracles that violate the conservation of energy. Cosmologist Jayant Narlikar poses a similar non-question when he asks, "where did the matter we see around us originate in the first place?" (Grünbaum, 1990, 92). For Grünbaum such questions are as meaningless as Descartes' question about why physical objects continue to exist and do not disappear even though no force appears to be acting on them to prevent this. As far as Grünbaum is concerned the existence of the universe and the matter in it ought to be taken as a brute fact just as the continued existence of the matter within it is. Grünbaum deploys this line of reasoning to expose the welter of what he considers meaningless questions that inform Bernard Lovell's claims to the effect that modern cosmology (whether based on the steady state or big-bang version) demands inference to divine creation in order to show that all such arguments are based on meaningless presuppositions.

Lovell, Grünbaum notes, presents his case in a series of papers, books and lectures dating from the late 1950s to the late 1980s. In that time period the cosmological sciences witnessed great advances in terms of both empirical discovery and theoretical change. That period, of course, saw the decline of the once quite prominent steady state theory, the advent of the early big-bang models and more recently the inflationary cosmologies that incorporate quantum theories of the vacuum into cosmology. Nevertheless for Lovell, modern cosmology is just as consistent with divine creation as earlier approaches. Indeed, Lovell later writing on the subject merely extends his early work over to the new domain and the central structure of his argument remains intact. Grünbaum takes Lovell's early argument presented in his 1961 book *The Individual and the Universe* as the point of departure of his critique. In that work Lovell argues that both the steady state theories and the big bang models each leave the problem of creation a mystery.

Lovell's arguments concerning the big bang are fairly straightforward; essentially he argues that this cosmology leaves the big bang unexplained and deals with only what happens immediately after. What caused the matter and energy to explode into being at the beginning of time? Lovell's answer is that the theory leaves the event unexplained and apparently miraculous, and hence in need of inference to divine creation. In spite of the obvious contrasts between big-bang cosmology and steady state cosmology, Lovell's argument for divine creation in this case is strikingly similar. Steady state cosmology was proposed in order to explain the observed red shift in distant galaxies, in other words to account for the fact that the galaxies seem to be flying apart from one another. In the steady state view, the density of the universe remains constant even though the universe expands because new hydrogen atoms are spontaneously created and form into new stars and galaxies that fill in the gaps left between the mutually receding galaxies. In the steady state theory there is no instant where the universe is created, it is infinitely old. However for Lovell the continuous creation of hydrogen atoms out of nothing is left miraculous and therefore in need of inference to divine creation. Lovell's more recent work extends this argument to modern inflationary cosmology wherein he argues that the false vacuum that is the cause of the rapid inflationary expansion stands in exactly the same need of external causation as the spontaneous creation of hydrogen atoms or the big bang did.

For Grünbaum all of these arguments are based on the tacit assumption that the question "what caused the universe to exist?" or in the case of steady state "where does its new hydrogen, and its state of expansion come from?" requires an answer, and therein lie Lovell (and other's) mistakes (Grünbaum, 1990, 96). For Grünbaum it is not enough that a questioner find a question to be "psychologically insistent" for it to be a meaningful well-posed question (1990, 96). Grünbaum's thesis revolves around the idea that when the questions and assumptions underlying a "divine creation position" like Lovell's or even non religious dissatisfaction with a particular theory that leaves "creation" unexplained are examined, they turn out to be unwarranted. It must be noted that Grünbaum does not criticise Lovell simply because he feels that Lovell has drawn incorrect conclusions from his analysis of cosmology, Grünbaum's critique of Lovell's work purports to show that the basic questions that it addresses are illegitimate pseudo-questions.

For Grünbaum then his conclusions apply not only to theists who try to utilise the "problem of creation" to make some room for Christian creation in cosmology, but also to commentators (philosophers or scientists) who find dissatisfaction with a theory because it leaves "the problem of creation" unanswered. Thus Grünbaum includes the dissatisfaction felt by many with steady state sympathies, like Bondi or Narlikar, toward the big bang theory as examples of the deployment of the same set of meaningless questions. Grünbaum makes his argument by first trying to show that, in general, arguments that are intended to support the necessity of a first cause must fail. He then applies these conclusions to the various cosmological theories to prove that no "problem of creation" exists either in the steady state cosmology, their big bang rivals or the more recent inflationary cosmologies.

For Grünbaum Lovell's erroneous assumptions about the problem of causation stem from adherence to illicit arguments about first causes that date back to the early middle ages. In these arguments the existence of any given thing stands in need of explanation. Whatever caused the existence of any given thing itself must have been caused and so on. For many medieval theologians this line of reasoning implied a "first cause" ultimately responsible for the creation of everything. That is to say, a divine creator who began the world and all the causal processes within it. In so far as the universe is a "thing," so this line of reasoning implies, the universe must have been created by this divine first cause. As Grünbaum points out this line of reasoning suffers from a series of fairly familiar series of errors. For one thing the idea that something was created does not at all imply that it had a creator, this error for Grünbaum stems from the connotations of agency that come with the idea of creation. Many causal processes occur without the conscious intervention of anyone, the melting of snow for example. Thus the inference to a creator can not be derived from the everyday observation that every event has a cause. In addition, those causal processes that we observe that involve conscious guidance do not create new entities out of nothing. The process of knitting a sweater after all simply changes existing matter and energy into a sweater it does not create a sweater out of nothing. Thus, ordinary experiences cannot warrant the inference to the creation of the universe out of nothing (Grünbaum, 1990, 98–100).

The second set of fallacies with traditional arguments from first cause is fairly obvious. Even if every event or thing is caused, this still does not warrant inference to a first cause. This would only be the case if the universe had only existed for a finite amount of time. That is to say if the universe was infinitely old, the causal chain explaining any given thing could stretch back forever without ever hitting on a first cause. A related point states that if the idea that everything has a cause is granted then the idea of a first cause seems to be an odd one. Does not the so-called first cause have a cause? The inference to divine or other first cause on the basis that every event or thing has a cause is therefore illegitimate. Grünbaum notes with approval Shopenhauer's identification of this mistake, "those who try to exempt God from their universal causal assertion treat causation like a hired carriage that is dismissed upon reaching its desired destination" (1990, 101).

The last dubious argument for first cause that Grünbaum identifies is the notion that a divine first cause is to be accepted on faith because the divine first cause "passes all understanding." Although it is unclear who is supposed to defend this view, Grünbaum argues that it cannot be convincing because if a "belief … is incomprehensible, what is being believed?" (1990, 102). It is of course no help to say that the incomprehensible can be called upon to explain the prosaic on the basis that God can understand such an explanation. This is so because the explanation is not being offered to God, it is being offered to ordinary humans with their limited capacity. For Grünbaum the arguments that stem from the "problem of creation" in cosmology suffer from a similar set of errors that the traditional arguments from "first cause" do.

For Grünbaum, just as the traditional arguments for first cause falter so too does the demand that creation in cosmological theories stands in need of explanation. In the case of the now outmoded steady state theory recall, "creation" takes place in the form of the spontaneous generation of new hydrogen atoms that preserve the overall density of matter in the expanding space-time. For Lovell, this creation, if it exists, requires divine agency. For critics of the theory, it is problematic on conceptual grounds because it leaves the cause of the central postulate, the creation of new matter, mysterious. However, for Grünbaum, this charge (or implication in the theistic interpretation) stands on the same incoherent ground that plague arguments from first cause.

For Grünbaum the central feature of the steady state theory is not left mysterious at all. In his view this spontaneous generation of new matter is postulated as the natural feature of the universe and should be taken as a brute fact that is neither conceptually incoherent nor standing in need of explanation. For critics of the creation of matter out of nothing, the question is begged about the universe's natural state. In this view matter and energy are conserved, that is, the amount of energy in the universe remains unchanged and the new matter thesis must *a priori* be problematic. However, why must this be so? Grünbaum argues that the steady state theory simply offers a different empirical thesis about what the natural state of the universe is. Steady state physics simply proposes that energy density is conserved, not quantity and the creation of new matter can be taken as natural and not in need of explanation.

Grünbaum points out that not everything stands in need of explanation and he appeals to some striking cases from the history of science to make this claim. For Aristotle, non-vertical sub lunar motion of any object required explanation in terms of an external force on the object in question. However, Galileo's experiments with inclined planes refuted this claim (from Aristotle's view, objects travelling down an inclined plane ought to stop when they reached the bottom, but they do not). In the Newtonian physics that replaced Aristotle's the natural tendency of any object is to remain in its non accelerated motion unless it is acted on by an external force. In Newtonian physics, this tendency to remain in uniform motion does not stand in need of explanation it is simply the empirically-verified, brute fact of the way things behave (Grünbaum, 1990, 101). In the steady state theory then, the conservation of density stands in no more need of explanation then Newtonian uniform motion or (contra Descartes' thesis) the tendency for material objects to not disappear. For Grünbaum, the problem with the steady state theory was not philosophical, nor if it were true would it support Lovell's claims. The steady state theory's view of a universe that was not significantly different in the past simply became harder and harder to reconcile with empirical discoveries of things like the cosmic background radiation or the confirmation that quasars are indeed cosmologically red shifted. However, no philosophical problems or explanatory gaps would have plagued the theory if it had turned out to be empirically adequate. Similar points about the "creation problem" are supposed to apply to both early big-bang theories and their inflationary successors.

For Grünbaum, the pseudo-problem of creation in the big bang models rests in the cause of the big bang itself. Narlikar, for example, describes it as a "sudden and fantastic violation of the laws of conservation of energy" (Narlikar, 1977, 196). Big bang cosmologies leave this violation unexplained. However, for Grünbaum, this demand for explanation misses the point. Nothing occurred before the big bang because there was no time for anything to occur in—time and space both originating at the "time = 0" of the big bang. In this sense every event in time does have a causal predecessor in the big bang models, there was no violation then of the laws of conservation to explain in so far as the universe has always had the same energy content. The question might remain as to why (rather than how) there is anything corresponding to the universe that obeys the laws that it does, but in this is as much a pseudo-question as what happened before time = 0. As Grünbaum argued with regards to the steady state theory, not everything stands in need of explanation (Grünbaum, 1990, 107–10).

Grünbaum does acknowledge that the recent inflationary cosmologies that rely on quantum theories of the vacuum do in a sense provide a causal "explanation" of the big bang. The idea is that at time = 0, a "false vacuum" existed. A false vacuum is not in its lowest energy state—a possibility allowed by quantum theories of the vacuum. General relativity implies that such a vacuum would expand at an accelerating rate. When the false vacuum decays into the lowest energy state the excess energy coverts into the radiation and energy the fills the universe today. This "inflationary" replacement for the early "hot big-bang" models has the virtue of explaining not only the big-bang but also many observed features of the universe. For example its "flatness" (small overall curvature), its isotropy (being the same in all directions) and the absence of magnetic monopoles (outré particles that are predicted by quantum theory but not observed, during the inflationary period of the early universe they are spread out so much that only a few are left in the observable universe) are all explained by the inflationary models (Grünbaum, 1990, 11; Linde, 1990, 239–48). Again for Grünbaum in this cosmology, creation is a pseudo-problem. The big bang is explained, so there is no "creation problem" there, and the observed features of the universe are concomitants of natural law, the initial vacuum state is supposed to be the brute fact that needs no explanation.

Grünbaum's ideas about he creation pseudo-problem with regards to cosmology have not gone without response. Narlikar for example has argued that Grünbaum's accusation to the effect that Bondi and himself have confused the creation problem with a finite temporal limit in their comments on the big bang cosmology are based on a poor analysis of the theoretical situation in cosmology. The core of Narlikar's critique rests on his observation that time (T) = 0 "has been given undue importance on the time axis ... that comes from a specific theory of gravity we happen to use ... that is inadequate in handling the situation at T = 0" (Narlikar, 1992, 366). Essentially Narlikar is pointing out that general relativity cannot account for the situation at the "singularity" which is supposed to exist at T = 0. Thus a more adequate account can be legitimately sought after, and such an account might well cover T = 0 or even eliminate a finite temporal limit altogether. And this he claims is exactly what occurs in more recent cosmologies that take quantum mechanics into account. Narlikar also expresses concern over Grünbaum's treatment of the steady state theory. Briefly, Narlikar feels that the creation of new matter might *not* need simply to be treated as a brute fact and sites research to the effect that physical explanations of the phenomena have been fruitfully sought after (Narlikar, 1992, 368).

To be sure Narlikar is correct that Grünbaum's treatment of the singularity in the big bang cosmologies tends to take poor account of the emerging quantum cosmologies that do extend their theoretical domain over T = 0. Furthermore, Narlikar is correct in his accusations to the effect that many of the phenomena that Grünbaum argues should be taken as brute facts might well become explanatorily transparent in light of new theory. However, Narlikar's critique restricts itself to the technical details of Grünbaum's reading of cosmology's treatment of T = 0. Essentially Narlikar argues that Grünbaum has missidentified his concerns over the inadequacies of big bang cosmology as pseudo-questions. He provides no critique of the central philosophical point underlying Grünbaum's argument; the idea that there *are* pseudo-questions that can be identified as scientifically meaningless. Moreover, while Narlikar does take effective issue with Grünbaum's identification of what can brook explanation, he takes no issue over Grünbaum's analysis of the role of explanation in science. Trenchant critique of Grünbaum then ought to address these philosophical aspects of his argument in addition to the details of his treatment of specific cosmological theories.

Demarcation, Methodology and Pseudo-Questions:

The core of Grünbaum's argument lies in his contention that it is not always necessary for a scientific theory to provide explanations for natural phenomena. For example, the non-accelerated constant motion in Newtonian mechanics is left unexplained, but no-one poses a "motion problem" for theories of non-accelerated motion. Furthermore, Descartes questions about the cause of the continued existence of matter are now seen as pseudo-questions. Matter simply remains in existence, and this, for Grünbaum requires no explanation—it is just a feature of the natural and observed behaviour of things like tables and chairs. For Grünbaum the various variations of the "creation-problem" that are sometimes applied to the three twentieth-century cosmologies discussed above, all demand explanations for what is presented by those theories as "natural and spontaneous" behaviour. The question Grünbaum does not address is this: how is one to know whether or not something should be taken as natural and unperturbed behaviour or as a troublesome *ad hoc* adjustment to get a theory to fit data?

Consider the case of Aristotle's claim that constant motion required explanation in the form of applied force. Aristotle's claims were, of course refuted by Galileo, but the fact that Aristotle's view had enough empirical entailments to stand for tests demonstrates that they were meaningful. In this sense Aristotle provided a theory to deal with observed motion that turned out to be empirically inferior to Newton's. Aristotle's views on motion were in the long run empirically unsatisfactory, but they were not based on meaningless assumptions stemming from pseudo-questions. In the end, of course, Newton's view does take non-accelerated inertial motion as an empirical primitive, but this was a decision taken after a many hundreds of years old debate that directly addressed the question as to whether or not this is the case. Why might queries about the "creation" of, say, hydrogen atoms in the steady state theory not be taken the same way? Grünbaum cannot of course respond that pseudo-problems rest at the base of unsatisfactory theories. Recall that the steady state theory was in Grünbaum's view philosophically unproblematic even if it was empirically unsatisfactory. Grünbaum's critique of the "problem of creation" in a sense accuses those who address the "problem" of begging the question that there are no brute facts to be accounted for but not causally explained.

However, even if such brute facts should from time to time to be taken as such, in the absence of some *a priori* characteristic of such primitives that permits their identification, Grünbaum seems to beg the question that "creation," as it appears in the various cosmological theories, is such a primitive. In other words, the fact that something is a primitive and without need of causal explanation is something that is decided by debate, scientific and philosophical. A global ban on such debate must rest on an arbitrary distinction between that should be explicated and that which should not. Grünbaum's arguments—if they are not to be hopelessly question begging and arbitrary—must rest on some demarcation between the scientifically metaphysical and the metaphysically meaningless. However, the existence of this demarcation is a long settled problem in scientific epistemology. Commentators as diverse as Carnap, Hempel, Feyerabend, Sellars and van Fraassen have all acknowledged that scientific language is theory-laden. That is to say that theoretical concepts in the sciences receive their interpretation not just in terms of observation but in terms of metaphysical and theoretical concepts as well. Science and metaphysics, then, blur into each other and there is no clear line between them. In this sense the degree to which science can address a question is not immediately obvious and must be determined through close scrutiny of the case in question. Grünbaum's ideas seem to require a return to the early and most obviously unworkable phases of logical positivism.

Indeed, Grünbaum's proposals about the nature of pseudo-questions in general, if adopted, would have a stifling effect on science. Consider the more recent inflationary cosmological theories. Grünbaum acknowledges that a great deal of their appeal lies in their explanatory fruitfulness with regards to things like the high degree of isotropy and the expansion of the universe itself. What would have been the need to entertain a new theory like cosmic-inflation when one considers the fact that much of its appeal lies in explanations to pseudo-questions? It is true that Grünbaum contends that the expansion has a temporal predecessor in these theories and therefore is not a pseudo-issue, but the creation of hydrogen atoms in the steady state theory also had temporal predecessors but stood in no need of explanation. What makes one a pseudo-question and the other not? Grünbaum has simply adjusted his own account of pseudo-problems in an ad hoc way to accommodate a set of theories that have gained a great deal of appeal that also answer questions that he earlier dubbed non-questions. Ideas of course are born with the help of a thousand midwives, and part of the motivation for the development of the inflationary programmes certainly came from attempts to study the implications of quantum theory for cosmology. Nevertheless it would be foolhardy to suppose that a great deal of the enthusiasm to pursue them did not stem from inflation's explanatory possibilities. However, if Grünbaum's vision of cosmology as simply accounting for and not trying to explain features of the universe, such as its expansion and even existence, were adopted as a methodological guide, much of the motivation to pursue these recent cosmologies would have been lost.

Methodology and a New Principle of Tolerance:

I noted at the beginning of this paper that the failure of Grünbaum's efforts to establish the nature of a scientific pseudo-question brings to mind Carnap's venerable principle of tolerance. The reason for this is precisely the remarkably restrictive and intolerant approach Grünbaum recommends for what should be taken as scientifically meaningful. The original positivist principle of tolerance was most fully articulated in the *Logical Syntax of Language*. In its original formulation this principal states that one is free to choose any linguistic framework from which to approach a problem. For example, in one framework numbers might be primitives but in another they might be classes of classes. In one, the question of describing nature and structure of a number is a pseudo-question, in another it is not. Mutual tolerance is implied because they are after all different frameworks and truth and meaningfulness are relative to the chosen framework (Earman, 1993, 12–15).

The original ideal failed because it requires an ultimate meta-language from which to make the delineations between the frameworks, and in this sense conflicts with Gödel's incompleteness theorem (Earman, 1993, 15; Friedman, 1992). So the original principle of tolerance is of no help in resolving questions of pseudo-questions.

However, Carnap did not long defend the strong meta-linguistically defined relativity thesis. In the end Carnap recognised, as he points out in "The Methodological Role of Theoretical Concepts," that scientific language must include much theoretical and philosophical content that can only receive "partial empirical interpretation" (Carnap, 1958). This is what might be described as an epistemologically liberal view with regards to what must be included in science. Under pressure from their inability to provide a definition of even partial-empirical interpretation, post logical-empiricist philosophers of science like Putnam and Sellars have abandoned even this minimal restriction on the degree to which philosophical or metaphysical concepts were meaningful in the languages of scientific theories. Given the open ended boundaries of the scientifically meaningful implied in this picture, a broad tolerance of what falls outside the current boundaries of a scientific theory is clearly implied. Given science's fluid boundaries, no philosophical theory can provide *a priori* reasons why metaphysical concepts might not become scientifically relevant at some point in the future. In other words, scientific change, or even just the meaningful motivation to investigate the possibility of scientific change, can come from many sources, even what at first blush seem to be obviously metaphysical or even religious sources.

The principle of tolerance contains what can be taken as a moral for deciding what the domain of science is. Many different approaches are possible and many different questions are possible to formulate, what might seem impossible to formulate in one approach might be possible in another. At the very least a charitable approach to alternative frameworks is implied. In the more fluid view of science (sketched above) that has replaced positivism, the clear delineation between the language of one theory and another, or even science and metaphysics becomes blurred. In this situation, tolerance is clearly implied and even to be recommended. As we have seen in the discussion of the plausibility of inflation, an open-minded approach to what can someday fall under the domain of science can lead to new theories and conjectures. Clearly this is a superior approach to Grünbaum's closed-minded and restrictive approach to what science can and cannot meaningfully discuss.

References

Carnap, R. 1958. "The Methodological Role of Theoretical Concepts." In *Minnesota Studies in the Philosophy of Science* Vol. 1. Eds. H. Feigl and H. Scriven.Minneapolis: Minnesota University Press.

Earman, J. 1993. "Kuhn & Carnap." In *World Changes*. Ed. J. Earman. Cambridge Mass.: MIT Press.

Friedman, M. 1992. "Philosophy and the Exact Sciences: Logical Positivism as a Case Study." In *Inference, Explanation and Other Frustrations: Essays in the Philosophy of Science*. Ed. J. Earman. Los Angles: University of California Press.

Grünbaum, A. 1990. "The Pseudo-Problem of Creation in Physical Cosmology." In *Philosophy and Physical Cosmology*. Ed. J. Leslie. New York: Collier MacMillan.

Linde, A. 1990. "The Universe: Inflation out of Chaos." In *Philosophy and Physical Cosmology*. Ed. J. Leslie. New York: Collier MacMillan.

Narlikar, J. 1977. *The Structure of the Universe*. Oxford: Oxford University Press.

———1992. "Concepts of 'Beginning' and 'Creation' in Cosmology." *Philosophy of Science* 59: 366–77.

Chapter 7

Are There Habitable Extra-Solar Planets? A Challenge for Religious Thought

George V. Coyne, S.J., Vatican Observatory

Introduction

The key word, it appears to me, in the title is "habitable," because, if we were to talk instead of "inhabited," this would be a very brief talk indeed, since there is **no** unequivocal scientific evidence for inhabited planets other than the Earth. Even to speak scientifically of "habitable" planets leaves a normal loquacious astronomer with little to say, unless rather basic assumptions are made. And, since I do want to say something so as to start the pot of religious thought boiling, I shall make those assumptions. I shall then, accepting those assumptions, discuss the scientific evidence concerning habitable extra-solar planets. At the end I would like to add a few thoughts on the religious implications which might be derived from the science.

Assumptions

I am going to accept as habitable the way in which the Earth is habitable, because, at this rudimentary stage of our scientific knowledge, hypotheses about other ways of living (for instance, non-carbon-based life) lead us into very unscientific pathways. I grant that this may limit our knowledge of the habitability of the universe, but I simply accept that limitation imposed by our assumptions. I further limit the conditions of habitability by taking, at these initial attempts at a scientific discussion, only the most rudimentary ones: (1) planetary systems form about some stars in the way in which they formed about the Sun; (2) the inner edge of the habitable zone in any planetary system is defined by the distance from the parent star at which water boils and/or at which we have a run-away carbon dioxide greenhouse effect; (3) the outer edge of the habitable zone in any planetary system is defined by the distance from the parent star at which water freezes and/or a thick carbon dioxide atmosphere develops. The conditions (2) and (3) are necessary, but not necessarily sufficient, conditions for life on the Earth, and so they define the minimum requirements for habitability within our assumptions.

The best model we have for the formation of planets about solar-like stars may be described as follows. A large interstellar cloud, typically containing 10^3 masses of the sun, fragments due to an interplay of kinetic, gravitational and magnetic energy. Each fragment that is sufficiently compact and stable begins to collapse by self-gravity and, like any normal gas, as it collapses it heats up. If it is sufficiently massive (more than about 0.1 the mass of the sun), it will raise the temperature in its interior sufficiently high, so that thermonuclear burning begins. At this point a star is born. (This is called a pre-main sequence star, since it is not yet completely stable.) For a star with a mass equal to that of the sun this process takes about 10^7 years. For more massive stars it is shorter, for less massive stars longer. The sun will keeping shining as it does today for about 10^{10} years and then it will explode and become a white dwarf. Note, therefore, that a star like the sun is born relatively (relating "gestation" to "lifetime") fast, some ten times faster than the birth of a human being! In the course of the cloud collapse there are stages which are important for the formation of a planetary system. As the star collapses, in order to conserve angular momentum, it rotates and this rotation causes a continuous flattening of the cloud until at the end of 10^7 years a disk has formed. There is also an intermediate stage after about 10^5 years at which a wind of high energy particles sweeps through the cloud and carries away much of the material left over from the collapse.

So, we have a solar-like star with a rotating disk of hydrogen gas and dust about it. How do planets form within this disk? As the disk continues to rotate the material in it begins to separate out into rings according to the mass distribution. Within each ring conglomerates begin to form due to elastic collisions, gravity and electrostatic binding. Eventually larger conglomerates, called planetesimals, of the order of 100 kms in extent are formed and then from these the planets are formed. During these processes the lighter elements are preferentially driven to the outer parts of the disk due to temperature of the parent star and the stellar wind. This explains why the outer planets in the solar system are more gaseous than the inner planets. Thus, for a star like the sun we have after about 10^9 years a stable star with a planetary system about it.

At this point it is necessary to repeat that we are still speaking of assumptions. The model just described for the formation of a planetary system is an assumption. How reasonable an assumption is it? I suggest two ways to address this question: (1) generate computer models and see how reasonable the results are; (2) compare what we predict with what we observe. The second approach takes us to the next part of my paper, but I wish to make a few general reflections here. When we examine the distribution of stars, according to their temperature and mass in our own Galaxy and in other galaxies, the model proposed for the formation of stars, appears to be reasonable. And when we determine the ages of stars and of galaxies by methods independent of the assumptions made in the above model of star formation, it all appears to be consistent. Even our knowledge of elementary particle physics, a totally independent field of research, supports what we have said about the thermonuclear processes installs. So, our assumption appears to be consistent with what we observe, but we shall say more of this shortly.

The first suggestion I made was to generate computer models, based on the assumptions, and see how well they fit with what we know of our planetary system. We do this by computer simulations, each of which represents 10^5 years of evolution. By "simulation" is meant applying the laws of physics (gravity, momentum conservation, etc.) to a cloud of gas and dust which has the following characteristics: the gas/dust density is the same at all distances above and below the plane of asymmetry of the evolving disk (this cannot be completely correct, certainly at the beginning of the disk evolution, but we accept it as a simplifying assumption); the gas/dust density is 6.2 grams per cm3 at 0.45 AU [AU = Astronomical Unit, the mean distance of the Earth from the Sun] from the parent star and it decreases with distance from the parent star. Why the magic inner edge of 0.45 AU? The answer: the star will capture any gas or dust closer to the star.

At the end we find the distribution of planets formed from the planetesimals at the end of 10^7 years. We note that in each case the resultant distribution of planets is similar to the actual distribution in our planetary system. The simulations presume that giant, gaseous planets (like Jupiter, Saturn, Uranus and Neptune) will be formed, but it does not calculate such evolution, since that is expected to be a much more complicated process.

We do the calculations twice: first we assume that the mass of the parent star is taken as the mass of the Sun and then in a second calculation 1.5 times the mass of the Sun. While this does not have a noticeable effect on the resultant distribution of planets, it has a serious effect on the location of the "Habitable zone" (HZ). The HZ, defined by the simple assumptions given in the first paragraph of this section, extends from about 0.8 to 1.4 AU for a solar mass star but from 1.8 to 3.2 AU for a star of 1.5 solar masses. This shift in the HZ is due principally to the larger surface temperature of the more massive star and, therefore, to the higher temperatures for the inner regions of the cloud.

The computer simulations, even with all of their simplifying assumptions, allow us to draw the following conclusions: (1) a planetary system like ours with a planet like the Earth located in a "habitable zone" is not unusual; (2) even stars more massive than the Sun may develop such systems; (3) it is unlikely that a planet like the Earth would exist in a "habitable zone" about a star much more massive than the Sun. It appears that an earth-like planet in an HZ can occur only about stars that have a mass not very different from that of the Sun.

We are still in the realm of assumptions. What observational evidence is there that the birth and death of stars occur as proposed and that planets form about some of them?

Observations on the Existence of Extra-Solar Planets

Only in the past decade have we been able to develop the sophisticated techniques required to discover planets about other stars. These planets have been discovered by analysing the systematic oscillations in the motion of the parent star. Only massive planets near to their parent star can be discovered in this way. So, the method is very limited. In no case, do we have an Earth-like planet in a habitable zone.

There are many difficulties associated not only with the discovery of extra-solar planets, but even with the definition of what we are seeking. The detection limit depends on the mass of the planet and its proximity to the parent star. Jupiter and Saturn, the most massive planets in the solar system, could not be so detected if we observed our own planetary system from the nearest star to the sun. Furthermore, according to their mass we can distinguish three kinds of objects: actual planets, "brown dwarfs" and real stars. To understand the difference among these objects we must recall the description of the birth of stars. If the collapsing cloud has less than about 0.1 solar masses it cannot raise the internal temperature high enough to start a thermonuclear furnace; so, no star is formed. The object still shines but not by thermonuclear energy. It has short-lived residual gravitational energy and is called a "brown dwarf"; "dwarf" because it is similar to the smallest stars known; "brown" because, since it does not have a thermonuclear furnace, it does not, as a star does, radiate much energy in the blue to red regions of the spectrum. The separation by mass between "brown dwarfs" and planets is ambiguous and it is difficult to separate out these objects. And yet they are very different kinds of objects. Planets form by the accretion of planetesimals, as we have described; "brown dwarfs" form like stars do by the collapse of a cloud fragment. So, the formation processes are very different; but the resultant object may lie on the observational borderline. This is even further complicated by the fact that the exact mass is uncertain, since we do not know the tilt of the orbit of the object about the parent star.

The conclusions to be drawn from the observations described above are: (1) the discovery of extra-solar planets by studying the motion of the parent star is promising, but the results thus far are few; (2) some of the objects discovered thus far may actually be "brown dwarfs"; (3) no Earth-like planets in a habitable zone have been discovered; (4) the discoveries made thus far do not complement the computer simulations we have discussed, but there is an observational prejudice to discovering massive planets close to the parent star. Some have proposed that the existence of massive planets close to the parent star is due to the migration of these planets towards the parent star after their formation in the outer zones of the gestating planetary system. This would, of course, change very much our discussion of habitable zones. However, since so little is known about such migrations, it seems of little use at this time to rethink our discussion of habitable zones. We must, nonetheless, confess to a great deal of ignorance in the matter. Other techniques, such as high-resolution imaging in space and from the Earth, spectroscopic detection of extra-solar planetary atmospheres, etc., are being developed. Within the next decade we will undoubtedly discover hundreds of candidates as extra-solar planets. We may also, based upon observations and our knowledge of the formation of planets and stars, pose some convincing statistical considerations.

Statistical Considerations

Since there are about 10^{11} stars in the Galaxy and 10^{11} galaxies in the universe, there are 10^{22} stars in the universe. From our knowledge of the distribution of stars by mass in the Galaxy, we can estimate that about 30% of stars are solar-like. We know that about 30% of stars are double or multiple, a fact that may, for dynamical reasons, exclude the formation of planets. It would be difficult to estimate the percentage of solar-like stars that would have developed a planetary system, but from our knowledge of the formation of the solar system and the computer simulations we have discussed, we know that the probability is neither zero nor one hundred percent. Let us say it is 10%. How many of these planets would be like the Earth: its mass, distance from the Sun, an atmosphere, etc. This may be even more uncertain, but, again, from geological knowledge of the formation of the atmosphere, we know that there is a finite probability. Let us say it is 2%. Now, if we put all of these considerations together we have, from these statistical considerations, 10^{17} Earth-like planets in the universe.

It is important to note the nature of this conclusion. It is based upon scientific facts combined with reasonable estimates which are themselves based upon scientific facts. Unless our scientific thinking is drastically wrong, this conclusion is acceptable and merits our further considerations about what it implies. I take it to mean at a minimum that the macroscopic physical conditions for life (an earth-like planet in a "habitable zone" about a solar-like star) exist elsewhere in the universe. We must also note that we have not spoken of extra-terrestrial life nor even directly of the conditions for extra-terrestrial life. Indirectly, however, we cannot ignore the question: if there is this degree of statistical certainty and at least some modest observational evidence that extra-terrestrial Earths exist, is there extra-terrestrial life? While, for various reasons, it is impossible here to address that question directly, the very asking has religious implications which we will soon discuss. One of the principal reasons for the lack of any direct approach to the question of extra-terrestrial life is the great uncertainty that still exists among geologists and biologists as to our scientific knowledge of the origins of life on the Earth. Lacking that knowledge, we can only speak directly of the macroscopic physical conditions for extra-terrestrial life and of what religious considerations are implied.

Challenges for Religious Thought

My considerations here are three: (1) Life in the Universe. Judging from what we know scientifically of the universe, the marvel is not whether there is life elsewhere, but that there is life at all; (2) Chance or Necessity? Did life arise by chance or by necessity and what does this say about God the Creator? (3) The God of Extra-Terrestrials. If there is intelligent life elsewhere, did Christ come to save them?

Life in the Universe

Evolution is an intrinsic and proper characteristic of the universe. Neither the universe as a whole nor any of its ingredients can be understood except in terms of evolution. And evolution is a daily happening. We, for instance, are constantly exchanging atoms with the total reservoir of atoms in the universe. Each year 98% of the atoms in our bodies are renewed. Each time we breath we take in billions and billions of atoms recycled by the rest of breathing organisms during the past few weeks. Nothing in my genes was present a year ago. It is all new, regenerated from the available energy and matter in the universe. My skin is renewed each month and my liver each six weeks. In brief, human beings are among the most recycled beings in the universe.

Life has made a relatively late appearance considering the total age of the universe. Life is thought to have emerged about three billion (3×10^9) years ago in its first microscopic forms. This was about twelve billion years after the Big Bang and about seven billion years after the formation of the first stars. Why did it take so long for life to emerge? In order to provide the chemical abundances required for life it is estimated that three generations of stars were required. It is only through nucleosynthesis in stellar interiors that the heavier elements can be created and at the death of a star this material is regurgitated to form the matrix for a new generation of stars. The lifetime of a star depends upon its total mass and can vary from several millions of years for a very massive star to tens of billions of years for lower mass stars. At any rate it took about ten billion years of stellar evolution to produce carbon, nitrogen, oxygen, etc. I repeat that the universe is by its nature evolutionary and it had to evolve to be big and old before it could contain us. I was tempted to say, "in order to contain us," but that would have introduced a finality which may not be justified scientifically.

The question is further complicated by the following consideration: as the universe evolved the appearance of life required a very fine-tuning of the various constants of nature and the laws whereby the universe applies those constants. Let me give a few examples. If the velocity of expansion of the universe at its beginning were one millionth greater or smaller than it was, we would not be here, because the universe would either have expanded so fast that no complex systems could come to be or it would have almost immediately collapsed in upon itself. If the mass of the proton and the electron differed by an extremely small amount, we would not be here, because stars like the sun would not have stable enough energy mechanisms to provide for the long time required to generate the chemical abundances necessary for life. If the energy level of the carbon molecule, which is created by two nuclear reactions beginning with four helium atoms, were only slightly less than it is, the abundance of carbon in the universe would be millions of times less than it is and totally inadequate to provide the chemical processes which led to life. Now all the constants of nature, a few examples of which I have just mentioned, are empirical values, discovered as it were in a laboratory. They could have different values and, if they did, we would not be here. Would you allow me to ask as a scientist: WHY are we here? To the best of my knowledge, no satisfactory scientific explanation has been given for this fine tuning of the universe. Life in the universe is a marvel; its origins are not completely understood scientifically.

Chance or Necessity?

Did the fine tuning of the universe and the consequent emergence of life happen by chance? The calculated probability is extremely small and not acceptable as a scientific answer. Granted that pure chance is not a satisfactory explanation, we might still ask to what extent chance played a role. The religious inclinations of Albert Einstein are not well understood. In his physics, however, he was clearly deterministic. In the debate over the meaning of quantum mechanical indeterminism he claimed that God does not play with dice. Recently an eminent biochemist has replied: Yes he does, because he is certain to win. In attempting to frame his conclusion in the context of Einstein's statement, what he was actually claiming is that intrinsic to the universe there is an interplay of determinism, chance and opportunity. His response to Einstein was to state that it is in the very nature of the universe that intelligent life inevitably come to be, although a long and complicated process involving laws, chance happenings and propitious opportunities was required. The important new consideration here is the notion of "opportunity." Neither chance nor necessity will succeed without it.

It appears to me that this state of affairs in our current knowledge of the universe and our place in it is an invitation to proceed beyond strictly scientific considerations to more transcendental considerations. The invitation, I would propose, comes from science. The ultimate answer to the "why" almost certainly will not.

Finally, it appears to me that, if we accept the invitation offered by this new scientific conception of the intrinsic struggles of the universe to realise itself in self-reflecting beings, we have a new way of using the process of analogy to come to a richer understanding of God through his creation. In our own personal freedom we participate in God's freedom. In an analogous way God has made the universe free. In its struggle to become it reflects God's loveliness, his tender care to allow us to be what we will be and in a universe which is always becoming what it will become.

The God of Extra-Terrestrials

This is the least scientific of my considerations thus far, so please permit a somewhat abrupt change in literary style. In his *Metaphysics* Aristotle states:

> It is owing to their wonder that men first began to philosophise; they wondered originally at the obvious, and then they advanced little by little to the greater matters, about the phenomena of the moon and those of the sun and the stars (*Metaphysics* II, 2).

Immanuel Kant likewise stated:

> Two things fill the mind with ever new and increasing admiration and awe: the starry heavens above and the moral law within (Kant, 1997).

Enrico Fermi recalls that one night while sitting under the stars he overheard a group of farmers nearby and remembers a robust voice stating: "What a nice sky! How can some people say that God does not exist?"

The thoughts or reports of these three eminent personages reveal the almost inevitable link in people's minds between the exploration of the Universe and thoughts about God. However, please note a progression from Aristotle's philosophising to Kant's moralising to the God of Fermi's farmer. While all three intellectual experiences are intimately linked, they are distinct and, with your indulgence, I have made a choice to talk about God only, and, indeed, about the God of Fermi's farmer. I do this because there is no doubt that the experience of Fermi's farmer is the most common one and, in my mind, the truest one. So I will not philosophise and I will certainly not enter into the mine-field of ethics, of what is right and wrong. I wish simply to say a few things about what farmers think about God in view of what cosmologists think about life in the universe.

How can there be human beings elsewhere in the universe? After all God sent his only son, Jesus Christ, true God and true man to this Earth. He was born in Bethlehem, he lived in Nazareth, and he was crucified on Calvary, outside Jerusalem. And God had only one Son. Now how could God send his only Son, who is truly a man, to other planets. Can a man exist on many different planets? But maybe Jesus did not have to arrive on other planets even though there are people with souls there.

The farmer knows his religion very well, so his musings are very incisive and, after listening to them for a long time, we are able to piece together the following sequence of hypotheses about the religious consequences of there being intelligent beings elsewhere.

Human beings have bodies which came forth after about 12 billion years in an evolving universe. Those bodies are very complex totalities, but most of all the human brain is the most complex organism we know. As a consequence human beings are intelligent, they can know themselves knowing and so they have a soul, a spiritual reality, and as such they were made by God. Are there other such beings, made by God, on other planets. We come to our first hypothesis. Yes, by assumption, we will call them by their traditional name of ETs.

At the very beginning human beings did something bad. They revolted against the God who had made them. Theologians call this "original sin." Even if we do not accept the Scripture story of Adam and Eve as historically true, "original sin" is an essential element in the theologians view of the relationship of humans to God. Did our ETs sin in this way? We come to our second hypothesis and, in order to keep the discussion going, we, of course, answer "yes, they sinned." Note that our second hypothesis is very different from the first. That we sinned is an historical fact and, therefore, quite contingent. It might not have happened. Whereas, ETs existing at all is not quite so contingent. In fact, many scientists maintain that, if life came to be at all, it MUST have come to be prolifically in this universe. There is a kind of necessity, although not absolute, about there being ETs.

God freely chose to redeem human beings from their sin. Did he do this also for ETs? Now we are getting ever more hypothetical, since we are determining what God, who is absolutely free, would freely choose to do. In fact, there are serious theological implications here for our understanding of God. With Fermi's farmer, who senses that God is good and passionate, the answer is "yes, God did save them." How could he be God and leave ETs in their sin? After all he was good to us—why should he not be good to them? With the farmer we are struggling to justify our hypothesis, but we accept it not realising that matters are going to get more difficult as we proceed.

God chose a very specific way to redeem human beings. He sent his only Son, Jesus, to them and Jesus gave up his life so that human beings would be saved from their sin. Did God do this for ETs? Or did he chose another way to redeem ETs? The theological implications about God are getting evermore serious. Surely God is completely free to chose his methods. He certainly did not have to send his Son to us. But once he chose to do so, did he have to chose to redeem ETs in the same way. There is deeply embedded in Christian theology, throughout the Old and New Testament but especially in St. Paul and in St. John the Evangelist, the notion of the universality of God's redemption and even the notion that all of creation, even the inanimate, participates in some way in his redemption. In his own way Fermi's farmer realises this and so he concludes that, if God is truly the God we know from how he revealed himself to us, then "yes, he sent his only Son to redeem ETs."

After this whole sequence of hypotheses, increasingly more difficult to make, we come to a serious responsibility to rethink some fundamental realities within the context of religious belief. What is the human being? Could Jesus Christ, fully a human being, exist on more than one planet at more than one time? We are obviously very limited today in our ability to answer such questions. We cannot rely, even theologically, solely upon God's revelation to us in the Scriptures and in the Churches, since that revelation was TO US and was received, therefore, in a very anthropocentric sense. We have come a long way since God revealed himself to us in a special way. And so, even theologians, if they are as wise as Fermi's farmer, must learn from the best of science, both the life sciences and the physical sciences, because they are an important ingredient in our continuing search to understand ourselves in God's universe.

References

Aritstotle. 1999. *Metaphysics*. J. Sachs, trans. U.S.A.: Green Lion Press.

Kant, I. 1997. *Critique of Practical Reason*. Ed. M. Gregor. Cambridge, MA: Cambridge University Press.

Chapter 8

Metaphors of Divine Love Through the Sciences

Yvon Provençal, CEGEP de Granby

Introduction

In a previous article (Provençal, 1997), I proposed an epistemological hypothesis which posits the existence of a structure much more complex than the human brain. This structure would be comparable to the whole set of scientific and philosophical conceptions in contemporary human society. As a form of consciousness, it has been described using the expression, "mind of society." Since this structure appears to exhibit rapid growth, I have supposed that, of all complex structures presently known to us, the young child's brain provides the best analogy. Contemporary human beings would, then, be analogous to the cells of this gigantic brain. The reader will excuse my use of the term "god" to designate something very different from the gods or God of the religious traditions. As a matter of fact, I am not concerned here with religious questions but with concepts and notions treated in an entirely rational way amenable to modern criticism. The reader will, I hope, pardon me again for presenting this paper somewhat as if it were a work of fiction.

However, it is not fiction but a real attempt at rational clarification using a bold hypothesis that is, on the whole, credible, particularly if we take into account all the information presently available to us.

This method, which I have called "ideometry," consists in looking at the ideas we have about real things rather than at the things themselves. An ideometric survey of contemporary ideas allows us to establish correspondences between concepts in various fields of knowledge ranging from mathematics, physics and biology to anthropology and social science. For example, paradoxes in ideas about the emergence of life in the pre-biotic universe correspond to those encountered in ideas about the emergence of human culture within the pre-human biological world. Ideometry appears, therefore, as a formalization of ideas. It allows us to look at existing ideas without having to presuppose anything about the truth or reality of these conceptions. In this way it is possible to establish striking correspondences between the most fundamental notions or questions in the above-mentioned domains. Ideometric correspondences appear as unsuspected regularities.

The "mind of society" designates the whole range of contemporary ideas throughout the various domains of science and, more generally, rational thought. Analogical correspondences are established by first taking this unusual "mind" and trying to state its most prominent characteristics and its changes, whether recent or to come. These are then related to the mind of the young child, to what it is and the way in which it develops mentally. The "child" thus becomes a metaphor of the whole of humanity. From an ideometric point of view, it makes sense to establish correspondences between the history of ideas as they occur in science and epistemology, and child psychology as a description of the stages of mental development. Taken globally, the history of human society corresponds ideometrically to the complete ontogenesis of the child from the state of conception through the embryonic, fetal, newborn, infant and other stages. Within this general framework of correspondences, the main points of connection, that is, the nodal points from which the lines of correspondence branch out, are linked to differences in determination relationships. This point needs clarification.

Correspondence of Determination Relationships

Physics, biology and anthropology are characterized by the concept of *complete structure*. This takes the form, respectively, of the atom, the biological cell and the human being. A complete structure is, by definition, the constitutive unit of a whole range of reality, such as is envisaged in any of the above-mentioned disciplines. Therefore, the notion of complete structure is a transdisciplinary concept denoting an ideometric relation that exists throughout these three domains at the same time. In this case we can speak about an ideometric *sequence*. From a formal point of view, this sequence is defined by the repetition of a relation endowed with the properties of anti-equivalence. In each instance, that is, at each level of complete structure, a given substructure appears as the epistemological focus for key issues in the related discipline. With the atom come the atomic nucleus and the problems of physical forces and elementary particles; the biological cell presents us with problems relative to DNA and the genetic code; and as far as individual human beings are concerned, we have the problems concerning the brain and mental capacities. Each of these problems constitutes the basis of research programs that are of crucial importance for the whole of contemporary science. We should point out here that each one of the above-mentioned domains exhibits a specific kind of determinism or line of determination. The differences between these kinds of determination appear as one of the main factors that researchers take into account when they attempt to gauge the importance of a concept or question for their own domain. For example, the distinction between physical and biological types of determination is fundamental for the biologist investigating the emergence of the first living cell. In the biologist's view, a problem exists inasmuch as biological determinations cannot be explained entirely in terms of physical ones. In ideometrical terms, this conceptual sequence can be expressed as follows: in terms of complexity, the human brain is to the living cell what the latter is to the atom. Here the term "complexity" must not be understood as applying to "real systems" but, rather, to the domain of rational conceptions and problems. The following table illustrates this situation:

Complete structure / Problematical substructure		
Physics	atom	nucleus
Biology	cell	DNA
Anthropology	human being	human brain
...	...	...

The suspension points indicate that the sequence could, in principle, be continued. This means that, formally speaking, nothing prevents us from considering the possible existence of a sort of complete structure exhibiting a higher level of complexity. I am referring to global human society. This immediately presents itself as the locus of an important class of problems relating to its origin, general meaning and direction. The level associated with this new type of complete structure will be called "meta-anthropological." The expression "theotic" (from the Greek *theos*, god) will also be used to qualify terms at this level, in order to bring out the supra-human level of complexity involved. The expression, "language of the gods" can then be understood as follows.

The "Language of the Gods"

Corresponding to each term in the sequence "biological/anthropological/meta-anthropological" is a type of determination, complexification and progressive organization that happens to be linked to a specific sort of "language." In biology, the expression "genetic code" designates the system that contains and uses the information at the root of all the existing life forms. Variations in genetic information, or changes in genomes over time, produce biological evolution. At the anthropological level, human languages exhibit ideometric correspondences to the genetic code. The arbitrariness of the linguistic sign corresponds to the arbitrary nature of the correspondence between amino and nucleic acids. The capacity to store and transmit information about cultural traits, whether these are transmitted orally or in writing, corresponds to the analogous genetic capacity for storing and transmitting genotypical and phenotypical characters of species. The elements of the genetic code are molecular: they comprise the four bases of nucleic acids and the twenty amino acids recognized by the theoreticians of molecular biology. The basic elements of human language are phonemes. These are the relatively few sound units from which all words and sentences are constituted. These sound units are determined by specific organs such as the tongue, larynx, etc. Their mode of production is essentially physiological and is linked, therefore, to biological complexity. In this respect, phonemes are more complex units than the basic elements of biological language, i.e., molecules. The mode of constitution of the latter derives essentially from physical laws. In human tongues we can recognize a kind of language which is clearly more complex than the genetic code, inasmuch as the living cell is more complex than the atom and biological determinations are more complex than physical ones. Following this approach, we can establish an ideometric sequence of language types, the terms of which represent an increasing level of complexity. At the meta-anthropological level, the basic unit must be more complex than a sound unit and reflect the specific type of complexity found at the anthropological level. The *ideas*, in the general sense of notions, concepts, theories, questions, problems, etc., appear to constitute the appropriate type of unit. Among these, a relatively small number of "fundamental ideas" represent the basic elements from which scientific theories or philosophical systems are elaborated. For example, notions like those of identity, difference, time, space, subject, object, etc. may be considered as the basic elements in several theories or systems. The following sequence then can be considered:

> *Biological organization*: the genetic code (based on nucleic acid *molecules*)
> *Anthropological organization*: human languages (based on the *sounds* emitted by the human voice, i.e., the phonemes)
> *Meta-anthropological organization*: meta-language (based on *works of human creation*)

According to this perspective, works of human creation appear as the meta-phonemes of a meta-language, that is to say, a kind of language more complex than any human tongue. The particular combination of these meta-phonemes is what creates the specific meanings of this new kind of language. Just like the arrangements of molecules in the genetic code or of sounds in human language, the combination of units at this new level must be *arbitrary*. The word "arbitrary" means not determined by an underlying substratum. According to biology, the rules of combination in the genetic code have been produced by "chance"—in other words, they are not determined by physical laws. Likewise, linguists hold that the sound combinations produced in human languages are arbitrary, in the sense that they are not derived from either biological or physical determinations. Finally, with respect to language of a higher order of complexity, arbitrariness at the meta-anthropological level signifies (and in a way that is consistent ideometrically) that the meta-significant combinations of ideas are not attributable to any cultural, anthropological, biological or physical determinations. In each one of the three cases (i.e., the biological, anthropological and meta-anthropological), there appears a type of ordering which is not determined by the underlying substratum. Rather, it appears to be arbitrary and, in some way, as attributable to "chance." However, at each level we are dealing with a type of chance that produces order and meaning and is responsible for new forms and kinds of evolution.

Let us suppose now that we want to understand what exactly it is we mean by the new kind of language we have referred to above as the "language of the gods." First, in what way could we appreciate the fact of its existence? A first step toward an understanding of this language (and perhaps indeed the only one) would consist in drawing an analogy with the situation of conceptual complexity that precedes it in the ideometric sequence. Our situation within global human society is analogous to that of neurons in the brain of a young child who is on the verge of speech. The emergence of linguistic meaning in the child's brain means that a new kind of regularity is transmitted and recorded by its neurons. This is not equivalent to ordinary sensory perception, such as visual or tactile experience. The combination of certain precise impressions transmitted through neuron networks in the child's brain produces the new phenomenon we call linguistic signification.

By using this analogy we can begin to understand why ideometrical meta-signification has not been acknowledged until now. Moreover, it helps us to grasp the idea of a new type of signification produced by the arbitrary combination of theoretical units. From the perspective of individual neurons in the young child's brain, the new regularities associated with language can only appear as an abnormal irruption. If we consider only brain function, these arbitrary regularities are, as it were, attributable to an improbable and even unexplainable form of chance since their genesis and development lie outside the child's brain. Likewise, ideometric regularities cannot be attributable to any of the scientific (i.e., physical, biological, anthropological) determinations, since they connect determinations of this type, taken as conceptions produced by global human society. Therefore, they disclose the existence of a language operating at a higher level than the human languages already known to us. This language, which is also profoundly different from these human languages, is theotic—a "language of the gods."

Just as a child learns much more about external reality and itself when it acquires language in addition to the data of its senses, human society should be capable of using this new type of language to discover a wholly new realm of reality. It should be capable of understanding itself better than it has ever been able to using the existing sciences and philosophies.

Who are the "Gods," or Theotic Structures?

At this point we should specify the precise meaning of the term "theotic," as well as the sense in which one has to understand the expression "language of the gods." Which "gods" are we talking about here? How exactly are they related to the gods or God of religious tradition? First of all, these "gods" must not be conceived as absolutes. Rather, they must be seen as being as limited, at their own level, as human beings, biological cells or atoms are at their respective levels. Indeed they amount to a type of complete structure, but one at a higher level of complexity. However, the adjective "divine" (or "theotic," if one prefers) remains a most appropriate way of designating these new structures, inasmuch as we are describing structures so much more complex than anything known until now that even the human brain is ridiculously simple by comparison. Ideometrically speaking, global human society is to the human brain what the latter is to one of its cells. Human beings are conscious in a way unknown to mere cells, and can do things that a cell could never do. However, neurons with their molecular and atomic constituents are complex to such a point that we can talk about them as containing the beginnings of a rudimentary consciousness. Also, biological organization can be seen as incomparably more powerful than lifeless matter. To be convinced of this, one has only to consider the diversity, mobility and evolutionary capacity of the numerous forms of terrestrial life. It is admissible, therefore, to speak about an *infinitely* greater complexity and power when we compare the living cell with a mere atom, or the human brain with a mere cell. Likewise, a theotic structure must be seen as infinitely complex, creative and powerful compared with a human being. Of course we have to accept the idea that an entity can be infinite and limited at the same time. This logical paradox arises from the ideometric approach: theotic structures are infinite compared with human beings, yet they are limited at their own level of reality.

Another logical paradox arises with respect to these theotic structures: we have to admit that they surpass human beings, yet are fully human. Ideometric correspondence leads to this contradiction, which is only an apparent one. Human beings and their cultures must be considered as being beyond the biological world and its laws inasmuch as the various features of cultural creativity are not determined by biological laws or principles. Nevertheless, human being are fully biological creatures and, as such, must be compatible with the principles of living matter. Similarly, human beings are physical and material entities yet they are, in some defined way, beyond matter. This is what leads us to say (and this is fully consistent with what we have said so far) that theotic structures are at one and the same time fully human—living and material—yet transcend the human and natural worlds.

How Does Theotic Language Appear to Us?

We must not confuse the first stammerings of theotic language with the sophisticated languages of contemporary human science. The kind of language that concerns us here exists at a very different level and, apart from formal ideometric features, has practically nothing in common with human languages or with the various scientific languages or jargons (including, for example, mathematical equations). It is now time to start identifying the shared features with greater precision.

Linguistics and child psychology will be particularly useful in helping us recognize these formal features. For language at the theotic level, such as it appears to us, corresponds to human language as practised by a very young child. Therefore, contemporary human society is engaged in a still naive use of this language. Human tongues share certain common features; these include a set of fundamental sounds called phonemes, which are the basic elements used to form the signifying symbols we call words. The combination of words in accordance with a limited number of grammatical rules allows for the construction of an unlimited number of sentences. A similar combinatory feature already exists in the genetic code. Nucleic acid molecules gather into "codons," which in turn gather into more complex units such as genes. Thus, here too we find certain fundamental constitutive elements of words that subsequently combine to make sentences. The repetition of these characteristics at such distinct levels of ideas is likely to be considered as a mere ideometric fact.

We should be able to find these characteristics again at a higher level, and in a more complex language. In this case the basic sounds are replaced by major works of human creation, and word combinations are replaced by arbitrary combinations of these basic works. Examples of the latter type of combination would include certain relations among disciplines.

It is striking that a central problem of modern linguistics consists in understanding how a child acquires the ability to speak its mother tongue. This question corresponds very closely to the one being raised here: how could contemporary human society develop its ability to speak the language at the level of complexity proper to it? As for linguists, the problem of language acquisition by the child is accentuated by the fact that the normal stimulus, i.e., that derived from the parents, seems too weak to adequately account for the phenomenon. It is the same for contemporary humanity ... theotic structures do not appear to provide a strong manifestation of their language, at least not in a way that is clearly discernible or understandable to contemporary science.

Child psychologists have established, however, that the most precocious function of spoken language is not communication but rather symbolization. Language is first of all useful to the child for internalizing and representing its thoughts. It gives the child a strategy for better structuring its thought, that is, its whole representation of the world and of itself. Theotic language seems to appear in the same way to humanity in the infantile stage, which uses it first for structuring its own thought. This takes the form of the existing scientific and philosophical ideas.

Theotic language may be further clarified by several aspects of language development that are covered in child psychology. The way in which children acquire language is almost invariably the same: parents speak to their child in a nearly normal way, although they know that a child of that age cannot comprehend what they say. The child does not understand, but tries to guess (Suzanne Borel-Maisonny, 1969, 8–10) the meaning of their words. We have to imagine a similar situation for humanity: if theotic structures were to "speak" to it, they would be content to address it in their own language. Undoubtedly they would not try to communicate with human beings in the latters' own tongues. To do so would be absurd; it would be as if parents tried to communicate with their child's neurons rather than with the child itself. In this sense, we must not be surprised that the "gods" have not yet made contact with us in a clearer manner. This is not ill will on their part!

God's Love as an Explanatory Principle

In this paper, I will also try to apply the same ideometric method, to the global history of scientific ideas and geopolitics. The use of God's love as an explanatory principle does not, of course, fall within the horizon of social science such as it is currently practised. However, the conceptual correspondence between humanity and the child can help us show that several problematic features of the history, particularly the recent history, of scientific ideas can be treated in a more rational way if we accept the existence of a kind of exterior effect corresponding entirely to that of the mother upon the child. Like parental love, the kind of influence we are talking about here is diffuse and indirect, yet essential and constant.

I am aware of the apparent incongruity of such an approach. However this claims to have an objective and profoundly rational character. My conception of rationality is not that of the theologians, who accept the *a priori* existence of an act of faith. Rather, it is a form of rationality which is in accordance with the critical sense of contemporary philosophers and scientists. Our proper subject here is ideas, that is, considered apart from any judgments about the reality they describe with more or less accuracy. Hence the relations between ideas, that is, ideometric relations, have an objective value, the validity of which depends only on data available in the existing corpus of scientific texts. Maternal love is a key concept in child psychology, as it has developed so far. According to psychologists and pediatricians, the mother has a profound effect upon the child's development. They affirm that the child needs her constant affection, and would not survive without the care she gives it. However, they also concede that the mother's influence on the physical and mental development of the child must be consistent with the progressive growth of autonomy in the latter. This means that the child must generally solve the numerous problems it confronts in the most autonomous way possible, and with the feeling that it does so by itself. Problems associated with the child's physiological growth must naturally be solved as they arise, using the resources of the child's own body. Cognitive problems, such as those associated with sensorimotor integration and the general intellectual development of the child, must also be solved by the child itself, that is, through the endogenic development of its own nervous system. It is also true that, without its mother, the child would have no chance to develop in this way. The mother's role is, however, essentially an indirect one. She must ensure the conditions required for the child's endogenic development by acting upon its surroundings and managing a whole set of physical and psychological factors that promote this development. We have to understand, therefore, that where humanity is concerned, the "mother's influence" is also indirect and implicit. History, as described by qualified authors, appears therefore as a realm in which human beings can only attempt to solve their problems on their own. They cannot rely on miracles, that is, on supernatural interventions of the divinity. Divine action must be conceived as directed toward the *possible* rather than toward the real.

Both psychology and pediatrics consider maternal love an important factor in child development. I propose to see it as analogous to an "explanatory principle" of what happens to the child. Many aspects of its person, including its existence and growth and the external factors that impact on its surroundings, can be explained only by taking into account that there is someone who loves it and takes care of it.

If we now consistently establish the correspondence with humanity throughout its history, it becomes possible to accept an explanatory principle of love. In this case, we are dealing with a "theotic love principle" which translates the conduct of a "theotic mother" towards a "theotic child." This conduct must be viewed as external to child-humanity and its whole conception of reality, the latter being equivalent to the child's for-itself. This exterior of reality is conceived of as a set of "possibilities." Human science and philosophy have only a very rudimentary idea of this set of possibilities. Expressions like "doing what is possible" or "changing what is possible" can still have only a very hazy meaning. They should, however, receive ample clarification in the relatively near future. A child who has not yet learned to speak has only a very rudimentary idea of the reality surrounding its own body. When its mother acts upon the objects it comes into contact with, the child generally does not know what she is doing, nor why. Only later does it become conscious of the more or less direct benefits it reaps from its mother's actions. And even then it is not aware of the causal relation between its mother and these benefits. Instead, it tends to believe, in a naturally egocentric manner, that what happens to it happens for no particular reason and is, as it were, its due simply for existing. Therefore child-humanity accepts "possibilities" as a matter of course, as entirely merited, but has no clear idea of what produces or transforms them. In ideometrical terms, it appears that the theotic mother constantly acts upon the possibilities available to child-humanity. But she does not act directly on reality itself (such as it is conceived by humanity, in correspondence with the for-itself of the child). Such action would correspond to that of a mother who intervenes unduly into matters affecting the child's own body or mind. Such direct action would be tantamount to the production of "miracles." Now, the theotic mother much prefers to act in an indirect way, letting child-humanity itself produce the effects it wishes or desires. The reason for this is clear: a loving mother will first and foremost attempt to help her child become autonomous and progressively more and more capable of providing itself with the means of its own subsistence and development. A baby, however, has a long way to go before acquiring complete autonomy. Nevertheless, we are dealing with a rapidly growing organism, and must measure its progress as much in relation to what it was (namely, an embryo and foetus with practically no autonomy whatsoever) as with respect to what it will be later on. This child corresponds to contemporary child-humanity, whose cognitive and technological capacities are enormous with respect to past humanity but doubtless ridiculously low with respect to what they should "normally" be in the future. I am referring to a time when child-humanity will have grown up, acquired greater autonomy and the capacity to fully acknowledge the existence of its mother and other theotic agencies. At that point, it will have fully recognized its possibilities for knowledge and action.

Let me clarify certain points concerning the actions of the theotic mother. The latter places possibilities at the disposal of child-humanity, letting it realize them for itself. For example, contemporary humanity has discovered new scientific and political possibilities which did not exist as such before the modern age. Indeed, in certain cases they did not exist before a more recent period, namely, the end of the twentieth century. This does not mean that the theotic mother "prompts" humanity by supplying it with answers when it comes up against problems. She does not "prompt" but contents herself with placing "possibility-objects" (i.e., "toys") within reach, so that child-humanity can handle and explore them.

What we have called "new possibilities" for humanity are generally interpreted as states of scientific or philosophical thought that result from "transformations" in history. The status and origin of these "transformations" are, however, not clear. A simple scientific view might attribute them to some change, such as, for example, a modification of cultural conditions. This situation corresponds, at a conceptual level, to the "egocentric" point of view manifested by the young child in relation to the objects placed at its disposal: for these objects are entirely "for it," and even "from it," since the child is still incapable of conceiving of alterity.

Thus these "possibilities" placed more or less within reach of child-humanity still appear very hazily to us. Currently, the best representation of them can doubtlessly be found in what we call mathematics. This appears to us as a very rich and inexhaustible set of "physical possibilities," which we call "theoretical models" or "models of possible universes." These models provide us with useful conceptual bases, especially in technology. They possess great practical worth, in addition to being immensely important conceptually, in the formulation of physical theories. Child-humanity explores these mathematical "possibilities" and discovers "reality" through them. This situation corresponds to that of a child handling the objects in its environment and thus discovering itself, that is to say, what it is and what it is capable of. However, mathematics as we currently know it undoubtedly presents only a very sketchy outline of what child-humanity might be capable of discovering in the future, especially with the help of theotic "language," which is still not at all mastered. The same holds for rational domains which do not belong to mathematics. Geopolitics, for instance, has specific explanatory models that have only gradually emerged from the realm of possibilites within the history of human ideas. What we call "cold war logic" or "the balance of terror" are based on the existence of new nuclear weapons and appear as the models of a new logic in history. In this case, humanity understands itself as "free" to realize or ignore these models, to put them into practice or not.

The explorations and discoveries of child-humanity are genuinely its own. However it is the "mother" who makes them possible. From the point of view of humanity, the theotic mother may appear as a "very powerful divinity." We are already familiar with the case of the "God of the philosophers," such as it was understood in the classical age. However, divinity in the modern sense would be a kind of matrix of the "possibilities" open to child-humanity. This divinity does not only actualize one universe from a set of possible universes. Rather, it goes much further, continually creating new possibilities. And it does this for the sole purpose of helping its child to actualize its potential.

The theotic principle of love may be expressed as follows: there is a type of causality that is essential, diffuse, constant and creative, and that acts upon humanity's actual possibilities but allows it to realize them itself so that it can evolve from the technological, scientific and philosophical standpoints.

From Equilibrium in the Child to Geopolitical Equilibrium

Although it is not clear initially whether such a method can apply to geopolitics, it will be shown that the ideometric approach is entirely compatible with the general aims of geopolitics, such as they are normally understood today. However, ideometry presupposes an entirely different understanding of rationality itself. We are dealing here with a more global type of rationality, that is to say, one more open to the search for the meaning of human thought as a whole. Geopolitics has already been defined as a rational undertaking that "attempts to correlate the main dynamic factors" which explain world organization at a given moment, and "results in an overview of an existing political situation and its possibilities" (Soppelsa, 1993, 1; my translation). This definition can be used just as it is. However, we may admit that these "possibilities" must be considered as open in an unusually broad manner. In our view, it is significant that experts in geopolitics are often primarily interested in "global equilibrium" rather than politics itself (*cf.* Touraine, 1995, 14). The notion of equilibrium will prove to be particularly important and significant within the framework of ideometry. What historians and sociologists refer to as global equilibrium in political, economical, technological and other matters corresponds with what psychologists and pediatricians describe as the overall equilibrium of the child in emotional, intellectual, physiological and other matters. Of course, we must constantly keep in mind the profound difference or alterity that exists between these two conceptual domains; for ideometric correspondences are established precisely on the basis of this alterity. Saying that humanity "corresponds" to the child means, first of all, that the former is irreducibly different from the latter, just as the the child is irreducibly different from its own cells.

The Equilibrium of the Child

Experts define the "equilibrium" of an organism in this way: "Equilibrium is the tendency of an organism to reach dynamic stability as an existing structure in which new events take place" (Seefeldt, Barbour, 1986, 394). The situation of the young child is characterized by a search for equilibrium that begins as early as the foetal stage. This equilibrium be physical, physiological, psychic, and so on. The foetus's search for the best position in its mother's womb is an attempt to obtain physical equilibrium. For example, the foetus' spine may end up close to that of the mother when she lies down, and this may cause some discomfort. Thus the baby kicks and twists in order to change its position (Warner and Rosenberg, 1976, 16). At birth, the child is even more physically unstable: its hands, eyes, neck and, indeed, almost its entire body, are ill-adapted to its surroundings. It enjoys practically no equilibrium, except when sleeping or feeding. Now the equilibrium of the child, as it is defined above, could also be that of child-humanity.

Humanity, as I stated in previous works (*cf.* Provençal, 1997), corresponds approximately to an eighteen-month-old child. At this age, the child still has all sorts of balance problems. Its psycho-emotional equilibrium is still precarious, as evinced by certain manifestations of anxiety such as prolonged bouts of crying without any apparent motive. It also has certain physical balance problems because this is the stage at which it is learning to walk.

Learning to walk

Walking is a precocious motor acquisition that rapidly develops into a complex function. This sets in motion a number of reflexes controlled by the brain stem, cerebellum and basal nuclei. But no specific center has been recognized for this function (*cf.* Rabischong, 1983). The physiological view of this matter is represented in the following statement: "Walking is an extremely complex activity. One need only observe a young child attempting this new activity to perceive the difficulties the potential walker must overcome" (Plas, Viel and Blans, 1983, 1, my translation). When it is about eighteen months old, the child can keep its balance in the standing position, but its balance is not stable. Falls are frequent at this stage. The child moves forward, spreading its legs for greater security. In addition, it opens its arms as if they were balancing poles designed to forestall possible falls. When the child wants to reach an object, it rushes forward and goes past it, often stopping when it falls to the floor (*cf.* Cohen, 1979, 90).

One of the salient points to remember from these descriptions is that the ability to walk sets in motion many mechanisms, some of which are unconscious actions. The situation of the budding walker is very different from the situation of the child who is learning to handle objects or coordinate its sense organs. Children learn to walk without being truly conscious of what they are doing. For instance, the cerebellum can learn and act autonomously, without any direct intervention on the part of the brain that responds to intention or voluntary consciousness. When children first learn to handle toys, for example, they are aware of what they are doing and their actions are completely willed or voluntary.

One aspect of the child's psychological situation appears as particularly important to some experts: the child must now assume responsibility for the consequences of its actions or decisions with respect to locomotion (*cf.* Stinson, 1990, 19). The child realizes that it can explore its surroundings by itself and reach places that were previously inaccessible. However, it also discovers that there is often a price to pay, which consists of relatively acute pain. This means that, for the first time in its life, it begins to understand that its freedom is great, so great indeed as to be apparently limitless. The child also realizes at this point that it can explore independently of its mother and can injure itself as a result of its own initiative. Thus it gradually learns from experience to foresee the consequences of its actions.

The Sufferings of the Child

The tears of the newborn child are generally interpreted as signs of physical or psychological suffering. They often seem to have no apparent or observable cause. It is generally agreed that a certain measure of equilibrium is lacking in the physiological or psycho-affective states of the child. Physiologists admit that suffering, by definition, implies continuity and duration, that it changes the whole attitude of a subject and transforms his/her relationship to the world. Pediatricians, of course, point out that babies often cry for very long periods, to the great distress of their parents. Existing theories on this matter are very limited. However, from our perspective, questions are as significant as good predictive theories.

At the conceptual level of ideometry, the psychological and physiological sufferings of the young child correspond to certain sociological and historical ideas. We are concerned here with violent conflicts and wars. These give rise, within human society, to an imbalance as significant as the pains felt by the young child. Qualified observers see in both of these a struggle to re-establish lost stability, a struggle that results in a new equilibrium or adaptation to the world. Sociologists of war, like those who study pain, deal with structures that exhibit catalysts and inhibiting agents, as well as development within certain thresholds or limits. In the respective cases, the conclusion is that war and suffering are part of a "normal" process. Physiologists believe that a pain is usually an alarm signal and that the very definition of suffering includes a positive element, a hope of relief. Some sociologists have advanced the hypothesis that wars serve sociological functions. They can, for example, constitute safety vales, providing an outlet for collective impulses and making it possible to re-establish demographic or economic equilibrium (*cf.* Cazeneuve, 1974). The suffering of the young child, as manifested in the shedding of tears, corresponds to socio-political conflicts such as violent struggles. These are ambivalent concepts. In one sense they are normal and functional, while in another they appear to be essentially intolerable. In both cases, some external factor operates to "normalize" (as much as possible) these intolerable states of affairs. The mother's actions tend to comfort the child and enable it to maintain its confidence in its own means. The corresponding role at the level of humanity as a whole is played by the *new possibilities* which appear before us. Like the child, humanity does not grasp the precise origin of what comforts it. New "models" constantly appear in knowledge in general, in the realms of science, technology and socio-political action.

Geopolitical Equilibrium

Geopolitics studies the conditions of international equilibrium. It is closely allied with the art of maintaining or modifying the balance of power between nations—tasks that usually fall to politicians and strategists. These disciplines are not exact sciences, since they have no true predictive capacity.

At the conceptual level, this situation corresponds to that of the child attempting to keep its balance while remaining largely unaware of the operative mechanisms that enable it to do so. For this is precisely what happens when the child is learning to walk. For the first time in its life, it comes up against the problem of adaptation which consists in its inability to become fully aware of all the actions required of its organism, a condition owing to the extreme complexity of the problems to be solved. In return, unconscious mechanisms originating mostly in the cerebellum allow it to accomplish what, from an external perspective, would seem to be incredible feats of balance.

Humanity, in learning to keep its balance on the geopolitical level, is in a conceptually similar situation. Human science corresponds to the child's incipient consciousness; the absence of scientific predictive capacity in the domain of international relationships corresponds, in a consistent manner, to the child's lack of awareness of its physiological mechanisms. The same consistency can be seen in the correlation between human beings' ability to overcome problems of international unbalance without the help of science and the child's capacity to overcome problems related to the complexity of locomotor mechanisms. Recent geopolitics provides eloquent and powerful illustrations of this correspondence, particularly in the situation created by nuclear weapons and the Cold War. Since geopoliticians normally claim to study global issues in a rational manner, this situation naturally appears to them as paradoxical.

The Paradoxes of Geopolitics

Experts in the field of geopolitics have remarked on a major paradox that has existed since World War II. I am alluding to the fact that international peace has been maintained through a plethora of conflicts. This paradox becomes more acute when we realize that global equilibrium is maintained *thanks to* particular cases of imbalance. For example, while their policies are ostensibly in favour of international peace, governments throughout the world have kept busy arming themselves (*cf.* Soppelsa, 1993, 6). It must be understood that the existence of nuclear weapons created a radically new situation, mingling deterrence with the possibility of massive and instantaneous destruction. As a result, the production of huge arsenals became a condition for the cessation of war (Touraine, 1995, 386). The arms race was spectacular in terms of quantity, quality and sophistication. Commentators spoke regularly about the "horizontal and vertical proliferation" of technology.

A few analysts concluded from this that nuclear proliferation was not destabilizing but, on the contrary, provided a guarantee of peace. Some of the most competent experts even used such astonishing expressions as "weapons of peace" to designate nuclear arms, and "lasting peace" to describe the very particular balance resulting from it (*cf.* Waltz, 1981). Others even described nuclear weapons as "life insurance" and the "ultimate guarantee" (*cf.* Touraine, 1995, 396).

That overall balance is achieved through a series of minor imbalances is a well-known theme in the physiology of walking. In order to walk, one must continually negotiate the lack of balance in one's own body. The peculiar dynamics of these minor imbalances are, paradoxically enough, sufficient to maintain balance during walking.

In other matters, none of the experts in geopolitics can find a truly reassuring balance in the present situation. They claim that arms proliferation increases the risk of danger, which pursues its own course (*cf.* Touraine, 1995, 392). What is certain is that, at the age at which children first begin to walk, a child who is able to keep its balance long enough to reach some of its objectives is still likely to fall, and the risk of injury increases the more it ventures forth.

During the Cold War, the two Great Powers maintained global geopolitical balance by constantly outdoing each other with respect to the size of their arms arsenals and armies, engaged, as they were, in an ongoing effort to compensate for presumed disadvantages in given areas. This kind of behaviour is more like the child's first clumsy efforts to maintain its balance, than the harmonious rhythms which come with total mastery of locomotor equilibrium. However, if we examine the major developments in the evolution of the Cold War, we may see that balance tends to become more and more complex and refined.

The Ideometric Meaning of the Cold War

The origins of the Cold War lie in a technological achievement based primarily upon an idea arising within modern science: the use of nuclear energy. This was a far-reaching discovery, and we are now just beginning to understand its effects on geopolitics. The previous situation was very different. Until World War II, technology generally led to increasingly brutal wars. A number of statements of Raymond Aron (1951, 31) are significant in this respect. According to Aron, attempts at negotiation were "doomed to failure" because of technology, which tended to promote a warlike attitude. The outcome of this tendency was World War II, "the first conflict to which one can attribute a true scientific dimension."

This geopolitical situation corresponds nicely to that of the child who is beginning to walk by itself. The first time it falls and hurts itself is also the first time it experiences pain due solely to its own personal and independent efforts. Previously, it passively underwent more or less painful situations of expectation and need that could never be attributed entirely to its own acts. When a fall results from the child's exercise of its will, this presupposes a clear awareness of its overall situation (even though the child is not conscious of the physiological details). Now the child's fall corresponds, at the conceptual level, to a "scientific" and potentially violent act on the part of child-humanity. Like the child who must learn to walk from experience without attempting to become aware of all the attendant details, child-humanity has to learn to develop its sense of balance in geopolitics and in dealing with the overly complex problems of human society. And it must do so without trying to find fully "scientific" solutions. A number of quite harmful pseudo-scientific theories, i.e., "ideologies," have resulted from such efforts.

In its new social, technological and other experiences, humanity employs trial and error in order to explore its new possibilities. These mistakes or errors are not "faults" or "sins," nor do they lead to "punishment" of any kind. When a child commits an error, the loving mother does not punish it but, on the contrary, strives to restore its confidence in its own abilities. She conveys messages of consolation and hope. In their present state the sciences, including mathematics and the natural and social sciences (with geopolitics among them), do not exactly convey the same message to humanity. Still, certain arbitrary regularities that appear throughout the separate fields of rational thought tend to suggest something that may really be equivalent to just such a message of love addressed to child-humanity.

References

Aron, R. 1951. *Les guerres en chaîne*. Paris: Gallimard.

Bachelard, G. 1949. *Le rationalisme appliqué*. Paris: Presses Universitaires de France.

Bailly, F. 1991. "L'anneau des disciplines." *Revue Internationale de systémique*, vol. 5, no. 3.

———1994. "The Characterization of System Identity in the Physical and he Biological Sciences." *World Futures: The Journal of General Evolution* 42: 11–20.

Blake, F. 1954. *The Child, his Parents and the Nurse*. Philadelphia: J. B. Lippincott Company.

Borel-Maisonny, S. 1969. *Perception et éducation. La parole et la perception des sons*. Neuchâtel, Switzerland: Delachaux & Niestlé.

Bourdil, P. 1989. *Le Dieu des philosophes*. Paris: Les Editions du Cerf.

Cazeneuve, J. 1974. "Guerre et paix." *Encyclopaedia Universalis*. Paris.

Cohen, J. P. 1979. *L'enfant de 1 à 6 ans*. Guide médical Nathan. Paris: Ed. Ferand Nathan.

Fromm, E. 1962. *The Art of Loving*. New York: Harper and Row.

Goldmann, L. 1978. *Epistémologie et philosophie politique*. Paris: Denoël-Gothier.

Lalande, A. 1983. *Vocabulaire technique et critique de la philosophie*. Paris: Presses Universitaires de France, 14th edition.

Mill, J. S. 1859. *On Liberty*. London: J. W. Parker & Son.

Pearce, J. 1989. *Worries and Fears*. New York: Thorsons Publishers.

Piaget, J. 1970. *Epistémologie des sciences humaines*. Paris: Gallimard.

Plas, F., E. Viel, Y. Blans, 1983. *La marche humaine. Kinésiologie dynamique, biomécanique et pathomécanique*. Paris, New York: Masson.

Popper, K. R. 1968. *The Logic of Scientific Discovery*. New York: Harper Torchbook.

Provençal, Y. 1987. "Une analyse de la notion d'objectivité," *Philosophiques*, Journal of the University of Quebec, Vol. XIV, No. 2.

———1997. "The Mind of Global Human Society. A New Approach to Investigating the Future," *World Futures. The Journal of General Evolution*, Vol. 47, pp. 121–42.

———1998. "The Mind of Society. Investigating and Using the Language of the Gods," *World Futures. The Journal of General Evolution* 52, p. 281–312.

———(forthcoming). "The Mind of Society. Investigating and Using the "Language of the Gods," *World Futures: The Journal of General Evolution*.

Rabischong, P. 1983. Preface to *La marche humaine. Kinésiologie dynamique, biomécanique et pathomécanique* by F. Plas, E. Viel and Y. Blans. Paris, New York: Masson.

Sampson, G. 1980. *Schools of Linguistics*. Stanford, California: Stanford University Press.

Schwartz, S. and J. Heller-Miller. 1988. *The Language of Toys. Teaching Communication Skills to Special-Needs Children*. Woodbine House.

Seefeldt, C. and N. Barbour. 1986. *Early Childhood Education. An Introduction*. Columbus, Toronto, London, Sydney: Charles E. Merrill Publishing Company.

Simon, H. 1981 "The Architecture of Complexity," in *The Sciences of the Artificial*, 2nd ed. Cambridge, MA: MIT Press.

Singer, I. 1984. *The Nature of Love*. Chicago and London: The Chicago University Press; 1st ed.: 1966.

Soppelsa, J. 1993. *Géopolitique de 1945 à nos jours*. Paris: Éditions Dalloz.

Stinson, W. J. 1990. *Moving and Learning for the Young Child*, ed. by the American Alliance for Health, Physical Education, Recreation, and Dance.

Sutton-Smith, B. 1986. *Toys as Culture*. New York, London:Gardner Press, Inc.

Touraine, M. 1995. *Le bouleversement du monde. Géopolitique du XXIième siècle*. Paris: Seuil.

Waltz, K. N. 1981. *The Spread of Nuclear Weapons: More May Be Better*. London: IISS, Adelphi Paper, No. 171.

Warner, S. and E. Rosenberg. 1976. *Your Child Learns Naturally*. New York: Doubleday & Co. Inc.

Section C

Science, Religion and the Environment

Chapters 9 to 12

Chapter 9

Science and Religion: Is Real Conversation Possible?

Cristina D. Vanin, St. Jerome's University

The question for this paper emerges from my ongoing work with the thought of Thomas Berry, a cultural historian who has been addressing ecological concerns for the past thirty years. Berry argues that, at its core, the ecological crisis is a matter of changing the very foundations of our thinking, especially about the nature of the world, and consequently, about the nature of human beings.

> We are seeing the earth's survival as simply another moral problem. In reality, this relationship of humans with the natural world is not simply another moral problem; it is a profound, ontological problem. It is a profoundly *religious* problem (1991, 72).

As an ontological problem, the crisis regards the very being of the universe and ourselves. Because it is also a religious problem, it must be responded to in the context of ultimate meaning and value.

For Berry, changing our understanding requires integrating the contemporary scientific knowledge about the emerging and developing universe with the religious or spiritual dimension of that understanding. To that end, he develops what he considers appropriate cultural symbols which can facilitate this change in thinking as well as in affectivity. He seeks to contribute to the development of an adequate functional cosmology for the present time.

In this paper, I indicate Berry's central arguments regarding the need to respond religiously to the ecological crisis. Berry's desire for an integrated account of the nature of the universe raises important epistemological and metaphysical questions. I also suggest that the work of Bernard Lonergan on epistemology answers such questions and provides a foundation for real conversation between science and religion. The metaphysics which emerges from Lonergan's epistemology distinguishes different domains of knowledge while indicating how they are related to each other in the larger work of understanding the universe and the place of the human within that universe.

One of Berry's overall concerns is to overcome the deleterious effects of the world view of mechanist determinism. He says: "[W]e are beyond the time when the scientific story of the universe could so identify the world of reality with the material and mechanistic aspects of the universe as to eliminate our capacities for that intimate communion with the natural world ... [We need to develop] an understanding of the most intimate aspects of the natural world" (Swimme and Berry, 1992, 2). Such intimate communion is possible if the universe is regarded as more than mere physical matter, that is, if its spiritual dimension is also considered.

The most significant problem which Berry sees with scientific knowledge is that, over the last two hundred years, its primary aim has been to analytically reduce wholes to their component parts.

> [T]he different sciences have developed an immense volume of information about the natural world in its physical aspects and a corresponding power to control it. Yet the earth is still seen as so much quantified matter. Life and consciousness as integral and pervasive dimensions of the earth ... found little understanding or appreciation except as more advanced phases of mechanistic processes (1980, 2).

This focus in the sciences is evident in cosmological studies, which traditionally were concerned to achieve a full understanding of the universe and of the role of the human in the universe. Unfortunately, cosmology came to be reduced to the level of a "mathematical cosmology," which meant that it could only provide empirically-based answers to questions regarding the size and age of the universe, the material of which the universe is made, and so on; for Berry, this is not a complete understanding of the universe.

Berry looks as well at Galileo who focused all of his attention on what he called "primary qualities," which he considered to be real and objective, while "secondary qualities," such as colours and sounds, were merely apparent. With the mechanist determinism that developed after Galileo, this distinction developed into a separation between an "objective world," or an "out there," as Berry says, and a "subjective world," an "in here." Science was concerned only with understanding the universe objectively; this was considered real. "Subjective" aspects such as feelings, spirituality, or psychic dimensions, were not regarded as part of the real world. In general terms, this meant that the scientist as subject came to be considered as separate from the universe that was being observed and investigated. Eventually, the universe that could be understood objectively was no longer thought to be alive.

A universe which is only understood in terms of mechanism is a world in which human beings can be known only as parts of a machine. There is little in the machine metaphor to suggest to human beings that they regard the universe as living, as having its own meaning and integrity. Instead, the metaphor has tended to regard human beings as quite separate from the rest of the world. The only kind of value and meaning that the universe had for humans, consequently, was as a material resource for human needs.

To the extent that mechanics was considered the integral science and a dualistic perspective was functioning, it was thought that ideas about numinous qualities or inner vital principles or spirituality belonged to a romantic, unrealistic and "subjective" tradition. Berry acknowledges, however, that scientific inquiry has headed toward the reversal of its own mechanist position.

> Our observational sciences, principally through theories of relativity, quantum physics, the uncertainty principle of Heisenberg, the sense of a self-organizing universe, and the more recent chaos theories have gotten us far beyond the mechanistic understanding of an objective world (*cf.*, Budenholzer, 1984, 351–68).

Part of the inadequacy of the prevailing cosmology is that it lacks the integration of scientific and religious insights into the nature of the universe. Either overcoming these dualisms between the objective and subjective, or between the material and the spiritual—or the integrating these different dimensions, makes it possible to retrieve the kinds of questions that were inherent in traditional cosmology.

The movement away from mechanist determinism includes confronting the problems of dualistic thinking about objectivity and subjectivity. That is, new kinds of questions, particularly questions about presuppositions, about the nature of knowing, and about what is known, have emerged; these are questions from which science itself is not immune. For help with such epistemological questions, we can turn to the work of Bernard Lonergan, Canadian philosopher and theologian, whose study of human understanding was for the sake of addressing perennial and fundamental philosophical problems (1957; 1972). Lonergan's work suggests that ultimately, there is no contradictory opposition between reason and faith or science and religion. Rather, we are dealing here with two complementary ways of gaining knowledge.

In order to arrive at an understanding of the complementarity, it will be helpful to look at some misconceptions that arise about both reason and faith (Crysdale, 1993). One problem has to do with what it means to know the facts. Is it simply a matter of taking a good look, even a highly technical look (Budenholzer, 1984)? A second issue has to do with the role that belief plays in our knowing and the assumption that believing only relates to morality or religion, that is, that it has little to do with facts or with reality.

With regard to the second issue, distinguish between what you have learned for yourself and what you know because you have trusted in the knowledge that someone else has. If I want to understand why the Niagara region and Toronto were hit so hard by recent snowfalls in comparison to Kitchener-Waterloo, I can turn to the meteorologists. When I take my car in to the garage, the mechanic lets me know what is wrong with my car. The pharmacist explains to me the side effects that may arise when I take certain drugs. While in each of these cases I have gained some knowledge, it is not knowledge that I have discovered for myself. Much, if not most, of what we know is a result of accepting what other people have discovered. Still, even if much of what we know we accept from others, we can also identify within ourselves a drive to ask questions, a persistent desire to understand things for ourselves.

The point here is that knowing involves two different movements and these two movements complement each other. The first Lonergan calls "the way down," or others (Crysdale, 1993) have called the "way of belief," or the "way of heritage" (Crowe, 1989, 151). The second way of knowing Lonergan refers to as knowing "from below upwards," or the "way of discovery" or "way of achievement." While we can distinguish these two ways of knowing, they cannot be regarded as contradictory. My knowing is always a mixture of these two ways. Whether one is a scientist or a theologian or a mechanic or a doctor, our knowledge of facts has as much to do with believing as it does with discovering things for ourselves.

When we pay attention to these two ways of knowing, we can no longer sustain the notion that reason is what is involved in discovering real facts and faith is merely about accepting opinions. There does not need to be a debate between faith and reason or belief and knowledge. The more pertinent questions we should be asking are: who should we believe? Why should we believe them?

Let us return to the first issue, namely, the notion that if we simply take a good enough look, the facts are clearly there for us to grasp. There is a tendency to presume that the "real" pertains to hard objects of experience and that knowing those objects has to do with getting a true picture of them. Knowing is identified with some intuitive sense, a biological sensation, that is analogous to looking.

The conception of reality which arose with the development of modern empirical science is still at the heart of religion-science discussions. From the distinction that Galileo made between primary qualities of matter—extension, shape, number, and motion—as objective reality, and other qualities—colour, temperature—as subjective, emerged a serious problem in the theory of knowledge. What Galileo argued is that the real has to do with extensions and motions of bodies. Reality was restricted to certain qualities that can be imagined and the criterion for truth became a certain intuition of the physical world. The idea that nature could be described exclusively in terms of the motions of particles was accepted by Newton. Frank Budenholzer talks about the consequences of this idea for religion and science.

> What is important is to realize that at this point the underlying conflict between science and religion had already emerged. The person doing science was expected to accept a metaphysics which envisaged reality

> as essentially an imaginable system of particles in motion. Within such a horizon God, and possibly the human mind, may be seen as exceptions to this materialist criterion of reality (see Descartes, 1968). Yet even if this is the case, the relationship of God to the world becomes problematic and religion becomes an inner matter to be verified in a way that is incompatible with scientific knowing (Budenholzer, 1984, 354).

Lonergan has indicated that the process of discovery is a much more complex process that involves a series of activities or operations. He distinguishes four different types or levels of activities that all people use as they come to know and to act. On a first level, we all have experiences of various kinds, including seeing, touching, tasting, feeling, as well as experiencing ourselves as conscious. When we experience, we spontaneously want to know about our experiencing. What is it? Why is it that way? In other words, on a second level, the data of experience raises questions. If my car suddenly stops, I want to know why. All kinds of possibilities may come to my mind. But I don't stop at postulating about possibilities. I also try to determine which of the possibilities is the right one. Is the car overheating? Is it out of gas? Is there something wrong with the transmission? On a third level, we continue to ask questions until all the pertinent or relevant questions have been dealt with and we make a judgment about what is happening. Then, on a fourth level, when we have the facts, we decide what to do. What Lonergan has identified and articulated here is an invariant and recurrent pattern of operations of human knowing which moves beyond merely looking to include understanding, judging, and decision making.

Is there any relationship between this way of discovery and coming to know by way of belief? Lonergan himself states that development,

> begins in the affectivity of the infant, the child, ..., the pupil, the follower. On affectivity rests the apprehension of values; on the apprehension of values rests belief; on belief follows the growth in understanding of one who has found a genuine teacher and has been initiated into the study of the masters of the past. Then, to confirm one's growth in understanding comes experience made mature and perceptive by one's developed understanding ... (1985, 180–81).

Both ways contain the same four elements but they work in opposite directions. The way of heritage is best illustrated by human development. As children, we have the potential to ask questions and make discoveries for ourselves. But, chronologically, we proceed through the way of heritage first, accepting what others give us as their knowledge and values. Because we are connected affectively to our parents, we accept certain values and ways of behaving as correct. We accept the judgments, the knowledge, that we are given, often because we trust the source of that knowledge. Over time, questions for understanding begin to arise because we want to understand what it is that we have accepted as true. As we understand more, our experience changes; we become more mature, more perceptive. We eventually begin to develop that inherent desire to know, to inquire, to discover for ourselves.

What is most important about this discussion of these two ways of knowing is the fact that they do not contradict each other. Rather, they are in a dialectical relationship; there is an ongoing revision and critique of both approaches. As Cynthia Crysdale states,

> So it is that the pursuit of truth and authentic living is an ongoing interaction between knowledge as received and knowledge as discovered. Neither faith nor reason has a monopoly on the truth. Rather, each is part of a self-correcting process of learning in which faith is challenged and enriched by creative discovery and reason is held accountable by the common fund of knowledge and its canons of accuracy (1993, 164).

We have been talking about two ways of coming to know. Yet, underlying this discussion is a more fundamental question about whether I can know anything at all. How do I know that anything is true? By paying attention to my own operations of knowing, I can realize or discover that, coming to know anything involves more than merely "looking" at the data. The very process of knowing itself becomes a matter for discovery. Lonergan refers to this process of discovering for oneself what knowing is, "intellectual conversion."

> Intellectual conversion is a radical clarification and, consequently, the elimination of an exceedingly stubborn and misleading myth that knowing is like looking, that objectivity is seeing what is there to be seen and not seeing what is not there, and that the real is what is out there now to be looked at. Now this myth overlooks the distinction between the world of immediacy, say, the world of the infant and, on the other hand, the world mediated by meaning. The world of immedi-

> acy is the sum of what is seen, heard, touched, tasted, smelt, felt. It conforms well enough to the myth's view of reality, objectivity, knowledge. But it is but a tiny fragment of the world mediated by meaning. For the world mediated by meaning is a world known not by the sense experience of an individual but by the external and internal experience of a cultural community, and by the continuously checked and rechecked judgments of the community. Knowing, accordingly, is not just seeing; it is experiencing, understanding, judging, and believing. The criteria of objectivity are not just the criteria of ocular vision; they are the compounded criteria of experiencing, of understanding, of judging, and of believing. The reality known is not just looked at; it is given in experience, organized and extrapolated by understanding, posited by judgment and belief (Lonergan, 1995, 238).

You can grasp what Lonergan is saying only by attending to yourself as a subject who knows. The evidence that you refer to is the evidence of yourself engaging in these activities of knowing. In other words, the key to intellectual conversion is self-appropriation, coming to know myself as a knower who engages in these different levels of activity, who comes to know in different ways.

It is precisely such self-appropriation that guards against the notion that theological claims or religious claims are "merely subjective." For inherent in the operations of knowing are norms of objectivity; the activities of knowing are part of an inherent dynamism in the human person to discover intelligibility, to ascertain truth, to know. The norms of objectivity are constituted by this very dynamism of knowing. This orientation toward intelligibility, truth, and value provides the impetus to question, to find out, to figure things out, to understand, to know. In contrast to suggesting that the norms of objectivity lie outside of us, in some external authority, self-appropriation leads us to know that being objective has to do with authentic subjectivity.

There is one point regarding "authentic subjectivity" that needs clarification. If you assume that knowing involves getting out of your own mind so that you can access the real that is out there, then the word "objective" means "reliable external facts" and "subjective" refers to arbitrary internal feelings or opinions. If, on the other hand, you discover that knowing is a much more complex process, then the question of objectivity is: "Am I authentically adhering to the internal exigence to understand clearly, to verify the truth, to know and create value?" This is very different from asking whether I am adhering to some external standard that exists "out there." This is not to suggest that knowing objectively is only an internal or intuitive process. We do indeed attend to data which is "out there" but the point is that this is not all that is involved in objective knowing. Vernon Gregson states,

> Whenever we use the full capacity of our subjectivity, all of our levels of consciousness, all of our desire to experience, our desire to understand, and our desire to find the truth, then our conclusions have a claim to objectivity. If we don't use all that we are, then our conclusions are merely arbitrary and "subjective" in the pejorative sense. Lonergan makes the point of the relationship between objectivity and subjectivity quite strikingly in his statement: "Objectivity is the fruit of authentic subjectivity." The full use of all of our capacities leads to objectivity, and nothing less than that leads to objectivity. Intellectual conversion is the recognition that this is true (Gregson, 1988, 27).

I set out in this paper to argue that real conversation between science and religion is possible if we correct some fundamental philosophical problems that have arisen since the emergence of modern science. Lonergan's study of human understanding and his critical realism provides a corrective to misconceptions about the real, objectivity, and knowing. Insofar as mechanistic determinism has perpetuated the notion that any ideas about spirit are simply "subjective" and therefore not really real, Lonergan's clarification of objectivity as authentic subjectivity, of the real as verified intelligibility, and of knowing as a complex pattern of activities, opens up the possibility of a true integration of religious and scientific insights into the nature of the universe and the place and responsibility of the human within that universe.

I agree with Thomas Berry that we urgently need at present to experience the universe as a sacred, beautiful, awesome, reality, such that we would be moved to seek to understand and to affirm the whole of the universe, in its material as well as spiritual dimensions. He says, in *Dream of the Earth,*

> To learn to live graciously together would make us worthy of this unique, beautiful, blue planet that evolved in its present splendor over some billions of years, a planet that we should give over to our children with the assurance that this great community of the living will lavish upon them the care that it has bestowed so abundantly upon ourselves (Berry, 1988, 72).

This shift in understanding, this intellectual conversion, that I have presented, is a foundational step on the road to addressing this profoundly ontological and religious problem of the ecological crisis. I trust that it helps scientists and people of faith, as they utilize the full capacities of their subjectivities, to dialogue together about the nature and meaning of the universe and our true role as humans in the cosmos.

References

Berry, T. 1991. *Befriending the Earth*. Conn.: Twenty Third Publications.

———1988. *Dream of the Earth*. San Fransisco: Sierra Books.

———1980. "The American College in the Ecological Age." In *Riverdale Papers VII*. U.S.A.: Riverdale Centre for Religious Studies.

Budenholzer, F. 1984. "Science and Religion: Seeking a Common Horizon." *Zygon* vol. 19: 351–68.

Crowe, F. 1989. "Interpreting Lonergan," In *Appropriating the Lonergan Idea*. Ed. Michael Vertin. New York: Catholic University of America Press.

Crysdale, C. 1993. "Reason, Faith, and Authentic Religion." In *The Struggle Over the Past: Fundamentalism in the Modern World*. Ed. William Shea. U.S.A.: CTS Pub-lication.

Gregson, V. 1988. "The Desire to Know: Intellectual Conversion," in V. Gregson ed. *The Desires of the Human Heart*, New York: Paulist Press.

Lonergan, B. 1957. *Insight: A Study of Human Understanding*. London: Harper and Row.

———1995. "Natural Right and Historical Mindedness." In *A Third Collection*. New York: Paulist Press.

Swimme, B. and T. Berry. 1992. *The Universe Story*. SanFrancisco: Harper.

Chapter 10

There Lives the Dearest Freshness Deep Down Things: Ecology, Transcendence, and Immanence

John Mitterer, Brock University

Introduction

The title of this paper springs from a line from **God's Grandeur**, an 1877 poem by Gerard Manley Hopkins. I find it prescient of my major themes, especially the human exploitation of nature and the immanence of spirit in nature. Hopkins seemed to feel nature was infinitely renewable, though. I wonder how this poem would have changed had he known just how much we have come to understand of nature's finite fragility:

> **God's Grandeur** (1877)
> The world is charged with the grandeur of God.
> It will flame out, like shining from shook foil;
> It gathers to a greatness, like the ooze of oil
> Crushed. Why do men then now not reck his rod?
> Generations have trod, have trod, have trod;
> And all is seared with trade; bleared, smeared with toil;
> And wears man's smudge |&| shares man's smell: the soil

Is bare now, nor can foot feel, being shod.

And for all this, nature is never spent;
There lives the dearest freshness deep down things;
And though the last lights off the black West went
Oh, morning, at the brown brink eastward, springs—
Because the Holy Ghost over the bent
World broods with warm breast |&| with ah! bright wings.

Let me properly begin this paper with some context. I am as guilty as the next person. I am selfish. I want to see all the species of birds in the world. I always thought the limiting factor would be my own life span but now I see it is something else. I can no longer think of the environment without thinking of the extinction of the birds. It is clear to me that the current environmental crisis has in no way been directly caused by the teaching of the Bible or by religions like the Roman Catholic Church. The real culprits, or causal variables, include unbridled capitalism and the population explosion. In this paper, however, I will not address some of the immediate concerns facing environmentalism; that is not my purpose here. Rather I will inquire into the relationship between our current environmental crises and our Western spiritual tradition. This relationship is better understood as having helped to create some of the background of Western thought within which we have reached world ascendancy. Along the way I will wonder aloud if our traditional metanarrative is capable of sustaining a truly helpful environmentalism. I will close with a discussion of alternative visions of spirituality and their potential for undergirding environmentalism.

I do not see traditional Western religions as the only segment of society failing to respond to the early alarm calls sounded by writers such as Rachel Carson (1962) or Paul Erlich (1971). We all slept. That other major "religion" of the modern West, science, has also not responded as well as we might, in retrospect, have hoped. Recently, Carl Safina (1998), a lecturer in the School of Forestry and Environmental Studies at Yale University and the Director of the Living Oceans Program at the National Audubon Society, wrote: "The crisis in the oceans is the latest in a long series of clarion calls about the perilous state of our environment. As with the other shifts in our world view in the past, academics with relevant expertise have a professional—and personal—obligation not to assume that some other responsible party will figure out how to preserve the resources on which we and future generations must depend." I want to add that, in my view, his call goes out to all scientists, regardless of the relevance of their expertise. As Richard Rorty (1998) has so powerfully argued, in this generation we have witnessed a general retreat of the intellectual political left from the social policy arena. This must end.

Ecology

Science HAS at least supplied the conceptual framework and most of the data within which the concept of "environmental crisis" has been formulated. Just how much of a crisis IS it anyway? Here I follow closely David Quammen's (1979) thesis that we are becoming a "Planet of Weeds." Let me outline his basic ideas.

Quammen begins by suggesting that there have been five major mass extinctions in geological history. For the record, they were at about 439 million years ago during the Ordovician period, 367 million years ago during the Devonian period, 245 million years ago during the Permian period, 208 million years ago during the Triassic period, and 65 million years ago during the Cretaceous period (the K-T event). During these mass extinctions, better than 50% (and as much as 95%) of the earth's biodiversity was lost.

According to Norman Myers (1979), we are currently extinguishing species at the same rate as the "great dying" of the dinosaurs. From 1600–1900, there were 75 known species extinctions due to humanity. From 1900–1979, there were another 75 known species extinctions, a rate above those known during Cretaceous. Based on known rates of deforestation during the 1980's from 63 tropical countries and a mathematical model of the relationship between decreasing habitat area and decreasing species diversity, the W.V. Reid World Resources Institute (1992) estimates by 2040 that 17–35% of tropical species will be extinct or doomed to be. According to Quammen, Stuart Pimm and Thomas Brooks, of the University of Tennessee have estimated that 50% of bird species will be gone by 2050 and that if previous trends continue, one-third to two-thirds of all species will be gone by then as well.

Sir Robert May (May and Lawton, 1995) has described five causal factors which account for most extinctions: habitat destruction, habitat fragmentation, overkill, invasive species, and the secondary effects of extinctions cascading through ecosystem. He estimates that most extant animal and bird species will last 200–400 years. Quammen quoted him as saying that "Much of the diversity we inherited will be gone before humanity sorts itself out."

According to Quammen, two key variables in these current extinctions are environmental degradation and human population growth. Environmental degradation follows a "landscape cascade" from wildlands to extensively used areas to intensively used areas to degraded land. According to The Population Division of the United Nations (1998), the human population of the earth is near 6 billion people and is projected to reach about 9 billion by 2050. Paul Harrison (1993) analyzes the environmental impact of people as being due to population size, consumption level, and technology.

Quammen summarizes the effects of this catastrophe as follows: "The species that survive will likely be like weeds, reproducing quickly and surviving almost anywhere." He likens the situation to the problem of invasive species, which are, generally speaking, "weedy" species. Such species survive at the expense of narrowly endemic species because they are "scrappers, generalists, opportunists." They tend to thrive in human-dominated terrain because in crucial ways they resemble humans: "aggressive, versatile, prolific, ready to travel." Familiar examples include the city pigeon, coyote, raccoon, white-tailed deer, brown-headed cowbird, starling, black rat, brown rat, cockroaches and houseflies. As Quammen concludes, "virtually everything will live virtually everywhere, though the list of species that constitute "everything will be small." And humans will, of course, be on the list since we are the consummate "weed."

Transcendence

What relationship do traditional Western religious ideas have with our current crisis? Simply put, these ideas have, to date, fueled the crisis, not muted it. In a previous work (1995), I outlined some ideas about the relationship between men and women. I want to lay out the highlights of those ideas because my treatment of the current topic is, as I see it, an extension. There I argued that in traditional patriarchy men and women related in a "psychology of domination," or, for those inclined to a softer view, a "psychology of stewardship." I argued that this relationship arose out of man's attempt to approach to God, to the infinite, to metaphysics. I argued that the relationship of man to woman was analogized to the relationship of God to man. More precisely, I argued that, in the classic metanarrative, man can never truly know God; he can only yearn for God. This sort of love is *eros*, a striving toward, in this case an idealization, a transcendent, perfect being. In addition, man also experiences *nomos* towards God; a submission of his will to God. In contrast, God, being perfect, cannot experience yearning and so does not feel eros toward man. He also cannot experience nomos. Instead God manifests *agape*, a downward flow of grace. (Granted there is also *philias*, brotherly love, but it does not figure into the relationship between God and man at all.)

It is inevitable then, that the relationship of God and man be inherently asymmetrical. No doubt about it, God dominates man. This does not, of course, mean that God need be without compassion or that God need be cruel. It is just that God is, of necessity, calling the shots. And so I argued quite simply that the relation of God to man is transposed onto the relation of man to woman, yielding a "psychology of domination" or, as Cora Twohig-Moengangongo (1999) put it, a "hierarchical dualism," in which it is essentially man's job to "care for" his woman. This sort of relationship between man and woman is explicitly addressed in the bible.

Not being a biblical scholar, I will simply adduce two standard references from the King James version on the relationship between men and women (parenthetically, I want to excuse my lack of Biblical erudition by claiming that my shallower reading corresponds reasonably well with what the infamous "common man" might deduce from the whole thing). There is, of course, the famous idea, from Genesis 2:20–23 where we see that Eve was created out of Adam to help him:

> [20] And Adam gave names to all cattle, and to the fowl of the air, and to every beast of the field; but for Adam there was not found an help meet for him.
>
> [21] And the LORD God caused a deep sleep to fall upon Adam and he slept: and he took one of his ribs, and closed up the flesh instead thereof;
>
> [22] And the rib, which the LORD God had taken from man, made he a woman, and brought her unto the man.

> [23] And Adam said, This is now bone of my bones, and flesh of my flesh: she shall be called Woman, because she was taken out of Man.

The other famous idea is from Ephesians 5: 22–24, where we see that as man's "help meet," woman is expected to obey him:

> [22] Wives, submit yourselves unto your own husbands, as unto the Lord.
>
> [23] For the husband is the head of the wife, even as Christ is the head of the church: and he is the savior of the body.
>
> [24] Therefore as the church is subject unto Christ, so let the wives be to their own husbands in every thing.

In fairness, I should note that Ephesians goes on (Ephesians 5: 28; 33):

> [28] So ought men to love their wives as their own bodies. He that loveth his wife loveth himself.
>
> [33] Nevertheless let every one of you in particular so love his wife even as himself; and the wife see that she reverence her husband.

In other words, that a woman must obey her husband does not license him to be cruel. Even in this kindness, however, we see that a man should "love" his wife and that she should "reverence" him. Nothing that I can find in the Song of Solomon, one of the kindest treatments of the relationship between men and women, suggests any different. One need not look far, even in these Godlessly feminist times to find this psychology of domination baldly stated. Consider the Promise Keepers—a Christian-oriented modern men's movement. In promising to remain in marriage and remain responsible for their children, this movement urges men to make just the kinds of promises that they should be making. However, the foundation is that of a psychology of domination.

As reported by Robert Bly (1996), the recommended conversation with a promise keeper's wife is this: "Honey, I'm going to take the leadership of the family back now. I'm not asking you about this, I'm telling you." Bly goes on to wryly note "For some women that will be satisfying; for others it will be intolerable. And the relaxed tone of the suggested conversation implies that men are completely out of touch with what women have achieved (179)."

So what is the problem? Why is it bad for the man to wear the pants in the family? Doesn't someone have to? Isn't hierarchy necessary and inevitable? As implied in those passages from Ephesians, a man must love his wife as himself. So stewardship can't be all bad, can it? To this I must reply with a story I attribute to B. F. Skinner. Apparently, in the British Navy of the sailing era, boredom was a problem during long stretches at sea. One commonly played "game" involved taking some number of cabin boys and lashing them by one wrist around one of the ship's masts. Imagine six or eight young boys lashed by their left wrists to the mast, aligned around it like the spokes around the hub of a wheel. Each boy was given a switch or stick and one was told to begin. The idea was that he would whack the boy ahead of him and when that boy felt the blow, he in turn would whack the boy ahead of him. So the entire perverse process would circle and recircle the mast. Setting aside the sheer sickness of such a "game," Skinner noted that it was inevitable that this "game" would spiral out of control; the boys eventually lashing at each other in complete savagery. The sight of such a spectacle was, presumably, what amused the bored sailors.

B. F. Skinner asked why these "games" spiraled out of control. After all, if all of the boys kept their blows at modest levels, they would not end up inflicting any real harm on each other. Why did they compete rather than cooperate? His answer was quite simple—it is almost impossible for us to feel the pain of the other as much as we feel ours ourselves. Even if every boy was determined to do no more than match the intensity of the blow he had just received, it is likely that he would deliver a more ferocious blow in return. In what sense, then, could we trust these boys to enter into a relationship of stewardship with each other? And in what sense could we describe the sailors as "stewards" of the boys? Simply put, then, it is hard for me to be your steward because it is hard for me to be as fully aware of your perspective or your issues, and so it is hard for me to uphold the priority of your claim over mine. In other words, it is very hard to truly "walk a mile in another's shoes." Politically, this wisdom was expressed by Lord Acton: "Power corrupts and absolute power corrupts absolutely." It seems to me that all of Western political democratic thinking follows from the attempt to ensure society against the rule of the tyrant.

What about the relationship of man with nature? Again it seems to me that the relationship of God to man is simply transposed onto the relationship of man to nature. Again, not being a biblical scholar, I will simply adduce a few standard references from the King James version. The most famous is undoubtedly Genesis 1:26–30, which clearly gives man dominion over nature:

> [26] And God said, Let us make man in our image, after our likeness: and let them have dominion over the fish of the sea, and over the fowl of the air, and over the cattle, and over all the earth, and over every creeping thing that creepeth upon the earth.
>
> [27] So God created man in his own image, in the image of God created he him; male and female created he them.
>
> [28] And God blessed them, and God said unto them, Be fruitful, and multiply, and replenish the earth, and subdue it: and have dominion over the fish of the sea, and over the fowl of the air, and over every living thing that moveth upon the earth.
>
> [29] And God said, Behold, I have given you every herb bearing seed, which is upon the face of all the earth, and every tree, in the which is the fruit of a tree yielding seed; to you it shall be for meat.
>
> [30] And to every beast of the earth, and to every fowl of the air, and to every thing that creepeth upon the earth, wherein there is life, I have given every green herb for meat: and it was so.

Man's dominion over nature is reiterated in Psalms 8:6–8 (and virtually identically in Hebrews 2: 7–8):

> [6] Thou madest him to have dominion over the works of thy hands; thou hast put all things under his feet:
>
> [7] All sheep and oxen, yea, and the beasts of the field;
>
> [8] The fowl of the air, and the fish of the sea, and whatsoever passeth through the paths of the seas.

More to the point, as, say, Genesis 2:5 & 9 makes clear, the point of having created nature is FOR man. There is no sense of nature having an independent existence. We see, for example, that anthropocentrically, the trees were either pretty to look at or good to eat:

> [5] And every plant of the field before it was in the earth, and every herb of the field before it grew: for the LORD God had not caused it to rain upon the earth, and there was not a man to till the ground.
>
> [9] And out of the ground made the LORD God to grow every tree that is pleasant to the sight, and good for food; the tree of life also in the midst of the garden, and the tree of knowledge of good and evil.

The same sort of anthropocentrism emerges in Psalms 104:15–15:

> [14] He causeth the grass to grow for the cattle, and herb for the service of man: that he may bring forth food out of the earth;
>
> [15] And wine that maketh glad the heart of man, and oil to make his face to shine, and bread which strengtheneth man's heart.

The Bible goes on to give man instructions about nature. Man's job in the Garden of Eden was, as Genesis 2:15 makes clear, to take care of things:

> [15] And the LORD God took the man, and put him into the garden of Eden to dress it and to keep it.

In Leviticus 3–5, we do encounter a gentle idea, that of conservation. Even so, we find no hint that it is for anything but the benefit of man:

> [3] Six years thou shalt sow thy field, and six years thou shalt prune thy vineyard, and gather in the fruit thereof;
>
> [4] But in the seventh year shall be a sabbath of rest unto the land, a sabbath for the LORD: thou shalt neither sow thy field, nor prune thy vineyard.
>
> [5] That which groweth of its own accord of thy harvest thou shalt not reap, neither gather the grapes of thy vine undressed: for it is a year of rest unto the land.

Management of flocks is extensively discussed in Ezekial 34:3–5. There, shepherds who are negligent pay the price. No notion of ecology is present here; the "beasts of the field" are just a nuisance:

> [3] Ye eat the fat, and ye clothe you with the wool, ye kill them that are fed: but ye feed not the flock.
>
> [4] The diseased have ye not strengthened, neither have ye healed that which was sick, neither have ye bound up that which was broken, neither have ye brought again that which was driven away, neither have ye sought that which was lost; but with force and with cruelty have ye ruled them.
>
> [5] And they were scattered, because there is no shepherd: and they became meat to all the beasts of the field, when they were scattered.

Good shepherds, in a covenant with God, can count on better results, as, for example, in Ezekial 34:25–26:

> [25] And I will make with them a covenant of peace, and will cause the evil beasts to cease out of the land: and they shall dwell safely in the wilderness, and sleep in the woods.
>
> [26] And I will make them and the places round about my hill a blessing; and I will cause the shower to come down in his season; there shall be showers of blessing.

Finally, in Isaah 3–6; 19–21, we even find what seems like a biblical prophecy of environmental crisis:

> [3] The land shall be utterly emptied, and utterly spoiled: for the LORD hath spoken this word.
>
> [4] The earth mourneth and fadeth away, the world languisheth and fadeth away, the haughty people of the earth do languish.
>
> [5] The earth also is defiled under the inhabitants thereof; because they have transgressed the laws, changed the ordinance, broken the everlasting covenant.

> [6] Therefore hath the curse devoured the earth, and they that dwell therein are desolate: therefore the inhabitants of the earth are burned, and few men left.
>
> [19] The earth is utterly broken down, the earth is clean dissolved, the earth is moved exceedingly.
>
> [20] The earth shall reel to and fro like a drunkard, and shall be removed like a cottage; and the transgression thereof shall be heavy upon it; and it shall fall, and not rise again.
>
> [21] And it shall come to pass in that day, that the LORD shall punish the host of the high ones that are on high, and the kings of the earth upon the earth.

So, as I see it, the Bible, the mainstay of the Western religious tradition, urges a psychology of domination of man over nature. There are so many ways to express it. We value our souls, not our bodies. We have souls, the animals do not; we are spiritual; they are not, we matter in God's grand scheme; they are a part of the set on which we play out our heavenward dramas. Bit players on the stage of life. And the Earth is no more than the backdrop for all human action, to be used as man sees fit, in his role as "steward" over the beasts of the earth and the fowl of the air. Really, what chance does nature have?

Let us add to this that the goal of man's erotic yearning toward God orients man's attention away from this world to one beyond it. Away from the immanent to the transcendent; from the physical to the metaphysical. As Brennan Hill, head of Theology at Xavier University, so appropriately puts it, "There's a tendency in Christian life to be otherworldly, to think, 'My true home is in heaven with God and I'm just a pilgrim temporarily on this earth'" (Schneider, 1998).

Let's face it, this metaphysic, this grand metanarrative—to lay bare my post-modernism—is incapable of spawning a truly reverent environmentalism. At best, we can ground environmentalism in conservation, the careful shepherding of our God-given resources, like "talents" to be invested for the greater glory of God. Where, here, are we to find anything with the power to halt the march of capitalism or the human population explosion? On the contrary, as Max Weber (1958) so cogently argued, Biblical values have been appropriated to undergird the expansion of capitalism. Also on the contrary, the Roman Catholic

Church's reluctance to take the idea of population control seriously makes it clear who will remain on Noah's Ark when the flood arrives.

So where, then, does all this leave traditional Western religion and environmentalism? Well, as strange bedfellows driven to reach out to each other by the fear that the planet is spiraling into an environmental crisis that neither constituency alone can halt. While traditional religious values such as reverence for living things, notions of stewardship and moral responsibility seem relevant to environmentalism, organized religion can be downright hostile. Some possible reasons have been articulated by Brennan Hill.

1. Some people claim ours is a fallen world; pollution is just one manifestation of it.
2. Some people believe that poor living conditions are the will of God and that suffering—spiritual and ecological—is sent to test us.
3. Apocalyptics think the world is not worth saving since it is destined to end in fire anyway.
4. Some maintain that religion is a private affair that should focus on spiritual issues, not social or political ones.
5. Most importantly, from my point of view, conservatives fear paganism and earth-worship (Schneider, 1998).

So in the end I think that traditional Western religion can do little to help the environmental movement besides adding the weight of environmentally aware members to the fray. This essentially political assistance may be invaluable, if enough concerned churches and church groups get active. As far as I can tell, this is indeed happening, from the Redwood Rabbis and the National Religious Partnership for the Environment to the Evangelical Environmental Network to Visions for the Earth. But beware, the churches may become more immanent in the process.

Immanence

To summarize to this point, I worry that no spiritual way out of our environmental crisis will be produced by our traditional spiritual values. That metanarrative is too domination-oriented and also otherworldly-(metaphysically-) oriented. The approach from the contingent to the absolute cannot provide a psychology of equality or of genuine ecology.

I can sense an alternative metanarrative gaining a toehold in our culture. You know, I really think a new religion(s) is (are) in the process of being born. Although I am not at all sure this new (or perhaps only recycled) metanarrative is, in the end, any better for any purpose, at least I think it has a better chance of spawning a more spiritual ecology, so I will end this paper with a consideration of it. Metaphorically put, God will have to come back down to earth and roll up her sleeves. And we shall have to get out of our heads and back into our bodies, as Morris Berman (1989) has argued, refocusing our deepest efforts in the here and now. As a postmodernist, I suspect that as the environmental crisis deepens, we will find that sort of metanarrative more congenial; necessity may truly become the mother of invention. This point of view is expressed directly in the title of David Suzuki's (1998) recent book: *The Sacred Balance.* It is what the Gaians would have us believe.

One way to express this difference has been articulated by Walter Truett Anderson (1992). In his vocabulary, the traditions I have been worrying about are "exoteric"—they are "institutionalized, reified and deified." Their public belief systems are expressly a metanarrative meant to explain reality and to serve as complete systems of social values and beliefs. Exoteric traditions are concrete and doctrinal. They are openly available in scriptures and other official teachings; there is nothing secretive about them. They present a publicly accessible body of knowledge to be learned. Their goal is usually transcendent—they seek to transcend this imperfect world. They are often expressed in hierarchies of power; spiritual, political, economic.

The other spiritual metanarrative is "esoteric" or mystical. Such traditions (such as, say, Sufism or Zen Buddhism) are primarily traditions of individual instruction, more secretive in their practices, with dramatically different ways of transmitting knowledge. Truth is something that each individual must discover for him or herself. Such traditions are more open to immanence, the notion that spirituality must be found here and now; that spirituality is a state of mind.

Esoteric traditions are more suited to the temper of the times and, as a post-modernist, I believe they will become more and more prominent. Traditional religions may well rediscover their mystical sides, the very same ones they sought to eradicate in centuries past. It appears to me that new esoteric traditions will also arise. Steeped in immanence, this development represents something more than a desire to save the birds. The tremendous spiritual hunger which so obviously haunts post-modern culture is not being fed by exoteric traditions. In a post-modern world, metanarratives can no longer make sweeping metaphysical claims, or be violently exclusionary, or distance people from direct contact with the holy. In a postmodern world, the Pope's claim to divinely inspired infallibility would be seen as a charming anachronism if it did not still sway so many.

Instead, immanence is called for. The sacred is within us. We find it, our spirituality, on a journey within, guided by the Bible, Carl Jung, the self-help literature, and even Oprah Winfrey. When we transcend, it is outside of ourselves only to our loved ones, to suffering humanity, and to our lovely planet Earth. There we also find the sacred. Or so we so passionately desire. This immanence is deeply personal; there are many paths to salvation. All metanarratives lead to salvation. Tolerance is the chief psychological virtue and partnership is the organizational model of choice; what Cora Twohig-Moengangongo referred to as "dialectical interconnectedness." If this dialectical interconnectedness extends to nature, and that is the intent of those busily spinning the Gaian metanarrative, then Nature may once again be experienced as sacred. This sort of psychology, a psychology of equality, and this sort of spirituality based on immanence, not the notion of stewardship, may help us develop a truly reverent ecology and just may help us get out of our current jam.

Until traditional exoteric traditions get this point and accept that they must adjust their metanarratives, they risk increasing irrelevance. I take heart from much of what has been recently written, in this volume and elsewhere, that just such an evolution from exoteric to esoteric metanarrative may indeed be occurring. I close by begging God to make sure it comes soon enough.

References

Anderson, W. T. 1992. *Reality Isn't What it Used to Be: Theatrical Politics, Ready-to-Wear Religion, Global Myths, Primitive Chic, and Other Wonders of the Postmodern World.* San Francisco: Harper Collins.

Berman, M. 1989. *Coming to our Senses: Body and Spirit in the Hidden History of the West.* New York: Bantam Books.

Bly, R. 1996. *The Sibling Society.* New York: Vintage Books.

Carson, R. 1962. *Silent Spring.* Boston: Houghton Mifflin.

Ehrlich, P. 1971. *The Population Bomb.* New York: Ballantine Books.

Harrison, P. 1993. *The Third Revolution: Population, Environment, and a Sustainable World*. U.S.A.: Penguin.

May, R. and R. H. Lawton. 1995. *Extinction Rates*. Oxford: Oxford University Press.

Mitterer, J. 1995. "Male and Female in the Modern World." In *The Nature and Pursuit of Love: The Philosophy of Irving Singer*. Ed. D. Goicoechea, New York: Prometheus Books.

Myers, N. 1979. *The Sinking Ark : A New Look at the Problem of Disappearing Species*. New York: Pergamon Press.

Quammen, D. 1998. "Planet of Weeds." *Harper's Magazine, October*: 57–69.

Rorty, R. 1998. *Achieving our Country: Leftist Thought in Twentieth-Century America*. Boston: Harvard University Press.

Suzuki, D. T. 1998. *The Sacred Balance: Rediscovering Our Place in Nature*. Prometheus Books.

Weber, M. 1958. *The Protestant Ethic and the Spirit of Capitalism*. New York: Scribner.

Chapter 11

The Return of the Sacred in Public Debates on the Environment: Secular and Religious Uses of "Transcendence"

David Seljak, St. Jerome's University

According to mainstream sociologists of the 1960s, one of the earmarks of modern society was the privatization of religion, the relegation of religion to the sphere of the private life of the individual, the family, or the ethnic community. Talk of the sacred or transcendence was banished from public debates on politics, economics, and society. Leading this programme of secularization were scientists (the new cultural embodiment of reason), democrats, and social reformers. It is ironic that now, in the face of the environmental crisis, scientists, environmentalists, and grass roots activists are calling for a re-entry of the sacred into public life. For example, the well-known English-Canadian biologist and environmental activist, David Suzuki; former development aid manager, David Korten; American vice-president Al Gore; mathematical cosmologist, Brian Swimme; and a collection of world-renowned scientists all invite religious leaders to become involved in the ecological movement. Furthermore, they argue that unless nature is regarded as "sacred," humans will continue to view the environment as a collection of resources whose only purpose is to serve our needs. This anthropocentric "disenchantment" has meant that other species can make no claim to survival in the face of our own claim, or even our consumerist whims (Suzuki, 1997).

This call for a re-entry of the transcendent into public debates is not a call for a return to a pre-modern (that is, pre-democratic and pre-pluralist) society nor is it a defense of the privileges of any religious group or institution. It is not a threat to democracy (Casanova, 1994). It is instead an attempt to balance the modern worldview's obsession with scientific control over nature for the purposes of economic growth with an ethic of self-limitation in the face of the majesty and value of the web of life which surrounds and supports us. Even so, this re-entry of the transcendent into public life poses certain dangers not addressed by scientists and environmentalists. By looking at recent papal documents, I will show that how the Roman Catholic tradition's understanding of the transcendence of God and the dignity of the human person can serve as a useful corrective to the sometimes vague and abstract understanding of "the sacred" displayed by many scientists, environmentalists, and social activists. The so-called "anthropocentric" approach of the Church serves to link the ecological crisis to a wider moral crisis, the domination and exploitation of human individuals and peoples. Furthermore, the Church's social teaching on justice and the common good can balance the excessively individualistic emphasis common to these environmentalists. Without a religious community, the call for the return of the sacred will remain an idealistic protest that will only reinforce further the individualism that makes collective action impossible. I believe that Catholics ought to engage these secular thinkers in a serious dialogue about transcendence and ecology since I believe both groups ultimately ground their positions in an affirmation of the absolute value of life itself. Consequently, there is much room for dialogue and cooperation on a solution to this crisis among people of good will. Secular scientists and environmentalists might learn more about rooting their conception of the sacred in more concrete terms of the common good and social justice whereas the Catholic Church might find itself developing a deeper anthropology as it ponders the interrelationship that modern science has discovered between human beings and the rest of the cosmos.

The Return of Transcendence

By the end of the 1980s, a large body of work written by Christians in response to the environmental crisis existed in English (see Scharper, 1997). In the early 1990s, two extraordinary developments occurred. First, the mainstream religious organizations in Canada and the United States developed concrete programs to stimulate debate at the level of congregations and parishes (Shibley and Wiggins, 1997). Simultaneously, scientists, environmentalists, and activists—who were traditionally suspicious of religion—began to see in organized religion a possible ally. While Christians have often sought to move religion back into public debates, it was remarkable that the invitation was now coming from secular humanists.

What was new in these developments is the invitation of the sacred back into public debates on the common good. One dramatic example of this phenomenon is the open letter organized by Carl Sagan, a well-known and respected physicist, to the world's religious communities and leaders asking them to overcome old suspicions and animosities to form a partnership with scientists in developing a new environmentally sane public ethic. The letter, released in January 1990 and signed by 33 scientists from the United States, Europe, and the USSR, recognizes the potential of religion "to influence personal conduct and commitment powerfully" (http://nrpe.org/open-letter.html, 1990). Furthermore, it argues that respectful behaviour toward the environment has to be rooted in an understanding of nature as "sacred." The scientists write:

> As scientists, many of us have had profound experiences of awe and reverence before the universe. We understand that what is regarded as sacred is more likely to be treated with care and respect. Our planetary home should be so regarded. Efforts to safeguard and cherish the environment need to be infused with a vision of the sacred (http://nrpe.org/open-letter.html, 1990).

While science has to provide a deeper understanding of the physical world, religious leaders and communities need to communicate the principle that the earth is sacred. Such a teaching would act as a counter-balance to the purely utilitarian mentality that has led to so much environmental destruction.

This sentiment is echoed in David Suzuki's 1997 book, *The Sacred Balance*. Suzuki, a geneticist, host of CBC's weekly programme "The Nature of Things," and perhaps the best-known environmental activist in English Canada, argues that there exists a "sacred" interdependence between human beings and the natural world. All that life itself along with all that sustains life—the air, water, soil, and energy that make up the earth's life support system—must be considered "sacred," of supreme value. Suzuki protests that we have lost this sense of sacred interdependence, so evident in the rich narratives found in the cultures of aboriginal peoples (Knudtson and Suzuki, 1993). This loss is the negative side of our greatest achievement, Western civilization, the creation of our rational, abstracting minds. This has led to a deep alienation both from nature and from our essential being.

Indeed, the world we have created is an extraordinary, unprecedented achievement, constructed out of the awesome power of our abstracting, pattern-making brain. But it has lacked the ingredient we discover we depend on to thrive—the idea of wholeness and connection we call spirit. Human beings have always believed in power beyond human power, life after death, and spirit-among-us (the sacred, the holy). But *our* cultural narrative does not include these beliefs, so our experience of them is stunted, truncated, painful. The consequences are threatening indeed—the denial of value, the negation of being (Suzuki, 1997).

The modern mind creates a double alienation: first from nature and secondly from the body itself. Suzuki celebrates the Romantic protest against modernity and its trust in the body's direct experience of nature (Suzuli, 1997, 203–4). It is our trust in our rationality and our belief that we are separate from nature that have led to our cavalier attitude towards the environment. He writes:

> Although we know who we are, where we come from, what we are for, we give that knowledge no weight; our culture tends to deny or conceal that insight, and so we are left alienated and afraid, believing the truth to be "objective" instead of embodied. A world that is raw material, resources, dead matter to be made into things, has nothing sacred in it. So we cut down the sacred grove, lay it waste and declare that it does not matter, because it is only matter. Just so the slavers of an earlier century declared their merchandise to be incapable of "proper human feeling." Just so generations of experimental animals have been sacrificed in the name of research (1997, 204–5).

Suzuki's book is dedicated to showing how humans are totally dependent on and entirely integrated into their environment. Chapters on water, air, earth, and fire demonstrate in scientific detail our dependence on the basic elements of the ecosystem. Another chapter on life shows our close relationship to the "web of life," upon which we depend for both short-term and long-term survival. Finally, Suzuki turns to our need for "spirit," for a sense of the sacred or transcendent that gives us a sense of wholeness and unity (Suzuki, 1997).

In practical terms, a newfound spirituality would teach us our true place in the cosmos. We would feel at ease thinking of ourselves as one species among many and dependent on many. This spiritual insight would lead in turn to a new ethos of self-limitation, a respect for other species and for the earth itself, a respect that is the heart of humility and wisdom (Suzuki, 1997, 208). The return of the sacred in public culture would allow us, Suzuki argues, "to reenter the world, restore its spirits and celebrate the sacred" (1997, 195). Considering life and the earth itself as being of ultimate value would lead us to rethink our current tendency to rely on "bottom line" thinking to define "value" solely in economic terms. He proposes a number of far reaching political and economic reforms that would reflect our belief in the sanctity of life (1997, 174–75).

Why This demand for the Return of the Sacred? Why Now?

What drives them to this unfamiliar territory, I believe, is the current context. Three factors in particular are most frequently cited: the size or magnitude of the problem, the magnitude of the shift in behaviour and consciousness required to overcome it, and, finally, the sense that we are accelerating our destructive behaviours instead of arresting them. David Korten's work identifies the runaway globalization of the free-market economy as the underlying context of these new calls for the return of the sacred into public life. The redefinition of all of human life in economic terms promotes consumerism and suppresses criticism of the market place. Individuals are persuaded—at the deepest level of their beings—that increasing production and profit is the goal of human life. Korten argues that only a rediscovery of spiritual meaning can counterbalance the current obsession with economic development. Voicing sentiments that remind one of recent Catholic social teaching,

Korten writes that spirituality teaches us the primacy of people and life over economic systems. It reminds us that "people-centred development" is the real purpose of life and that the economy "is but one of the instruments of good living—not the purpose of human existence" (Korten 1995, 7). The return to the sacred is a strategy to counterbalance the globalizing and totalizing claims of the new world order, the certainty of the economic "science" that justifies it, the impersonality of the bureaucracy that implements it, and the cold rationality that guides it. The Catholic theologian Gregory Baum explains how he has come to the same insight:

> In contemporary culture, largely defined by capitalism, global competition and the struggle for survival, the metaphysical claim of human beings and the rights derived from this dignity will not be effectively defended against the logic of the market unless this dignity be recognized as sacred and hence untouchable; that is to say, as grounded in the divine transcendent. Similarly, I am tempted to propose that in contemporary culture, marked by individualism and utilitarianism, the self-restraint and social sacrifices necessary for protecting the global ecology will not be made unless universal human solidarity, embracing the generations still to come, be recognized as a sacred value, derived from the divine transcendent (Baum, 1994, 14–15).

Even if some of them do not develop the idea so fully, I would argue that these scientists, environmentalists, and social activists have come to the same conclusions.

The Dangers of the Return of the Sacred

Reintroducing the sacred into public debates poses certain dangers. In an earlier day, one might have cited the danger of a return to theocracy or the inherent threat to pluralism and democracy that public religion in the past has posed. I doubt that the new emergence of the sacred in the public sphere poses these dangers. The authors distance themselves from any one religious tradition or institution. They are democrats and do not call for the rejection of scientific reason, only a conversation between technology and ethics. The dangers of this strategy are more likely to lie in its abstractness and idealism. The authors cited above distance themselves from all particular communities, so that their call for a return to the sacred remains abstract and powerless. The scientists led by Carl Sagan only appreciate the power of "religious teaching, example and leadership to influence *personal* conduct and commitment powerfully" (my emphasis). Suzuki's book is addressed to individual readers; he makes no reference to community. Without community to debate and refine the concept of the sacred—and what that concept means to concrete living—the concept will inevitably inspire much personal religiosity but little communal action. Moreover, because this invitation of the sacred into public life does not seem to be informed by an historical consciousness, the authors seem unaware of the possible political dangers. The use of the sacred in public debates has often led to the absolutization of political, economic, and cultural positions, protecting them against criticism or reform and raising the stakes in conflicts with other positions. The sacralization of nature could easily degenerate into the absolutization of a green movement or the goals of the environmental movements of the countries of the North over the needs for justice and development with respects to the countries of the South. Finally, the globalizing economy tends to generate a mirror-image, globalizing ecological movement rooted in the same norms of so-called "universal" rationality. Rooting the command to respect the environment in "the sacred" begs the question: who gets to define the sacred? I would argue that, if we want to avoid a new form of cultural or ideological imperialism, each community must define for itself a conception of the sacred and root its ecological *praxis* in that particular tradition. In light of the interconnectedness of human communities, this effort must take place in a spirit of openness and dialogue. But a vaguely defined understanding of "the sacred" is too weak a foundation for a new environmental praxis.

Papal Teaching on the Ecological Crisis

Pope John Paul II has begun to address the ecological crisis in light of the Roman Catholic definition of "the sacred." Although done out of a particular tradition and on behalf of a specific community, this work does not represent a return to a pre-modern Christianity. It is rooted in a respect for pluralism, democratic politics, and civil liberties—and in fact criticizes the dominant forms of political and economic development for not being concerned enough about these principles. It is necessary to situate the Church's attempt to participate in this public debate in its long history of trying to introduce the concept of "transcendence" or "the sacred" into public debates. Before the Second Vatican Council, the Church's introduction of the sacred in public debates was often a protest against modernity and a defense of the privileges of the Church. As such, the Church's forays into public debates often violated the norms of pluralism, democracy, and civil liberties. Since the Council, the Church's public performance on social and political issues has been more open to pluralism, democratic politics, and the human rights tradition (Casanova, 1994, 69–73). Its social teaching has rested on two main points: the transcendence of God and the dignity of the human person that is rooted in that transcendence. Its insistence on God's transcendence means that no human social order can be considered perfect. Each needs to be perfected so that it will protect and promote the welfare of every human being. This orientation has introduced a prophetic dimension into Catholic social thought, so that the papacy has been very critical of all ideologies and systems that claim total allegiance. In his most recent message on world peace (1 January 1999), John Paul II identifies the materialistic consumerism that lies at the heart of the dominant form of modern development as one such ideology. Like Marxism, Nazism, Fascism, racism, nationalism, and ethnic exclusivism, it encourages people to pursue their self-interest without regard for the damage done to others (John-Paul II, 1999). It is in this context that the pope addresses the ecological crisis.

While other popes have addressed the ecological crisis in passing, John Paul II has addressed it squarely and much more frequently (Vaillancourt, 1997, 234–38). Like the scientists, environmentalists, and activists discussed above, he too argues that without a correct understanding of "the sacred," no solution to the crisis is possible. However, the Catholic tradition understands the "sacred" in terms of a God who not only prohibits selfish behaviour but also calls us to a more fully human way of life based on solidarity and compassion. The ecological crisis, the pope argues, is essentially a moral crisis rooted in the negation of the humanity of the majority of persons. Consequently, he does not separate the exploitation of the natural world from the exploitation and oppression of the poor. In each context, the dominant system, legitimated by the dominant ideology, affects both. To solve one crisis is to solve the other. For this pontiff, the solution is summed up in the word "solidarity," the key to assuring the common good and justice for the marginalized, exploited and oppressed.

Theocentrism, Anthropocentrism and Biocentrism

While Catholics might agree that for the protection of life, the concept of "the sacred" needs to be reintroduced to public debates on the environment, they would have some difficulty identifying nature itself with the transcendent. Pantheism is explicitly rejected; nature is part of God's creation; its sacred character comes from its relationship to the creator, who alone is holy. Humanity's obligation to respect nature and the natural order of the cosmos is rooted in God's command. John Paul II explains in his 1987 encyclical *Sollicitudo Rei Socialis* that humans were given dominion over other creatures and "nature" because they were inherently superior, made in the image and likeness of the Creator. Consequently, humans should use the gifts of God, the stuff of the cosmos, to fulfill their unique mission of self-perfection. They have the mandate of being co-creators with God; it is their right to shape the world. This higher spiritual calling is the basis of their power over nature and their right to its proper use. In the modern world, this right is expressed in "development" which the pontiff identifies as part of God's plan. While development presents humans with the constant temptation of idolatry and infidelity to God's will, humans are meant to be its chief protagonists. They are defined by their work that transforms the natural world (John-Paul II, 1987).

However, dominion in this sense is not "anthropocentric" but "theocentric." John Paul II writes:

> The dominion granted to man by the Creator is not an absolute power, nor can one speak of a freedom to "use and misuse" or to dispose of things as one pleases. The limitation imposed from the beginning by the Creator himself and expressed symbolically by the prohibition not to "eat of the fruit of the tree" (cf. Gen 2:16–17) shows clearly enough that, when it comes to the natural world, we are subject not only to biological laws but also to moral ones, which cannot be violated with impunity (John-Paul II, 1987).

Thus when humans use the gifts of nature to higher ends they conform to God's will which is to redeem both humanity and all of creation in

Christ. The idea that "man" can "make arbitrary use of the earth, subjecting it without restraint to his will" is rooted in a widespread "anthropological error" (John-Paul II, 1987). The modern attitude is idolatrous because humans have set themselves in God's place, making their desires absolute.

It is at this point that John-Paul II comes closest to the thinking of deep ecologists (Vaillancourt, 1997, 326). Nature, he argues, has its own order, "its own requisites and a priori God-given purpose" (John-Paul II, 1987). Consequently, human will is limited by the absolute claims of other beings and the natural world. The pope warns against using "with impunity the different category of beings, whether living or inanimate" for economic ends. "On the contrary," he writes, "one must take into account the nature of each being and of its mutual connection in an ordered system, which is precisely the cosmos" (John-Paul II, 1996, 34). This order is marked by "mutual interdependence." The world is not chaotic; it is marked by a fully integrated order that has its own integrity, an integrity that must be respected. Indeed, the pontiff goes so far as to suggest that nature has its own "subjectivity." He notes that the rest of creation "is called to join man in praising God." In 1979, he named St. Francis of Assisi patron of those who promote ecology. The pope explained that he did this with the hope that the saint would "help us to keep ever alive a sense of 'fraternity' with all those good and beautiful things which Almighty God has created" (John-Paul II, 1987, 16). The idea that the created order "praises" God and has in some sense a "fraternity" with human beings raises the issue of the subjectivity of nature, a concept which is by no means fully developed in papal writings. It suggests that, like human beings, the myriad of beings, both animate and inanimate, has an innate dignity and right to exist according to its own nature.

Sin, Human Dignity, and Solidarity

Despite these overtones of deep ecology, papal statements on the environmental crisis are closer to social ecology than to any other school. Like social ecologists, John Paul II sees the ecological crisis as the result of wider moral crisis in social relations (Vaillancourt, 1997, 326–27). The "natural" human relations of mutuality, cooperation, and solidarity mandated by the creator have been destroyed and replaced by those of domination and oppression. The modern systems of development in their various forms all absolutize their goals and marginalize, exploit, and oppress individuals and whole peoples. At the heart of this loss is sin, not only personal sin but social sin or institutionalized forms of domination, violence, and theft often perpetuated by nations, blocs, classes and other groups. At the heart of all sin are the desires for wealth and power "at any price"—even the cost of the lives of fellow human beings. The sinners absolutize their desires and pursue their satisfaction without concern for the consequences of their actions for others (John-Paul II, 1987, 37). Furthermore, they objectify their brothers and sisters, reducing them to mere instruments to be used and discarded in the pursuit of their goals. This brutal reality is disguised by sophisticated rationalizations, but behind the decisions of these groups are "real forms of idolatry: of money, ideology, class, technology" (John-Paul II, 1987, 37).

In terms of the ecological crisis, the Pope suggests, this sin expresses itself as the pursuit of human projects without concern for the destruction of the web of life that sustains us all. He writes:

> The most profound and serious indication of the moral implications underlying the ecological crisis is the lack of respect for life evident in many patterns of environmental pollution. Often, the interests of production prevail over concern for the dignity of the workers, while economic interests take priority over the good of individuals and even entire peoples. In these cases, pollution or environmental destruction is the result of an unnatural and reductionist vision which at times leads to a genuine contempt for man (John-Paul II, 1990, 7).

The pontiff correctly identifies the modern economic project as the real culprit in the ecological crisis. This system is not really anthropocentric because it does not take into account the whole of humanity and the whole of the human person. Those in poverty are excluded from development. Those who enjoy the material benefits of progress are culturally oppressed by a system that defines development in narrow economic terms. When this economic programme puts the needs and wants of capital over the basic welfare of whole peoples, it is a sign of collective and individual greed and selfishness which are "contrary to the order of creation, an order which is characterized by mutual interdependence" (John-Paul II, 1990, 8).

The ecological question can not be extricated from the question of social justice. The pontiff recognizes that there are two sides to the ecological crisis: the underdevelopment of the so-called Third World and, much more seriously, the "superdevelopment" of the First World that promotes an unsustainable consumerist lifestyle. The "structural forms of poverty" such as the unjust distribution of land in poorer countries that leads poor people to exploit and destroy marginal lands and the global economy which encourages irrational development among heavily indebted nations need to be addressed. War, with its great potential to destroy the environment, must be avoided. Finally, the consumerist lifestyle of the wealthy has to be completely rethought since it is, he argues, the driving force behind the destruction of the environment (John-Paul II, 1990). When humans wantonly use and misuse the earth's resources to increase their power and wealth, they forget that the earth is "a common heritage, the fruits of which are for the benefits of all" (John-Paul II, 1990, 8). The idea of the earth as a common heritage for all means that environmental damage is both a sin against the poor and against all future generations (John-Paul II, 1987, 34).

Like his analysis of the crisis, John-Paul II's proposed solution is centred on the human person. Because he has made the teaching on the dignity of the human person rooted in God's transcendence the foundation of his social teaching, he has become an advocate for human rights. The ecological crisis, he argues, is a human rights issue. In his first full message on the ecological crisis, he stresses the point that the environmental question is a moral question, one of right relations between human beings, relations based on solidarity, recognition of each other as brothers and sisters who belong to and rely on each other. He labels these right relations "solidarity," a commitment to the common good and social justice based on the recognition of the God-given dignity in each person (John-Paul II, 1987, 34). Solidarity is the foundation of all human rights, but especially the right to life. Since humans need a healthy environment in order to live, the right to a safe environment is a fundamental human right. International action is needed, he argues, to enshrine it as such "in an updated Charter of Human Rights" (John-Paul II, 1990, 9). In his 1999 message on world peace, he includes the right to a safe environment in a list of other fundamental rights: the right to life, religious freedom, participation in society, self-determination (for peoples), self-fulfillment, and peace. For this pontiff, a commitment to the environment involves a commitment to human development—the whole person and the whole of humanity.

Here the pontiff's emphasis is its most anthropocentric. He writes that "Respect for life, and above all for the dignity of the human person, is the ultimate guiding norm for any sound economic, industrial or scientific progress" (John-Paul II, 1990, 7). Human well-being can not be defined against the good of creation. Nor can the good of the natural world be separated from the good of humanity. He writes:

> The world's present and future depend on the safeguarding of creation, because of the endless interdependence between human beings and their environment. Placing human well-being at the centre of concern for the environment is actually the surest way of safeguarding creation; this in fact stimulates the responsibility of the individual with regard to natural resources and their judicious use (John-Paul II, 1999, 10).

But at his most anthropocentric point, the pontiff reveals that the question is not so cut and dry. The future of humanity depends on the safeguarding of creation, as he explains, "because of the *endless interdependence between human beings and their environment*" (my emphasis). Here the pontiff opens himself to a new anthropology, one that might well develop in new directions in conversation with the most recent science. Given John-Paul II's openness to reexamining the anthropology of the Church in light of theories of evolution and the origins of the cosmos, such a dialogue could enrich the Church's understanding of what it means to be human.

Dialogue for the Sake of Life

To defend human life then is to defend the whole "web of life" (to use Suzuki's term). The two are inseparable. When anthropocentrism is pushed to its logical conclusion, it becomes synonymous with biocentrism, since "real" divisions between humans and the biosphere are social constructions. We are made up of the air, water, soil, and energy that make up the rest of creation (Suzuki, 1997, 130–31). While the pope makes great efforts to distinguish human beings (and their special status, rights and duties) from nature, he is forced to admit in ever-increasing increments our total interdependence. Meanwhile Suzuki and other environmentalists frequently assert that we *are* the water, air, soil, and energy that make up the earth's life system but also say that we are something more. We are also spirit, they say, without defining precisely what they mean. John-Paul II, the spiritual leader, is led to contemplate our interrelation with nature; Suzuki, the geneticist, is led to contemplate our spiritual nature. Scientists, environmentalists, and social activists who take this approach and Catholics interested in the ecological crisis have much to learn from one another. More than this, the two groups have a solid basis from which to form a coalition against the forces of death and destruction at the heart of the ecological crisis. In both groups, one senses a visceral commitment to life. The Catholic tradition comes to respect the web of life via its fidelity to the divine command to respect the dignity of the human person. However, the scientific reality of humanity's integration into the environment moves the Church from theocentrism to anthropocentrism to biocentrism. Suzuki and fellow scientists and environmentalists begin with a commitment to protect the web of life so that humans can survive. The search for an absolute foundation for their values in a world dominated by market values leads them to "the sacred." Start where you want and you find yourself debating the right relationship between humanity, nature, and the sacred. It is remarkable that these two groups, so utterly different, sometimes historically defined as enemies, agree that this right relationship is at the heart of the solution to the ecological crisis. They agree that the ecological crisis is a moral crisis rooted in our most basic values and our understanding of what it means to be human, what it means to "succeed," and what it means to "transcend." While they define the specifics of the sacred very differently, they agree that the dominant form of development can only be opposed effectively by rooting our commitments in "the transcendent." For those committed to life, these preliminary points of agreement serve as the basis for a new and fruitful dialogue *for* life and of a coalition *against* the forces of death that the ecological crisis embodies.

References

Baum, G. 1990. "The Grand Vision: It Needs Social Action." In *Thomas Berry and the New Cosmology*. Ed. Anne Lonergan and Caroline Richards. Mystic, Connecticut: Twenty-Third Publications.

———1994. *Essays in Critical Theology*. Kansas City, MO: Sheed and Ward.

Casanova, J. 1994. *Public Religions in the Modern World*. Chicago: University of Chicago Press.

Gore, A. 1996. *Earth in the Balance: Ecology and the Human Spirit*. New York: Plume.

John-Paul II, 1987. *Sollicitudo Rei Socialis*. Vatican City: Vatican.

———1990. "The Ecological Crisis: A Common Responsibility. Message of His Holiness Pope John Paul II for the Celebration of the World Day of Peace, 1 January 1990." In *This Sacred Earth: Religion, Nature, Environment*. Ed. Roger S. Gottlieb. New York: Routledge.

———1996. "Message to Pontical Academy of Sciences on Evolution," Origins, 26: 349–52.

———1999. "Le secret de la paix véritable réside dans le respect des droits humains. Message de sa Sainteté le Pape Jean-Paul II pour la célébration de la Journée Mondiale de la Paix, 1er Janvier 1999."

Korten, D. 1995. *When Corporations Rule the World*. West Hartford, C.T.: Kumarian Press.

Scharper, S. 1997. *Redeeming the Time: A Political Theology of the Environment*. New York: Continuum.

Shibley, M. and Wiggins, J. 1997. "Greening Mainline American Religion: A Sociological Analysis of the Environmental Ethics of the National Religious Part-nership for the Environment." *Social Compass* 44, (1997): 333–48.

Suzuki, D.1993. "A Personal Forward: The Value of Native Ecologies," In *Wisdom of the Elders*. Eds. Peter Knudtson and David Suzuki. Toronto: Stoddart.

———1997. *The Sacred Balance: Rediscovering Our Place in Nature*. Vancouver: Greystone.

Swimme, B. 1996. *The Hidden Heart of the Cosmos: Humanity and the New Story*. Maryknoll, N.Y.: Orbis Books.

Vaillancourt, J. 1997. "Les prises de position, du Vatican sur les questions d'environnement." *Social Compass* 44: 324–28.

Chapter 12

Environmental Decline and Christian Contemplation: Thomas Aquinas and Thomas Merton

Mark S. Muldoon, Brock University

> And the most pitiful thing of all is that, in the name of God, Christians who ought to know better are busy blessing and praising the disease on the ground that this is a matter of "openness to the world" and "adjustment to modern times."
> Thomas Merton, *Conjectures of a Guilty Bystander*

In his now classic text on eco-theology, *The Dream of the Earth* (1988), Thomas Berry argued that "Western religious traditions have been so occupied with redemptive healing ... that they tend to ignore creation as it is experienced in our times" (Barry, 1988, 25). As a result, he adds, "traditional Western spiritualities have not enabled their followers to mitigate or even to understand or protest the terrifying assault of American society on the natural world" (Barry, 1998, 25). The central message of Berry's thesis is that we must re-establish a spiritual "intimacy" with the earth since, given the gravity of the present environmental crisis, "we will die" (Barry, 1988, xiv).

What Berry refers to as spiritual "intimacy" here is "the sublime expression of the deepest mystery of the universe: the revelation of the divine" (1988, 125). Such intimacy is urgently needed to balance our overly scientific-technological relationship to the earth. It is this latter relationship with its emphasis on objectivity, analysis, and instrumentality that have led to the crass degradation of our air and water resources upon which we depend for our biological existence. Berry's hope is that as we enter this new "ecological age" we awaken to the numinous powers ever present in the phenomenal world and our genetic endowment and "renew our human participation in the grand liturgy of the universe" (1988, 215).

Almost ten years later, David Suzuki, in his book, *The Sacred Balance: Rediscovering Our Place in Nature* (1997), makes the same urgent plea concerning the environment. Unlike Berry, however, who is a Catholic theologian, Suzuki is a secular scientist. What is interesting in Suzuki's case is that he too devotes a chapter to the need for a spiritual dimension to further combat environmental degradation. Like Berry, Suzuki has come to the conclusion that scientific narratives and warnings of environmental decay alone are incapable of generating a change in human behaviour and orientation toward nature. Scientific pronouncements alone do not have the motive power to radically awake us from our autistic slumber in the midst of the earth's demise. In this light, both Suzuki and Berry call for a re-visitation with wisdom traditions that honour spiritual values in nature.

However, in making such a clarion call, both authors admit that the environmental crisis is, at heart, a crisis of our humanity. This latter crisis is a crisis of human identity endemic to our post-modern era. In the late twentieth century, the human person is often characterized in the literature as a disenfranchised self, one who is set free from fixed social roles, constraints of duty to a community, and lastly, set free from any recognition of being dependent on the limited resources of the earth (Griffin, 1988; Taylor, 1991). Given the absence of any purpose but material ones, the post-modern self seeks fulfilment through ecologically damaging consumerism that is fuelled by the morality of utilitarian individualism. As such, answers to our environmental problems will not be technical ones alone, but must include a fundamental transformation in explaining to ourselves the purpose of life and our relationship to the earth. Such a transformation appeals therefore to the spiritual dimension of our humanity, a dimension that is cultivated through various forms of contemplative behaviour.

In the course of this paper, I would like to address these two very large themes, namely, our present environmental crisis and Christian contemplation. In the first part of the paper I will detail, from a "second-wave" perspective, the environmental crisis as it manifests itself with respect to both water and air in my immediate bioregion—the Great Lakes basin. Second, I will briefly describe Aquinas' world-view, and his notion of philosophical contemplation. I will contend that the inaction toward the environment by many Christian believers today is a function of the fact that their world-view is still informed by Aquinas' anthropology which does not encourage an ecological awareness in the least. This will be followed by a contrast, in the final part, with the thought of Thomas Merton who, at the end of the twentieth century, sees political action as one of the essential fruits of contemplation. This contrast is important because many of the eco-theologians today appropriate Aquinas and not Merton. Yet, in what I will present, it is Merton's sense of contemplation that offers the corrective direction called for by both Berry and Suzuki.

Part I

I concur with Berry when he states that at the end of the twentieth century, "interhuman tensions" are secondary to "earth-human tensions" (1988, 218–19). Never before has the global population lived under the threat of its own destruction from the very fact it has sullied the air and fouled the water it needs to subsist biologically (see e.g., Dyer, 1998). In the last several years, there has been a discernible shift in environmental organizations and their mandates. Traditionally, their focus as been on conservation and preservation of natural habitants, delicate and unique ecosystems, biodiversity, and the cessation of emissions of all kinds that deteriorate air, water, and land. At present, the focus has shifted from conservation to preventing human health effects from all levels of toxic contamination. As will be shown shortly, the literature now linking health effects to toxic contamination is substantial, robust, and convincing. Consequently, we are in a period of *second-wave environmentalism* where the stakes are much higher. The challenge now is to protect basic human health given that our biosphere is almost *completely* toxified (Mitchell, 1997, 26–36).

Yet, many remain oblivious to the potential crisis of human health that creeps ever closer as we continually increase the toxic loads to our water and air resources—not to mention the growing menace of both global warming and the depletion of the ozone layer.

What accounts for our societal indifference to the state of our health from environmental degradation? Part of the problem is that the topic is not considered important by the media services we depend upon for such information. In his introduction, Suzuki cites one glaring example.

On November 18th, 1992, some five months after the largest gathering of heads of state in history at the Earth Summit in Rio, a document was released entitled "World Scientists' Warning to Humanity." It was signed by more than sixteen hundred senior scientists in seventy-one countries including half of all Nobel Prize winners still alive at the time. It was one of the most unprecedented consensus ever made by the intellectual elite in the world. The warning was eloquent but blunt. No more than a few decades remain before current human practices make human life, as we know it on the planet today, unsustainable. Despite the credentials of the report and the gravity of its message, when the warning was released to the press, Canada's national newspaper and television network ignored it, while in the United States, *The Washington Post* and *The New York Times* rejected it as "not newsworthy." Suzuki goes on in his summary to note the types of items that did make front page news on November 19th—mostly political and financial reports. In his own words, he states,

> Behind the silence—and partly because of the silence—the eco-destruction continues, compromising the future for all the coming generations. That is our true challenge today—not debts and deficits or global competition but the need to find a way to live rich, fulfilling lives without destroying the planet's biosphere, which supports all life. Humanity has never before faced such a threat: the collapse of the very elements that keep us alive (Suzuki, 1997).

Let me begin to detail this eco-destruction as it pertains specifically to the Great Lakes Basin since I believe it is absolutely important to be informed and aware of what is happening in one's local immediate environment. While this summary could include water, air, soil, and biodiversity, I will restrict my presentation to the water and air only.

a) Water Contamination

Approximately 40 million people live in the Great Lakes Basin and over half of this population depend on the Lakes as a source of drinking water. At present, the most conservative estimate of toxic releases to the air and water of the entire basin are 126,364 tonnes per year (International Joint Commission's Agreement Public Forum. 1997). This does not include those toxins that are transported by air through what is known as "the grasshopper effect" (Baker and Eisenreich, 1990, 342–352; Hillery, et el., 1998, 2216–24).

The Great Lakes are such a large, slowly circulating water system that a drop of rain entering the upper lakes can take a century or longer to reach the St. Lawrence and the ocean. This means that the Lakes retain contaminants far longer than a quick flushing river system, and toxic contaminants build up more rapidly than they would in the vast, open ocean. Because of this unique geography, the Great Lakes represent an early warning system for toxic pollution impacting the planet as a whole. What is important to note is that the present toxic contamination of the Great Lakes is not necessarily a cosmetic one. It is arguably true that since the later 1970s, water clarity in all the Lakes has in fact increased. However, toxic pollution is not necessarily connected with large algae blooms associated with the process of eutrophication, or with surface sediments and murky water. In fact, the irritating thing about toxic contamination is that it is invisible except in its toxicological effects on organisms high in the food chain. The important expert, therefore, is no longer the biologist or naturalist but the epidemiologist.

The work on toxic contamination in the Great Lakes Basin is some thirty years old with early research being done on general physiological defects and reproductive problems in small mammals, local bird and fish populations. That work took a vital step forward in the early 1980's with the results of research from Wayne State University confirming a connection between human injury and toxic pollution of the Lakes.

The chemicals that are of very great concern today because of their impact on human health are generically known as Persistent Organic Pollutants (POPs). These chemicals resist breakdown by natural processes for long periods of time, and are thus persistent in the environment. These chemicals are all organochlorines; they include dioxins, furans, PCBs and hexachlorocyclohexane (HCH), DDT, chlordane, heptachlor, aldrin, dieldrin, eldrin, toxaphene and mirex (these eight latter ones being pesticides). Most POPs enter the Great Lakes as airborne fallout from industrial smokestacks and incinerators, while others enter from pesticides and volatile synthetics that move on wind currents that circulate between air, land, and water.

Most of us today who live in the Great Lakes Basin, and indeed world-wide, are exposed to Persistent Organic Pollutants, and our bodies, in varying degrees, contain such contaminants. They are mainly ingested through what we eat. Persistent Organic Pollutants (especially, the organochlorines) are fat-soluble and they tend to accumulate in fatty tissues of the body. The combined characteristics of being fat-soluble and persistent make their presence even more problematic because of the processes of bio-magnification and bio-accumulation. This means that there is a build-up of contaminants in an organism over time; when an organism eats another organism lower on the food chain, the higher organism inherits the entire contaminant load of the lower organism. Interestingly, both Health Canada and Environment Canada treat the bodies of Beluga whales that wash ashore in the Gulf of St. Lawrence as hazardous waste and treat their disposal in an appropriate manner.

In the last year, The United Nation's Environmental Programme Governing Council have prioritised 12 Persistent Organic Pollutants because of their known toxicity to human health. These particular twelve Persistent Organic Pollutants are important because they are all known to be endocrine disrupting chemicals, or sometimes, more commonly known as hormone disruptors.

Presently, Canada's Great Lakes Basin has the dubious distinction of being one of the best-documented areas with regard to the effects of hormone disruptors. The persuasive effect of endocrine or hormone disruption in both wildlife and humans has been galvanized in part by the work of Dr. Theo Colborn. Thirty years of research has been summarized recently in her book, *Our Stolen Future* (1997).

Why are hormone disruptors so worrisome? Hormones, such as estrogen, testosterone, and thyroxin act as chemical messengers and provide detailed instructions for neural development, sexual differentiation, and the development of the immune system, sperm production and ovulation. These hormones operate at extremely low concentrations (in some cases in concentrations of *trillionths* of a gram). The studies of Colborn and others have shown that persistent organic pollutants can mimic, block, and/or interfere with functions of naturally produced female and male hormones in tissue cultures and laboratory animals. Laboratory animal studies reveal that fetuses and infants are especially susceptible to bioaccumulating and hormone disrupting chemicals because exposures occur during critical periods of early tissue and organ development. One of the current controversies is the contaminant exposure to infants from maternal milk. Current surveys show that for some human infants, the daily intake of PCBs, dioxins, and dioxin-like contaminants from breast milk may exceed established guidelines (Jonson, 1997). The average breast-fed baby in Canada presently exceeds the World Health Organization's maximum "tolerable daily intake" for dioxin by a factor of 15 (Allsopp, Stringer and Johnston, 1998). In the most highly exposed populations in the Canada, namely, the Arctic, the level of contamination of breast milk is several times higher again (Arctic Monitoring and Assessment Program, 1997).

More specific studies have indicated that children whose mothers consumed large amounts of Great Lakes fish showed reduced intellectual development, reduced growth in size, and neurobehavioral impairments. Furthermore, research points to a distinct decrease in the sperm quality and quantity as well as reduced testosterone levels in men (Allsopp, Stringer and Johnston, 1998).

Where earlier studies reported effects following relatively high exposure to these chemicals as a result of accidental or occupational exposure, newer studies indicate that such effects may occur at tissue levels which are at, or near to, those currently found in the general population as a consequence of unavoidable everyday human exposure to these compounds.

The debate about levels of Persistent Organic Pollutants in breast milk and what to do about it, however, remains highly politically charged. International studies reveal that Persistent Organic Pollutants are found at significant levels in the breast milk of women world-wide (Allsopp, Stringer and Johnston, 1998). In some industrialized countries, the average level of contamination of human breast milk by PCBs, for example, is near the legal limit for cow's milk sold commercially.

I have not dealt with the problem of drinking water from the Great Lakes. Let it suffice to say that there are two central controversies of public concern. One is the presence of microbes found to be resistant to most local drinking water disinfection processes, especially encysted forms of protozoan parasites such as *Cryptosporidium.* Second, there is serious concern of the toxic by-products of drinking water disinfection itself—namely the problem of trihalomethanes (International Joint Commission's Agreement Public Forum, 1997).

b) Air Contamination

Today, like never before, our industrialized country depends on fossil fuels as a major source of energy for automobiles, electricity, and industrial processes. The result is the creation of a mix of air pollutants such as carbon monoxide, oxides of nitrogen, ozone, sulphur dioxide, volatile organic compounds, and small airborne particulates (what are now commonly called PM 2.5 and PM 10). In the last five years the effects of these pollutants on human health have taken on a new urgency. The Canadian government under the auspices of both Environment Canada and Health Canada now estimates that eight per cent of all non-traumatic deaths, approximately 16,000 per year, are attributable to air pollution (Last, Trouton and Pengelly, 1998, 32).

In the Ontario Regional Municipality of Hamilton-Wentworth, the estimated number of premature mortalities (particularly on bad-air days) range from 90 to as high as 321 (Regional Municipality of Hamilton-Wentworth, 1997, 21). In comparison, Ontario's Smog Plan Working Group (1996) has estimated a total of approximately 1800 premature mortalities and 1,400 hospital admissions per year province wide due to the effects of the inhalable particulates alone (Regional Municipality of Hamilton-Wentworth, 1997, 20).

In the last year, Health Canada statistician, Dr. Rick Burnett, states that the correlation between the number of premature deaths and the daily rise in certain air pollutants has been replicated not only in most major cities nationally, but internationally as well. Models are now available for predicting precisely the number of deaths expected in certain cities should the temperature rise to a certain point given the presence of certain pollutants, especially PM 2.5s and PM 10s. For example, if current levels of particulate matter were slightly increased in Hamilton over a year, this would mean an additional 92 deaths, 74 hospital admissions, 37,444 asthma days, 559,820 reduced activity days and 1,735,488 acute respiratory symptoms (Last, Trouton and Pengelly, 1998, 24).

However, it should be recognized that these serious outcomes of hospital admissions and deaths are just the tip of the iceberg. These pollutants lead to a number of other morbidity effects, as for example, adult chronic bronchitis, hospital emergency room visits, asthma symptom days, restricted activity days, acute respiratory symptom days, and bronchitis in children (Regional Municipality of Hamilton-Wentworth, 1997).

Presently, those most vulnerable to air pollution are children, the elderly and people with existing illness, especially heart and lung diseases. Between 1980 and 1990, for example, hospitalization of young children in Canada for asthma increased by 28 per cent among boys and 18 per cent among girls. In Ontario, the number of infants admitted to hospital for pneumonia, bronchiolitis and bronchitis in the summer months increase by 20 per cent when ozone and sulphate levels increase (Last, Trouton and Pengelly, 1998, 27).

Dr. Burnett (1998), indicated that Health Canada is having great difficulty in managing this information. It is finding it extremely difficult to state the results in non-threatening manner, namely, how does such an agency formulate a policy statement saying that at current ambient concentrations, urban air pollution may pose a serious health risk. In short, on hot summer days in urban environments, breathing for many has become a health liability.

What has been stated above should be put into a wider context, namely, that on the whole, the Great Lakes Basin in losing on another front, namely, biodiversity. As traditional agricultural practises move toward practises of agri-business, there is a predicted increase of toxic substances due to the use of pesticides and herbicides that will, in turn, potentially decrease bird and wildlife populations. Furthermore, there is the replacement of the Great-Lakes mixed Decidious forests with pine monocultures, the increasing loss of wetlands to urban and industrial development, and the cultivation and replacement of fish stocks with only selected genotypes which need large amounts of chemical support for their unnatural production.

This decrease in indigenous plant and wildlife species in the basin must be seen against an even wider background in that a newly established Living Planet Index has recently estimated that one third of the natural world has been destroyed by human activity in the past 25 years (McCarthy, 1998).

This fall in biodiversity is ultimately a health issue. At the shallowest level, there is the regret for the loss of species whose potential utility to humankind is yet to be discovered. At another level, species loss is worrisome because certain species act as "indicator species" of the state of nature, much in the same way canaries did for the state of air in coal mines. In other words, when such species disappear, they indicate that the planet as a whole may have become less habitable in a way that may be relevant to humanity.

Let me finish this first part by stating that reliable sources are presently announcing serious and quantifiable health concerns to human beings because of environmental degradation (Goddard-Hill, 1998). In many cases, large urban centres in Canada can no longer guarantee safe drinking-water and uncontaminated air to its citizens. People in certain sub-groups are dying and various environmentally related illnesses are becoming more apparent locally, and across the general population.

At the end of such a summary, the key question that needs to be addressed is this, is it acceptable that we permit the ongoing ingestion into our bodies of such toxic pollutants "involuntarily" and accommodate ourselves to their effects without ever addressing the cause, the consequences, and possible solutions?

The obvious answer is no, but the silence on part of the general public, legislators, and policy-makers is resounding. In our culture, what could possibly lie at the root of such a silence?

Part II

In order to address these questions, I would like to jump to another plane of analysis. Owing to the lethal impact of environmental decline, I am interested in knowing why, for example, such questions as above are not part of our common discourse today as a nation, or a local community, regardless of the presence of many earnest Christians who, by and large, are virtuous and would not harm others intentionally?

In this section, I would like to discuss Thomas Aquinas' notion of contemplation. For the most part, Eurocentric Christians today still live under the long shadow cast by Aquinas' metaphysics and theology as it informs us of how we fit into creation and our purpose therein. In this light, St. Thomas's thought is also a world-view. By world-view, I mean the collection of images, ideas, attitudes and beliefs that attempt to locate the person in the larger scheme of things, in the cosmos, along with the meaning and values that human beings attribute to that location. Aquinas' notion of contemplation should be understood as a fundamental component to the world-view articulated in his works. This will be the chief distinction in the next section, when I discuss Merton's notion of contemplation. Merton's reflections do not supply our generation with a world-view as much as his notion of contemplation, ultimately, reacts to a world-view not of his own making. It is this reaction that makes the contrast between these two Christian thinkers striking and why it is Merton, I will argue, who is the better candidate for eco-theologians to promote in advocating a new Christian concern for nature.

St. Thomas Aquinas (1225–1274 C.E.) is one of the central Doctors of the Catholic Church. His theological naturalism was constructed on the basis of many philosophical influences and perhaps none greater than Aristotle. St. Thomas's systematic approach to the theological and philosophical questions of his day has been both an explicit and implicit mainstay of Catholic thought up until today.

One of the great problems with Aquinas' thought is that it was too quickly reduced to a technical vocabulary and turned into an "-ism" known variously as "Thomistic scholasticism" or simply "Thomism." His thought, subsequently, became the purview of only experts and the scholars. Some of Aquinas' more vibrant and revolutionary spirit has been captured by only a few. Ones who come to mind are Père Marie Dominic Chenu, Josef Pieper, Athanasius Weisheipl, Etienne Gilson, Jacques Maritain and even G. K. Chesterton.

However, let me make reference to a new interest in St. Thomas on the part of theologians and scholars, most of whom see creation as the first order of revelation and therefore add a theological dimension to the present environmental debates.

Today, for example, some eco-theologians, such as Matthew Fox, have conscripted the thought and vision of Aquinas in order to show the consistency of an ecological promise inherent in Christian theology. Fox, once a Dominican priest like Aquinas, goes so far as to claim that "Aquinas represents a giant step forward in the West's rediscovery of the ecological consciousness" Fox, 1992, 32).

The central theme that re-occurs in some literature (e.g., Haugt, 1993, 81) is that Aquinas, in following Aristotle, turns toward the world and gives to thirteenth-century Christian thought a respect for nature, for the physical, and for the concrete reality of the universe. The theology of Aquinas is seen as a reaction against other theologies that denature nature by engrossing itself in allegorical and symbolic systems. St. Thomas, rather, returned to the realities that the symbols were intended to signify. For the eco-theologians, Aquinas' argument on the order, design, and variety in creation conveys a type of rightness ordained by God that demands a reverence for it on our part. One of the oft-quoted passages from the first part of Aquinas' magisterial work, the *Summa theologiae* (1266–74 incomplete) reads:

> For he [God] brought things into existence so that his goodness might be communicated to creatures and re-enacted through them. And because one single creature was not enough, he produced many and diverse, so that what was wanting in one expression of the divine goodness might be supplied by another, for goodness, which in God is single and all together, in creatures is multiple and scattered. Hence, the whole universe less incompletely than one alone shares and represents his goodness (Aquinas, 1963, Ia. 47.1).

Stated in more modern terms, the very bio-diversity of the planet is inherently good and beholds a divine purpose; it is an onto-theologically necessity. Again, from the *Summa theologiae*: "Creation is none other than the relation of the creature to the Creator as to the principle of its very being" (Aquinas, 1963, Ia. 45.3c). This refers to the fact that Aquinas conceived of creation as a universal hierarchical structure where the graduations of the hierarchy of being define an ontological link between the spiritual and the material. As such, nearest to God are the purely angelic creatures; next, human creatures, or embodied spirits with rational souls; then come animals, plants, and material elements. This hierarchical structure is a valuable insight in that it gives a foundation for reverence of other creatures as brothers and sisters sharing the relationship of divine recognition and dependence. Human beings, because of their rational souls, have the added pleasure of working toward their ordained end, which is happiness (*beatitudo*) and is achieved in the contemplation of God (Aquinas, 1960, 191).

For Aquinas, therefore, the act of contemplation is embedded in his metaphysical scheme and is central to the gap often observed in Aquinas between the philosophical and theological concepts of human happiness. Contemplation is the end point of a process of analogous reasoning that starts with the sense world. By higher and higher levels of intellection, the human being finally realizes that God alone satisfies the intellect's desire to seek the good. The intellect arrives at this point by the gradual elimination of objects other than God. Then theology intervenes, and insists there is yet a higher state to attain which surpasses the powers of our rational nature. This higher state is given by grace. The "blessedness of abstraction" is replaced by the "blessedness of vision."

As such, the universe as represented by Aquinas is not a mass of inert bodies passively moved by a forces which pass through them, but a collection of active beings each enjoying the efficacy delegated to it by God, Actual Being. A taste of that joy is attainable by the most rational of embodied beings—the human being—in the act of contemplation.

What is stated above, however, is only the inner dynamic of a much larger dynamic expressed in the *Summa theologiae.* The first part of the work articulates the emanation of all things (the *exitus*) from God, who is here the Principle of being. The second part of the work depicts the return (the *reditus*) of things, each according to its nature, to God, who is the end, the *telos* of being. All creatures, particularly human creatures, and all events, particularly human events, are framed between two causes, the efficient cause of creation and the final cause of God glorified.

Perhaps it is Bettini's engraving of *Monte Sancto di Dio* (1477) that best depicts the Medieval world-view espoused by St. Thomas (see figure 1). In this figure, the human subject is immersed in the natural world with its sole purpose of existence being to ascend from the created world by way of virtuous behaviour and contemplation to union with God.

In the Christian narrative of salvation history, the image of the mountain is very important. One can easily make a list of key events that take place on high places in the Bible—Mt. Carmel, Mt. Zion, Mt. Sinai, Mountain of the Beatitudes, Mountain of the Transfiguration, Mount of Olives, and so forth. It is perhaps Mircea Eliade who explains best this image in that the sense of the sacred mountain is an *axis mundi* (the centre of the world). The verticality of the mountain—as opposed to the horizontal—is a crucial symbol in trying to situate oneself in a world that is understood at once as divinely bestowed and sustained by the same divine nature. It is a thoroughly theocentric world-view (Eiade, 1957).

Associated with the key symbol of the mountain are the metaphors of ascent and the metaphor of fecundity, abundance, and plenitude. As a created being, the human being is immersed in the plenitude of creation surrounded by plants, birds, animals, and the grandeur of the seemingly inanimate elements. Yet, the proper end of the human being is to ascend from the material world, first through contemplation, and then consummation, in order to achieve an ultimate union with the Godhead. Notice that in Bettini's piece the ladder is chained at the bottom end. The note says that the climber is blind until he or she at least attains the first four virtues; the mountain itself is tiered (hope, faith, charity), and there is always the potential of failure given the presence of evil (bottom of figure) and human weakness.

As such, the created world for Aquinas becomes a stepping stone first for our contemplation *of* God and than our final consummation *in* God. The mountain becomes the median point between the world of pure form and the world of form still attached to matter. While God is present in all creatures, God is also removed from all creatures according to their place in the hierarchy of being. This is why Gilson called Aquinas' world "an ordered discontinuity" with an impassable abyss between the freely created universe and God the Creator (Gilson, 1956, 361). This sense of ontological discontinuity becomes the key to the ultimate value and disvalue one sees in the created world. Chenu summarizes the dilemma well for the 12th and 13th century Christian when he says, "The Christian contemplating the world is torn by a double attraction: to attain God through the world, the order of which reveals its Creator, or to renounce the world, from which God is radically distinct" (Chenu, 1968, 36).

Hence, it is this "ordered discontinuity" that ultimately makes Aquinas' appropriation by modern eco-theologians very difficult. While on the surface there is something appealing about the interconnectedness between created being and a celebration of created diversity fused with the human desire for union with God, there is a gnawing inner ambiguity about the earth and its integrity. Let me summarize this ambiguity in three short points (Santmire, 1985, 91).

First, the weight of the hierarchy of being for Aquinas is not with material creatures but with the angelic. Aquinas was not called the Angelic Doctor for naught. In the *Summa* he writes, "... angels, even as they are immaterial substances, exist in exceeding great number, far beyond all material multitude" (1963, Ia 50.3). Hence, in terms of proportion, Bettini got it right in devoting at least one-half of his piece to the angelic immaterial realm.

Second, although all creatures are ordained to the divine goodness as their end, Aquinas says that "some are closer to the end than others, and so participate in the divine goodness more abundantly" (Aquinas, 1958,

157). Hence, lesser creatures, having a smaller share in the divine goodness, "are in some way subordinated to higher beings as to their ends." More specifically, "lower beings realize their last end chiefly by their subordination to higher beings." Then, Aquinas points to the concrete order of the universe itself: "As we observe ..., imperfect beings serve the needs of more noble beings; plants draw their nutriment from the earth, animals feed on plants, and these in turn serve man's use. We conclude, then, that lifeless beings exist for living beings, plants for animals, and the latter for man." Further, in the same passage, Aquinas argues that since intellectual nature is superior to material nature, "the whole of the material nature is subordinate to intellectual nature." This means, in turn, "that the whole of material nature exists for man, inasmuch as he is a rational animal" (1958, 158). Aquinas concludes on this more accurately when he states in the *Summa* that "the less perfect fall to the use of the more perfect" such that the life of animals and plants is preserved not for themselves but for man (1963, Ia 96.1). Consequently, for Thomas, when our ascension is complete "in the consummation of the world,"—when our animal life ceases—the visible and tangible world of animals, plants, minerals, and all the mixed bodies, will not be renewed because they are incapable of renewal (1963, III supp. 91.5).

Aquinas' anthropocentrism here is not yet that of a Descartes, for whom knowledge is essentially, power over nature. Nor is it by any means the anthropocentrism of later industrial society, according to which nature is a storehouse of resources available for human exploitation. Yet, Aquinas' view is not totally dissimilar from these approaches to nature either (Santmire, 1985, 91). When he sees nature, he sees something created essentially to satisfy basic human needs and to aid the human ascent toward God. Nature is seen more as an object for human use, which satisfies biological needs and serves spiritual knowledge, than as a subject in its own right.

Third, there is the ambiguity between the priority that Aquinas allots to the common good and the individual good (Porter, 1990, 125). In the second part of the *Summa*, Aquinas insists, as strongly as any good Marxist, that the common good takes precedence over the good of the individual, just as the good of the cosmos as a whole is a greater good than the good of any one creature, however exalted (Aquinas, 1963). Yet, in the previous section of the *Summa*, Aquinas already affirmed the duty of self-love and the irreducible worth of the individual just as strongly. In deed, Aquinas insists that each person is under serious obligation to seek his or her own good correctly, that is, by pursuing the fundamental inclinations of human life in a way that respects their intrinsic ordering (Aquinas, 1963).

Consequently, if eco-theologians wish to conscript Aquinas' for their ends, and attempt to make the point that there is a poignant ecological promise latent in Christian theology, especially in Aquinas, then they must take Aquinas as a whole. Santmire summarizes the dilemmas by saying that "we are offered a onto-theology that both affirms nature and denies nature: one that stresses, under the rubric of creation, the overflowing goodness of God, yet which highlights, under the rubric of redemption, the nature-denying finality of fulfilment in God" (Santmire, 1985, 94).

Let me make it clear, for Thomas, creation is ordered, purposeful, and teleological. Human beings have a place in it; we know our place, and our ends. The ladder of virtue is perfective of our rational natures permitting us the contemplation of God and actualizes our intended happiness. However, the price for Aquinas' vision seems to be a type of indifference if not exploitation of the created world for the exclusive use of our redemption alone. Aquinas' sense of contemplation, while edifying, does not necessarily lead one to take the created world seriously, respect the earth's integrity, and to take responsibility for its well-being. While St. Thomas's metaphysical system and theology may be the most cohesive world-view ever written, I do not think it encourages the type of moral behaviour and action needed to confront our wilful destruction of the biosphere today.

Part III

In jumping to the twentieth century, let me address another Christian author whose fame and literary output makes him as well known to many as Aquinas' reputation had been in the previous centuries. I am speaking here of Thomas Merton, a Catholic Trappist monk who is perhaps one of the most important contemporary authors in the area of Catholic spirituality this century.

Merton was born in France in 1915, lived the life of a gypsy student, converted to Catholicism, entered the cloistered life of a severe Trappist monastery in Kentucky, and died, accidentally in Bangkok, Thailand, in 1968. Precisely one half of his fifty-four years was lived outside the monastery and one half inside. He became recognized internationally in 1948 with his autobiography entitled *The Seven Story Mountain* (1948). Perhaps his most celebrated text on spirituality is entitled *Seeds of Contemplation* (1949). As a monk, he published some 51 different books ranging from historical tracts, to poetry, to social commentary.

Above all else, Merton is the consummate observer of life, especially his own, with all of its existential trials and tribulations being so well documented in his voluminous diaries and journals. The last of these was just recently published under the title of *Turning Toward the World: The Pivotal Years* (Merton 1996)—an accurate title in terms of what I will say about Merton's thinking in the years leading to his death.

In these journals, one finds Merton contending with his human experience as a student, a teacher, a postulant, a priest, a monk, and a social activist. His first appeal to make sense of such experiences is not Christian theology necessarily. He passes them through, rather, the prism of his own introspective solitude and then enriches them by contrast and in discussion with the early Church fathers, the eremite tradition, Catholic theology, Eastern philosophy, as well as both fictional and non-fictional literature. For those who have read Merton's journals, one finds someone in constant communion with physical nature. He is forever walking in the forest, commenting on the birds, trees, and natural settings where he takes many of his guests to sit and talk (Merton, 1992, 214–22).

Unlike, Aquinas, Merton does not provide a well-formulated metaphysics, a doctrine of natural law, or a theory of moral virtue. Rather, he takes much of Aquinas for granted and radicalizes it. What does this mean? In his autobiography, *The Seven Story Mountain*, Merton had already studied Aquinas before his vocation as a professed religious began officially (Merton, 1976). In the epilogue to *The Seven Story Mountain*, he engages Aquinas in a long discussion concerning *contemplata tradere*, loosely translated as *what comes after* or *the fruits of* contemplation. Here he conflates Aquinas' more philosophical appreciation of contemplation with the profoundly spiritual practice of contemplation and concludes that *no one* is excluded from the need to contemplate and to share the fruits of this practise.

> This means, in practice, that there is only one vocation. Whether you teach or live in the cloister or nurse the sick, whether you are in religion or out of it, married or single, no matter who you are or what you are, you are called to the summit of perfection: you are called to a

> deep interior life perhaps even to mystical prayer, and to pass the fruits of your contemplation on to others. And if you cannot do so by word, then by example (Merton, 1976, 419).

Hence, not unlike Socrates who encouraged everyone—at a price—to examine themselves interiorly, not only to deepen and enrich their own lives, but that of the *polis* as well, Merton, in 1948, expands the practice of contemplation for those outside of a strictly religious vocation. In the last several years of his life, I would suggest, he further expanded the boundaries of contemplation beyond personal conversion and self-discovery to include political activism as well.

For Merton, contemplation is not an act of intellection alone (Merton, 1972, 4). Whereas Aquinas situates contemplation in his larger metaphysical schema of the individual soul seeking a level of imperfect happiness in the possession of God through theoretical reason, Merton's notion of contemplation issues from the larger properly mystical tradition of *vita contemplativa*. In this tradition, the presence of God is experienced as a type of awakening, a sudden gift of awareness of being able to witness the Real within what is empirically real. It is an awareness of our contingent reality as received, as a present from God, as a free gift rooted in the experience of solitude, thoughtful concentration, and openness to the world as it is lived (Merton, 1961, 1–13). In very crude terms, where contemplation for Aquinas is a philosophical "looking up," for Merton, contemplation is an existential "looking around" with an ever deepening sense that the physical world is not merely present to us in a detached manner, but that we are undergoing a deeper experience of "presence."

In an early biography released shortly after Merton's death (on which Merton had himself collaborated), Dennis McInerny breaks Merton's life into three periods (McInerney, 1974, 59). First, prior to his entrance into the cloistered life, Merton is the nascent critic of the world having lived both in Europe and America and seeing the Continent come to the brink of war. Writings from his student days at Columbia focused on poverty, the disparity of wealth, and the impotence of political systems to deal with such problems. Second, upon entering the monastery, his writing takes on an "other worldly" attitude with works devoted almost entirely to the monastic life and the lives of the saints. Merton admits that he had assumed, naively perhaps, that upon entering the thick walls of the monastery he had left the mad world happily behind. The third period begins in 1955 when Merton returns to questions of a "this worldly" nature starting with the book, *No Man is an Island*. These writings take on an urgency with a poignant focus on political and social issues as Merton attempts to come to grips with his response as a Christian to a world that seems to have embraced both potential annihilation and chaos. Hence, where once he had written books strictly for spiritual edification such as *The Waters of Siloe* (1949), *Thoughts in Solitude* (1956), we now see the appearance of such texts as *Seeds of Destruction* (1964), *Conjectures of a Guilty Bystander* (1966), *Faith and Violence* (1968), *The Non-Violent Alternative* (1971), *Contemplation in a World of Action* (1971).

The gist of these later texts express a "this worldly" attitude and deal with a Christian's life in and obligations toward the world. The theme is clear: "if the Christian was ever justified in turning his [or her] back on the chaos of the times, he or she could do no longer in good conscience. He [or she] must confront the chaos head-on and do what [one] could to ameliorate it" (McIernery, 1974, 62). Hence, Merton himself becomes an outspoken critic of the Vietnam War, the nuclear arms race, and a supporter of the civil rights movement. However, he does not stop there but goes on to write, more consistently than another theme, a constant critique of modern American society and the danger it poses to the spiritual growth and maturation of the human person.

In one of his last books, *Conjectures of a Guilty Bystander* (1969), Merton admonishes his readers not to be bystanders. The quintessential reason why most of us have been rendered bystanders is a loss of what Merton calls our authentic identity and being and here Merton reflects directly on the worth and value of Aquinas' sense of created being for the modern world (1968, 203).

"The real root-sin of the modern person," Merton argues, "is that, in ignoring and condemning being, and especially one's own being, we have made existence an affliction and disease" (1968, 224). What stops us "from living humanly is our own deeply ingrained habit of delusion" that arises from ... "the sham, the unreality, the alienation, the forced systematization of life" that compromises our humanity (1968, 256–57). The compromise starts with the contrived belief of popular culture that, at bottom, sees the individual as a completely free autonomous self with unlimited possibilities. This attempt to be "as a god," Merton warns, does nothing but squeeze the individual into a "spiritual and psychic cramp" devoid of any anchorage in love of being, love of community, and love of God (1968, 224). The result is a deep inner anguish that is expressed outwardly as resentment toward life as if life were a problem to be solved and not a mystery to be embraced.

If I had to choose a certain piece of art to depict Merton's sense of the alienated self in the modern world, I would point to Edvard Munch's "The Scream" (1893). This piece is often used to express the existential crisis of the post-war world in which, for various reasons, the human being is found isolated and alone in the cosmos. It expresses the sense of nihilism and all the angst of being cast into a world willy-nilly without any ontological and theological anchorage. The human being, now claimed a dispirited free and autonomous being, is unable to find any communion with beings (noting the distance of others on the boardwalk), and in the end, becomes a mere speck on the banal and formless background of the physical world de-spirited by science. If there is meaning, it shifts, arises, and disappears like distant ships seen on the horizon. Lastly, alienated from any positive notion of being, the contemporary individual screams from—as noted above—"the psychic and spiritual cramp" of thinking itself a god but yet remains powerless to soothe its own anguish.

For Merton, in losing touch with our authentic being, and thus with God, we become children of despair as we fall into a senseless idolatry of production and consumption as substitutes for mystery, grace, and gratitude. The consequence of this idolatry of the strictly temporal is the illusion that mechanical progress means human improvement. We have convinced ourselves, en masse, Merton argues, that our life can only be made better "if we have a better car, a better TV set, a better toothpaste, etc., such that we condemn and destroy our own reality and the reality of our natural resources" (1968, 222). In the name of embellishing this false goal of self aggrandizement through material goods, there are two consequences—a further loss of self and the destruction of creation. Merton enunciates this eloquently in *No Man is An Island*:

> Those who love their own noise are impatient of everything else. They constantly defile the silence of the forest and the mountains and the sea. They bore through silent nature in every direction with their machines, for fear that the calm world might accuse them of their own emptiness.... There are some men for whom a tree has no reality until they think of cutting it down, for whom an animal has no value until it enters the slaughterhouse.... These men can hardly know the silence of love: for their love is the absorption of another person's silence into

> their own noise. And because they do not know the silence of love, they cannot know the silence of God, who is Charity (Merton, 1955, 257–8).

With this observation in mind, it is little wonder that Merton was fascinated by Rachel Carson's *Silent Spring* (1962)—the seminal text for the contemporary environmental movement—and links his thesis of the alienated self in the modern world with environmental degradation. In a journal entry dated December 11, 1962, Merton writes:

> I have been shocked at a notice of a new book by Rachel Carson [*Silent Spring*], on what is happening to birds as a result of the indiscriminate use of poisons.... Someone will say: you worry about birds: why not worry about people. I worry about *both* birds and people. We are in the world and part of it and are destroying everything because we are destroying ourselves, spiritually, morally, and in every way. It is all part of the same sickness, and it all hangs together (Merton, 1985, 274).

In short, the nuclear arms race, environmental degradation, racial prejudice, and war, are deep symptoms of our spiritual capitulation to the idols of the modern world and a rejection of any ontological truths that cannot be bought, purchased, or owned by any one individual's will-to-power. Said in other terms, when our modern identity is no longer rooted in God's love for us, but in the images of modern advertising and the fads of the day we are at war with ourselves (*agonia*) and ultimately with creation itself (see Merton, 1961, 51–68). Consequently, evils of sorts in the world are almost entirely our own doing (Merton, 1968, 222).

The only way to reclaim a deeper sense of personal authenticity is through earnest desire and the rediscovery of God's love at the source of all personal identity. For this, contemplation is the key. Contemplation here is not a pain-killer, a form of escape, or the product of calculated ambition. It is the on-going process outwardly exhibited through the disciplines of prayer, solitude and moderation in order to undergo the inner conversion (*metanoia*) that frees us from our own confusions and obsessions. For Merton, the whole of Christian theology and its sacraments are designed preeminently to decenter and recenter the self in God. The result is a grounded identity that enlivens the capacities of the intellect, the imagination, and the intuition to see the world as mystery; to see our individual lives as redeemed; to see the role of the Christian as prophetic. Contemplation as such does not lead to a new interior perfectionism for its own sake but, rather, a new orientation toward creation.

Unlike Aquinas, the orientation of contemplation for Merton is not only vertical but horizontal as well. "The Seeds of Contemplation" lead to "The New Man" who does not step out of the world but one who engages it. This is the theme that captivates Merton for the latter part of his life. In works starting in 1955, the fruits of contemplation is a "turn[ing] to the world" which includes "respect for one another as well as living and growing things" (Merton, 1955; 1968). However, this respect is not a mere aesthetic or romantic appreciation but a *form of behaviour* that is at once confrontive and dissenting.

> ... I think there remain creative possibilities for those who can recognize some other source of hope and understanding than that which is offered by society speaking through the mass media. One who can exchange the refusal to live for an intelligent and creative social dissent may perhaps discover ways of [their] own out of the general confusion. But in any case these ways will open themselves to [us] as providential gifts (1968, 226).

As is well known, Merton himself became active politically in his latter years earning him criticism from both Church authorities and his readers. While he spoke out eloquently against the Vietnam war and the curse of racism, he spent his deeper passions on illuminating our unconscious complicity to an industrial-military complex that rendered injustice, oppression, and war as acceptable means to ensure our cultural pursuit of happiness. In an essay entitled "Christian Action in World Crisis" (1980), Merton is most blunt yet nuanced. "Beliefs and politics can no longer be kept isolated from one another" (1980, 223). There is no longer the luxury of the edifying ourselves with quaint pietism and pure intentions alone. Rather:

> Christians have got to speak by their actions. Their political action must not be confined to the privacy of the polling booth. It must be clear and manifest to everybody. It is crucially important for Christians today to adopt a clear position and to be prepared to defend that truth with sacrifice, accepting misunderstanding, injustice, calumny, and even imprisonment and death (1968, 223).

As such, Merton takes contemplation down from Aquinas' philosophical mountain and turns it into weapon against the despair of the world and ultimately its injustices. But, in adding this political dimension to the edifying practises of the Christian faith, Merton is quick to nuance it, as if he foresaw the abuse that unbridled fundamentalism might unleash. First, Christians should keep their heads and refuse to be carried away by wild projects of fanatics who seek over simplified and immediate solutions by means of inhuman violence (1968, 223). Second, when resistance or even civil disobedience is called for, it must always be non-violent. At the end of his life, many of his last writings are based on developing a form of Christian non-violence in light of Gandhi's example. However, one may ask isn't non-violence a rather ineffective tool for the sorts of things Merton has just rallied us to fight? For Merton, non-violence is useless if it is merely pragmatic. The whole point of non-violence, he argues, is that it rises above pragmatism and does not consider whether or not it pays off politically. Non-violence is defence of and witness of *truth*, not efficacy (1968, 223).

Let me emphasize here that for Merton non-violence does not mean non-action or quietism. These latter categories are not options for him. "What is wanted now is therefore not simply the Christian who takes an inner complacency in the words and examples of Christ, but who seeks to follow Christ perfectly, not only in his own personal life, not only in prayer and penance, but also in political commitments and in all his social responsibilities" (1980, 222). As such, there is no gap between our individual need for redemption and concern for the common good. They are all of one piece.

Hence, to conclude, if I had to reconstitute a saintly Christian from the past as a patron saint for the crisis we now face environmentally, I would choose Merton. Merton recognizes that the modern individual exists in a metaphysical vacuum. In that vacuum, many of us remain dislocated identities who, against our better intentions, unwittingly permit an increasing intensity of immoral activity to take place in our very midst, that is, the continual destruction of air and water resources (the necessities of life). Merton, in encouraging each of us to excavate the deeper resources of the self through contemplation, encourages us to be prophetic voices in the world. He does this by indicating through his own thought and actions that the fruits of contemplation can lead, eventually, to political action. In adding the political dimension to contemplation, Merton challenges the Christian ethos that has become lazy and indifferent to its accommodation to the world as such, and he ultimately demands that we confront the difficult injustices of our day.

As I framed it above, one of the most pressing injustices of our day is the question: *is it acceptable that we permit the ongoing ingestion into our bodies of toxic pollutants "involuntarily" and accommodate ourselves to their effects without ever addressing the cause, consequences and possible solutions?* For Merton, not to ask the question and confront it politically would be a failure of the contemplative spirit he so passionately defended.

References

Allsopp, M. and Stringer, R. and Johnston, P. 1998. *Unseen Poisons: Levels of Organochlorine Chemicals in Human Tissues*. Exeter, UK: Greenpeace Research Laboratories.

Aquinas, T. 1958. *Compendium of Theology*. Trans. Cyril Vollert. London: B. Herder Book Co.

———1963. *Summa theologiae*. Trans. Thomas Gilby. London: Eyre & Spottiswoode and McGraw-Hill Book Co.

———1963. *The Pocket Aquinas*. Ed. Vernon J. Bourke. New York: Washington Square Press.

Baker J. and S. Eisenreich. 1990. *Environment, Science and Technology* 24: 342–52.

Berry, T. 1988. *The Dream of the Earth*. San Francisco: Sierra Club Books.

Rachel Carson, R. 1962. *Silent Spring*. Greenwich, Conn.: Fawcett Crest Books.

Colborn, T., et al. 1997. *Our Stolen Future: Are We Threatening Our Fertility, Intelligence, and Survival*. New York: Penguin Books.

Chenu, M. 1968. *Nature, Man, and Society in the Twelfth Century: Essays on New Theological Perspectives in the Latin West*. Ed. and trans. J. Taylor and L. K. Little. Chicago: Unversity of Chicago Press.

Dyer, G. 1998. "There's Still Time to Avert Disaster," *Toronto Star*, November 18, 1998.

Eliade, M. 1957. *The Sacred and the Profane: The Nature of Religion*. New York: Harper & Row.

Fox, M. *Sheer Joy: Conversations with Thomas Aquinas on Creation Spirituality*. New York: HarperCollins Publishers.

Gilson, E. 1956. *The Christian Philosophy of St. Thomas Aquinas*. L. K. Trans. Shook. New York: Random House.

Goddard-Hill, A. C. 1998. *Environmental Epidemiology of the Great Lakes Basin: Human Health Effects of Industrial Pollutants, Effluents and Toxics*. A paper presented to the Canadian Association of Physicians for the Environment, Oakville, Ontario, and November 23, 1998.

Haught, J. 1993. *The Promise of Nature, Ecological and Cosmic Purpose*. New York: Paulist Press.

International Joint Commission's Agreement Public Forum. 1997. *State of Knowledge Report on Environmental Contaminants and Human Health in the Great Lakes Basin*. Niagara Falls, Ontario: International Joint Commission's Agreement Public Forum.

Indian and Northern Affairs Canada. 1997. *Highlights of the Canadian Artic Contaminants Assessment Report: A Community Reference Manual*. Ottawa: Indian and Northern Affairs Canada.

Johnson, B. et al. 1998. "Public Health Implications of Persistent Toxic Substances in the Great Lakes and St. Lawrence Basins." *Journal of Great Lakes Research* 24: 698–722.

John, L. et el. 1998. *Taking Our Breath Away: The Health Effects of Air Pollution and Climate Change*. Vancouver: David Suzuki Foundation.

Marcel, G. 1949. *Being and Having*. London: Darce.

McInerney, D. 1974. *Thomas Merton: The Man and His Work*. Washington, D.C.: Consortium Press.

Merton, T. 1996. "Turning Toward the World: The Pivotal Years." in *The Journals of Thomas Merton, vol. 4, 1960–1963*. San Francisco: Harper Collins.

———1972. *New Seeds of Contemplation*. New York: New Directions Books.

———1955. *No Man is An Island*. New York: Harcourt Brace.

———1980. "Christian Action in World Crisis." in *The Non-Violent Alternative*. New York: Farrar, Straus, Giroux.

Porter, J. 1990. *The Recovery of Virtue: The Relevance of Aquinas for Christian Ethics*. Louisville, Kentucky: John Knox Press.

Regional Municipality of Hamilton-Wentworth. 1997. *Hamilton-Wentworth Air Quality Initiative, Summary Report*. Regional Municipality of Hamilton-Wentworth, Hamilton, Ontario.

Suzuki, D. 1997. *The Sacred Balance: Rediscovering Our Place in Nature*. Vancouver: Greystone Books.

Taylor, C. 1991. *The Malaise of Modernity*. Concord: Anansi.

Section D

Science, Religion and Ethics

Chapters 13 to 18

Chapter 13

The Indefensibility of Callicott's Subjectivist Environmental Ethic

Darren Domski, York University

Introduction

J. Baird Callicott's subjectivist environmental ethic stands as one of the landmark meta-ethical positions in environmental philosophy. Grounded in the works of David Hume, Charles Darwin, and Aldo Leopold, it remains one of the most prominent and carefully thought out alternatives to the various objectivist positions that have also been offered to account for the non-instrumental, non-anthropocentric value of natural entities. Callicott's theory, inspired by Leopold's Land Ethic, has its original basis in the Humean concept of moral sentiment, in which moral judgement is founded on internal sense or feeling rather than reason. It is scientifically reinforced by Darwin, who claimed that altruistic moral sentiments were naturally selected for and made universal in human evolution, and subsequently expanded by Leopold to include as objects of those sentiments not just fellow humans but the entire biotic community. Over the years, many interesting and perplexing problems have been raised with respect to this communitarian ethic. I will show that although many of these criticisms can be shown to be harmless, three of them, including an original criticism of my own, prove to be much more serious. In short, I will argue that Callicott's theory has three unavoidable flaws: that it is either unacceptably immune to cognitive criticism because it is biologically determined or else hopelessly relativistic; that it commits the fallacy of equivocation; and that its emphasis and focus on the kinship relation in is entirely unacceptable in the first place. Because of these flaws, I conclude that Callicott's meta-ethical position, though it may possibly compliment an adequate environmental ethic, cannot provide the grounds for such an ethic.

Callicott's Environmental Ethic

Before Callicott's theory can be assessed, it must be summarized and explained. On this note, the fundamental groundwork of Callicott's theory of environmental ethics is laid out by Hume's moral subjectivism. According to Hume, moral value is not founded in reason but instead on the feelings or sentiments that we project onto the world. Values, therefore, are nothing but "referred or projected feelings or sentiments which originate with and depend upon a valuing subject and do not really belong at all to valuable objects" (Callicott, 1992, 160). Whether an action is good or bad depends not on any objective or rational criteria, but on whether the action elicits pleasure or pain in the person who observes it. For Hume, there is a sharp distinction between the world of facts and the world of values; the first is objective and observer-independent, and the second is subjective and observer-dependent. Facts exist whether or not human beings ever come along to discover them, but values are human constructs based on our emotional constitution, and exist only when humans value something. Hume believed that not all of our sentiments are self-oriented (Callicott, 1984, 304). Some of our sentiments are genuinely other-oriented, meaning that they are not derivative of the self-oriented ones. As a result, Hume posits as brute psychological fact the existence of not just selfish but also altruistic passions, and it is in these universally shared altruistic passions, rather than in fact or reason, that Hume grounds his subjectivist moral theory.

Whereas Hume provides the axiological framework for Callicott's environmental ethic, Darwin legitimizes it by grounding it in evolutionary science. According to Callicott, Darwin does Hume one better by not just positing but accounting for the heretofore unexplained existence of moral sentiments in terms of natural history. In doing so, he not only provides the explanation of how Humean altruistic sentiments would arise in a hostile, competitive world, but he also explains how those altruistic sentiments might be pressured to expand beyond their original limits. As Darwin (1904) explains, parental and filial affections are clearly selected for in evolution, particularly in mammals. The prolonged parental care that such affections provide is clearly conducive to reproductive success. Once established, such sentiments would be pressured by natural selection to broaden their scope, since the small social units that such sentiments would allow would be reproductively advantageous. According to Darwin, the greater the frequency of social instincts such as sympathy within a social group, the greater the reproductive success of that group, and, conversely, the more quarrelsome and disagreeable a group was, the less likely they would be to have reproductive success.

> Thus, not only was there selective pressure for more intense sympathy and affection within group boundaries, there was selective pressure for more widely cast social sentiments, since in competition among most internally peaceable and cooperative groups the larger will win out (Callicott, 1992a, 149).

As our concept of community broadens the target of our moral sentiments broadens with it. As a result, ethics naturally progresses toward and culminates in the universal application to all human beings, a common ethics of humanity. For Callicott, Darwin's explanation of the origin of ethics builds upon and validates Hume's subjectivist axiology, thus bringing subjectivism and biological science together.

According to Callicott, Leopold takes Darwinian/Humean subjectivism to its next logical step. Working within a Copernican world view, whereby "the Earth is perceived as a very small, lush, blue-green island in a vast desert sea of space" (Callicott, 1992a, 150), Leopold expands our sense of community to include all of our evolutionary kin. Leopold explains that when we realize the ecological fact that we belong to a biotic community consisting in plants, animals, soils, waters, and human beings, we will naturally extend our sentiments to all members of that community. He insisted that "to those who are ecologically well-informed, nonhuman natural entities are inherently valuable—as putative members of one extended family or society" (Callicott, 1992a, 162–63). The next step in our social-ethical evolution, he claims, is to realize that "nature as a whole is inherently valuable—as the one great family or society to which we belong as members or citizens" (1992a, 163). Leopold accepts that the social sentiments posited by Darwin are set by natural selection, but he emphasizes that they are nevertheless "often blunt as well and blind instruments," capable of being influenced by cultural representation (Callicott, 1992b, 192–93). When we recognize ourselves as members of not only a human but also a biotic community, this information will cause us to naturally extend the sentiments that we evolved for members of the former onto members of the latter. Thus, Leopold's Land Ethic, which forms the basis of and inspires Callicott's environmental ethic, represents in Callicott's opinion the culmination of the subjectivist axiology formed by Hume and grounded by Darwin.

In addition to its "legitimate ancestry in the Western philosophical canon" (1992b, 184), Callicott believes his environmental ethic has clear advantages over competing theories. To begin with, it allows for the existence of not just instrumental but inherent value in nature. In Callicott's opinion, an environmental ethic that does not allow for this would, as Regan claims, collapse into a mere management ethic for the use of the environment (Callicott, 1992a, 157). Callicott places altruistic sentiments on an equal footing with selfishness, and so things can be not only valued instrumentally for the ends they provide but also for their inherent worth. Things can literally "be valued for themselves, quite independently from the satisfying aesthetic, religious, or epistemic experiences they may occasion in nature aesthetes, nature worshipers, or natural scientists" (Callicott, 1992a, 163). Although value is anthropogenic, since it is necessarily conferred on the world by human beings, it can nevertheless be nonanthropocentric because it need not be human-centred. Callicott's ethic therefore avoids the difficulties he associates with the ethic of Holmes Rolston III, who attributes consciousness-independent, intrinsic value to nature (Rolston, 1988). Value, in Callicott's opinion, can only exist when there is a valuer, and so the only viable way to rescue nonanthropocentric value is by making it inherent rather than intrinsic. Hence, Callicott's environmental ethic succeeds in the most crucial task of establishing the existence of non-instrumental value in the natural world.

Various other aspects of Callicott's theory make it, in his opinion, superior to competing ethical theories. For one, his environmental ethic is in line with our commonly held scientific world view. It is therefore easier to uphold his theory than a theory like J-Theism, which is linked to the stewardship interpretation of the Judeo-Christian world view, because it does not conflict with scientific naturalism. Although Callicott recognizes J-Theism as a powerful environmental ethic, he acknowledges that it is only available to those, like John Muir, who are open to such a strongly theocentric orientation. Put simply, Callicott's bio-empathic ethic is more appealing than J-Theism because it does not require any super-natural commitments.

Callicott's ethic also has the advantage of providing for the ethical standing of not only individual organisms but also of superorganismic entities such as species and ecosystems. Individualist theories, even when they accommodate the value of plants, as is the case with conativism, a theory based on some version of reverence-for-life, still cannot adequately value species. At best, conativists can only incidentally protect a species by attaching value to the individuals of that species. For Callicott, this "intractable atomistic or individualistic bias" (Callicott, 1984) is unacceptable because it ignores our intuition that species themselves, and not just their individuals, also have inherent value. An environmental ethic that cannot place inherent value in species as well as individuals is simply inadequate, and, because Callicott's moral theory avoids this problem, he claims that it is clearly preferable.

Lastly, Callicott asserts that his environmental ethic is superior to theories like holistic-rationalism because it can provide for the inherent value of the current ecosystem to which we presently belong. According to Callicott, holistic-rationalism, which defines as valuable that which exemplifies or embodies a good such as organic richness or biodiversity, cannot differentiate between the good of the Earth's present ecosystem and that of some future ecosystem. As Callicott explains, our current stage in the evolution of life on planet Earth is temporally infinitesimal. In the greater scheme of things, no matter how badly we destroy our current ecosystem, the Earth will no doubt rejuvenate and in time produce another complex ecosystem. The current Age of Mammals was only made possible by the termination of the Age of Reptiles, and even if we as humans end the current age, evolutionary forces will in time produce another to take *its* place, one that perhaps will embody even more Good than the present one. Whereas Holistic Rationalism cannot place inherent value on "*our present* ecosystem, its component parts and complement of species" (Callicott, 1984, 304), Callicott's environmental ethic can. He explains:

> Our social affections are extended to our fellow members and to the social whole of which we are part ... this is the biotic community of which we are a part, these are our companions in the odyssey of evolution, and it is to them, not to any future complement, that our loyalties properly extend (Callicott, 1989, 182).

Thus, another mark of the superiority of Callicott's environmental ethic is its ability to place inherent value specifically in the *current* biotic community, rather than in biotic communities generally.

Some Lesser Difficulties

As confident as Callicott is that his theory is the best available, numerous problems can and have been raised in responce his subjectivist environmental ethic. One that immediately arises, and one which Callicott anticipates, is the threat that his ethic inevitably degenerates into radical relativism. According to this objection, because subjectivism places value solely in subjects who presumably have differing value judgements, value cannot be universal. Hume's analogy between aesthetic judgement and moral judgement seems almost to invite the charge that a subjectivist moral theory is as radically relative as our appreciation for art. If ethics "is ultimately a matter of taste ... then there can be no objective standards of conduct, no moral norms" (Callicott, 1989, 189).

Callicott deals with this objection quite handily by appealing to our shared subjectivism. His response, therefore, is similar to Hume's own solution to the problem of relativism. For Hume, there is a shared humanity in human beings. Because "the humanity of one man is the humanity of everyone" (Hume, 1957, 112), a subjectivist ethics can be firmly grounded. Near objective norms can still exist because moral judgement is nearly universal among human beings. Darwin only strengthened this defence by grounding this universality in natural selection. As Callicott explains, mankind has evolved moral sentiments that "vary within a range of normalcy" (Callicott, 1992b, 190). While our sentiments may not be identical, they are tolerably similar, and this similarity allows us to give meaningfulness to our moral claims. Radical relativism, therefore, is not a worry.

Another lesser charge that has been laid on Callicott's environmental ethic is that it is historically misinformed because it is, in fact, anti-Humean. As James Fieser explains,

> Callicott's claim that moral sentiments can be triggered by things other than valuing subjects is not supported by Hume's own position. Instead, Hume stresses that a spectator's moral sentiments arise only in response to an agent's mental qualities and intentions, which inanimate objects clearly lack (Fieser, 1993, 173).

One might point out that Hume, whose subjectivist axiology is utilized by Callicott in the construction of his environmental ethic, himself would not have supported Callicott's theory. Hume was clearly set against extending our sentiments to non-humans, and because Callicott historically connects his theory to Hume, this disagreement seems significant. As Fieser explains, "this historical connection falls apart ... since Humean moral sentiment fails to do what Callicott claims" (Fieser, 1993, 174). That Callicott employs Hume's subjectivism in ways that Hume clearly did not approve could thus be seen as a problem.

This difficulty, however, is easily avoided by pointing out that Callicott takes Hume's subjectivism as merely the starting point of his axiology. When Callicott claims that Leopold took the Humean/Darwinian theory to its next logical step, he clearly does not accept Hume's subjectivism as complete in itself. Fieser, after raising the difficulty, tries to show that it is not a very big problem by granting that "on a theoretical level ... Callicott's misconstrual of Hume is not as significant. We can take him as simply reviving the theory of moral sentiment in a revised form" (Fieser, 1993, 174). What Fieser fails to realize is that there is no problem there to downplay in the first place. Callicott is not reviving Hume's theory in a revised form. On the contrary, he is taking Hume as a starting point, as a first step in the construction of a communitarian environmental ethic that goes above and beyond Hume's actual communitarianism. Callicott is not revising Hume but using him as the first stage in the evolution of a Humean/Darwinian/Leopoldian land ethic. As a result, the fact that Hume would not approve of Callicott's environmental ethic becomes unimportant.

Another charge that has been raised against Callicott's theory is that it has no normative force. The basic idea is that Callicott's environmental ethic is in trouble because it is merely descriptive, and cannot rationally compel us toward moral action. As Warwick Fox explains, "while some readers might think that Callicott's Hume-Darwin-Leopold axiology has normative and not just explanatory force, Callicott does not actually claim this, nor can he" (Fox, 1985, 185). Kristin Shrader-Frechette also raises this problem with Callicott's theory:

> Callicott's use [of] biology to undergird his environmental ethics ... destroys the normative dimension of his ethics. He avoids relativism by postulating that ethical uniformity/unanimity is achieved by means of natural selection.... [but] behavioral uniformities explained through natural selection are descriptive not normative (Callicott, 1992b, 185).

The criticism is that, according to Callicott's theory, we can only describe what sentiments we actually have. In some sense, one would expect a true ethic to guide our ethical behaviour and rationally compel us toward certain actions and not others. All that Callicott's ethic can provide is a description of our inclinations.

Although Callicott's non-normativity at first seems quite problematic, the difficulty is much less serious than it appears. When Callicott responds to it by denying that we have any reason to uphold the modernist tenet that ethics needs to be normative in the first place, the charge becomes much more manageable. As Callicott explains, the traditional deontological and utilitarian ethical theories of Kant and Bentham are radically different from the subjectivism originated by Hume. For both Kant and Bentham, egoism is taken as a universal primitive. Either because I am rational or because I am sentient, I demand consideration or respect, and, in order to remain consistent, I am required to consider and respect others who share the same characteristic. As Callicott phrases it, "I am compelled ... by the logic of my own moral claim upon others to grudgingly grant their similar claims upon me" (1992b, 187). Morality is normative for both of these schools because it demands of us certain morally appropriate behaviour. Why, Callicott asks, are we required to follow this prevailing modern paradigm? Callicott's subjective axiology "does not regard egoism as the only genuine and self-explanatory value. Selfishness and altruism are equally primitive" Callicott, 1989, 149). As a result, his environmental ethic does not *need* to be normative. Callicott explains that normative force, though common to nearly all modern moral philosophy, is simply not required. Like Plato and Aristotle, Hume did not believe that humans were individualistic egoists who had to be made to act morally by normative force. It was only more recently that this belief entered meta-ethical circles. In the end, the charge that his theory does not have normative force is for Callicott equivalent to the charge that it does not fit the standard modernist paradigm. His response is to ask why it needs to.

The last of the less serious attacks on Callicott's environmental ethic are the charges that it is unacceptably monistic, according to Christopher Stone, and unacceptably anthropocentric, according to Holmes Rolston, III. The basis of Stone's attack is his belief that our various moral concerns for people, for sentient animals, and for the environment cannot be handled by one ethical theory (Stone, 1987, 133–34). He claims that in our moral considerations, each area of our lives should be guided by the moral theory that seems most applicable to it. To expect us, as Callicott does, to uphold a single, monistic ethic in our moral decision-making, is for Stone totalitarian nonsense. According to Rolston, Callicott's environmental ethic, because it does not allow for value that it completely independent of any valuer, places far too much importance on the human being doing the valuing and not enough importance on the thing valued (Rolston, 1988, 112–17). For Rolston, the difference between anthropogenic and anthropocentric value is not significant; both focus too much on the subjective valuer. Without the concept of intrinsic value, defined as value that is completely independent of all consciousness, one cannot have a truly ecocentric environmental ethic. In Rolston's opinion, Callicott's "is not yet a genuinely biological or ecological theory of value" because the cash value of his ethic amounts to the following:

> "Let the flowers live!" really means, "Leave the flowers for humans to enjoy" after all, because the flowers are valuable—able to be valued—only by humans even though when properly sensitive humans come along they do value these flowers for what they are in themselves (Rolston, 1988, 112–17).

According to Stone and Rolston, Callicott's subjectivism, because it is too monistic and too anthropocentric respectively, is unsuitable as an environmental ethic.

I do not find either of these attacks on Callicott's position very problematic. In Callicott's debates with Stone and Rolston over the monistic and anthropogenic character of his environmental ethic, I see no reason why the ethic cannot hold its own. Although Stone clearly sees merit in one's upholding intrapersonal pluralism, Callicott's assertion that such pluralism would make ethical decisions difficult and would lead to a life of perpetual self-contradiction, "the philosophical equivalent of ... a multiple personality disorder" (Callicott, 1994, 52), seems a fair rebuttal. It seems at least plausible to say, with Callicott, that, unlike the sciences, our moral life cannot be compartmentalized. "Duties to friends and strangers, to institutions and abstractions, to animals and to the biosphere may all come into play simultaneously" (Callicott, 1994, 52), and, in order to weigh these various considerations coherently, it seems perfectly reasonable to pursue a monistic ethic. Thus, though I am unsure how to react to the Stone's criticism, Callicott's own reaction seems perfectly legitimate.

As for Rolston's charge that Callicott's subjectivism is intolerably anthropocentric, I again believe that Callicott can hold his own. Although I greatly respect Rolston's motives, his belief that intrinsic value can exist independently of all consciousness is itself quite contentious. Although I can understand the draw that such a concept would have, and although I admit that an environmental ethic ground in objective intrinsic value would be extremely strong, it is simply far from clear that such an objective theory is obtainable. When Callicott responds that value cannot exist unless there is a valuer, there is no clear way to undercut this response. However advantageous it would be for environmental ethics, Rolston's intrinsic value is, for many, too difficult to swallow, and it is precisely Callicott's avoidance of that problematic concept that makes his theory appealing to many philosophers. Certainly, though there is some force to Rolston's objection, the force is not sufficient to make his criticism a strong one. We clearly have an important consideration to note in examining Callicott's position, but that is all that can be said for certain. Anything else we might say depends too much on our other meta-ethical convictions. As a result, Rolston's charge against Callicott's position also fails to bring the position down, for though Rolston makes a potentially strong point, its strength depends too much on which of two perfectly viable meta-ethical orientations we adopt.

Some More Serious Problems

Although many of the charges brought against it can thus be turned aside, there are some difficulties with Callicott's environmental ethic which seem much harder to extinguish. Even when Callicott has had a chance to offer his rebuttal, these difficulties seem unwilling to go away. One such problem, as raised by Fox and Shrader-Frechette, is that Callicott's ethic is unacceptably immune to cognitive criticism because it is biologically determined. Because Callicott's theory "provides us with no means of criticizing the medical-like descriptive norms derived from common innate moral sentiments" (Callicott, 1992b, 191), we are left with an ethic that cannot be modified. In essence, we are biologically "stuck with a set of inflexible moral norms determined by our biology" (Callicott, 1992b, 192). This seems highly undesirable, especially for an environmental ethic that hopes to modify our inter-species sentiments and apply them to the entire biotic community.

Callicott has responded to this problem by claiming that although our sentiments are biologically determined, they are by no means set in stone. Callicott points out that our evolved emotions, though set by natural selection, are nevertheless "blunt as well as blind instruments" (1992b, 192–93). Our altruistic feelings are extremely vague, and there is more than enough room for culture to massage and form them in certain directions. Because our moral sentiments are sufficiently plastic and malleable, to whom they apply, and in what behaviour they result in, can be culturally determined. Whereas this solution might spawn worries of cultural relativism, where irresolvably different and incommensurable values would be formed by different cultures, this, claims Callicott, is not the case. His reason is that, though our moral sentiments are formed by culture, "a culture's values and ethical ideals rest upon and are justified by suppositions of fact and supposed relations among supposed facts" (Callicott, 1992b, 195). Although certain cultures in human history have upheld morally repugnant values such as racism or sexism, Callicott asserts that cultural values are not fundamentally relative because culture is in principle informed by fact. Cultures, as they purge themselves of the false facts that allow repugnant values to exist, can therefore arrive at nonrelative values. Although it is not the normative force of the modernist paradigm, Callicott believes his environmental ethic can nevertheless have a kind of normative force, one based not on coercion but on fact-based reason. Hence, Callicott attempts to balance his subjectivism between the extremes of biological determinism and cultural relativism, hoping to find a happy medium.

I am not convinced, however, that disagreements between various cognitive cultures over appropriate values really can be resolved by reference to facts. In order to truly avert cultural relativism, one seems forced to accept the apparent conclusion that every set of possible values except for one contains at least one factual error. Callicott mentions examples such as racism and sexism, and explains that because these cultural values are not properly based on true facts, they can legitimately be dismissed. By debunking the non-facts on which such error-laden values are based, we can eliminate them and thus avoid relativistic pitfalls. I believe, however, that Callicott oversimplifies the nature of cross-cultural value disagreements. Although racism and sexism might be based on factual errors, it is not at all clear that non-vegetarians and loggers, or for that matter vegetarians and non-loggers, make factual mistakes. Even when non-vegetarians become vegetarians (or vice-versa), they usually do not cite a misconstrual of the facts as the reason for their decision. It seems to me simply unacceptable that all disagreements between cultural communities arise because of factual errors. Facts simply do not seem capable of doing the normative work that Callicott requires them to do, and so his theory seems stricken with either biological determinism or else cultural relativism.

Interestingly, it would seem that even if Callicott can escape both determinism and relativism, the escape can only succeed at the cost of hurting the original foundation of the theory. In order to make the escape, Callicott would have to successfully ground his environmental ethic in evolved sentiments that are nevertheless blind and blunt instruments, capable of being amended. In other words, reference to facts would have to somehow form a normative standard according to which our inherited sentiments could be evaluated and modified, and, as I have explained, I do not think that it can. However, even if such reference to facts *can* form a normative standard according to which we can evaluate and modify our sentiments, it would seem that this normative standard would threaten to make the bio-empathic element of Callicott's theory entirely superfluous. The dilemma would seem to be this: either facts are of no use to Callicott's theory because they fail to rescue the theory from relativism, or else they are of too much use, entirely extinguishing the original niche that the sentiments occupy in the theory. After all, if we have a superior normative standard by which we can judge, adjust, and modify our often misguided moral sentiments, why do we need the sentiments in addition to that standard? Callicott seems capable of avoiding relativism only by detracting from his original Humean/Darwinian/Leopoldian orientation, since any standard capable of correcting and realigning that orientation would seem just as capable of entirely replacing it. As a result, Callicott's balancing act between biological determinism and cultural relativism seems a hopeless mess. Either he cannot escape the relativist threat, or else he makes the sentiments extraneous in his escape.

Another serious problem raised against Callicott's environmental ethic is that the logic of its argumentation is fallacious and therefore non-compelling. Ernest Partridge draws attention to this problem when he insists, contrary to Callicott, that the stretch to apply our moral sentiments to the entire biotic community is simply too much. He argues that, contrary to Callicott's assertions, "Humean moral sentiments are more likely to incline one to anthropocentrism than to Aldo Leopold's land ethic" (Partridge, 1996, 149). According to Partridge, our moral sentiments, though expandable to larger and larger groups of sentient human beings, cannot be legitimately expanded to include the non-human community because they then cease to be *moral*. A moral community, in his opinion, can only consist of moral agents capable of reciprocating moral attitudes consciously. It is not enough that members of our moral community be in some sense our kin; they must be kin of a certain sort, capable of some form of moral deliberation. Callicott is therefore wrong: we *are not* required to extend our moral sentiments to non-humans.

> It is just the differences between human and natural "communities" that cause me to reject this extension. Extend out from human communities, and you leave the domain of cognition and reciprocation among equals, to that of mere sentience, and then, into the domain of insentience and nonlife. As you do, you shed the stringency of your moral imperatives. Thus, as my neighbour cares how I treat him and his property, so then must I respect his concerns, as I demand that he respect mine.... But that redwood and that river don't care in the least (Partridge, 1996, 154)?

For Partridge, a morality extended beyond at least sentient beings can no longer properly be called a morality. The way he sees it, "*personhood* is not only the source of [our] moral sentiments but also its limit"

(Partridge, 1996, 153). As a result, the only truly moral community to which we can belong is the human community. According to Partridge, Callicott's environmental ethic should be rejected because it requires that we expand the bounds of our moral community beyond their meta-ethical limit.

Of course, Callicott has argued that we do in fact have compelling reason to apply our moral sentiments to more than just human beings, that the logic of his position is not just sound but compelling. He claims that we should accept his environmental ethic

> because (1) we all generally have a positive attitude toward the community or society to which we belong; and (2) science has now discovered that the natural environment is a community or society to which we belong, no less than to the global village (Partridge, 1996, 159).

This argument can be meticulously expanded:

> (1) we (i.e., all psychologically normal people) are endowed with certain moral sentiments (sympathy, concern, respect, and so on) for our fellows, especially for our kin; (2) modern biology treats *Homo sapiens* (a) as, like all other living species, a product of the process of organic evolution; and hence, (b) people are literally kin (because of common ancestry) to all other contemporary forms of life; (3) therefore, if so enlightened, we should feel and thus behave ... toward other living things in ways similar to the way we feel and thus behave toward our human kin (Callicott, 1989, 125).

The greater biotic community, humans included, turns out to be just as morally subject as the human community, for when kinship is taken as the criterion of membership, we are no less a member of the former as we are of the latter. For Callicott, we have clear and argumentatively persuasive reason to expand our moral sentiments to our ecological kin: we are already disposed to value our kin, and so when we learn that all living things on Earth are literally our kin, it is only logical to extend our valuation.

But when we say that we have learned that all living things on Earth are literally our kin, to what extent are we being metaphorical? This seems to be the central question. When we say that all earthly beings are our kin, do we really mean what we mean when we say that all human beings are our kin? What Partridge's anthropocentrically oriented attack on Callicott's position makes clear is that Callicott is guilty of equivocating on the meaning of the term "community." It is the same kind of equivocation that we would be guilty of if we were to say that human beings share a kinship with the community of all atoms, since we and atoms share in some sense a common causal history in the big bang. Granted, there is a shared natural history between evolved life forms, and this shared history does seem to fully justify the claim that all earthly living beings form a community *of some sort*. What is open for debate, it would seem, is how much attention we should pay to the phrase "of some sort." The key point is that no matter how we deal with the problematic phrase, we are clearly unjustified, as Callicott's position seems to require, in just dropping it from our moral consideration altogether. Whereas "community" is a term that ordinarily incorporates many concepts, Callicott requires that we forget about all of them, save shared natural history. Callicott, in short, commits the fallacy of equivocation. The natural community is simply different from the human community, and so Callicott's reasoning is invalid.

It is important to make this criticism clear. Notice, for instance, that it is irrelevant whether or not we actually do attribute moral standing to non-humans. Although Partridge does not, this fact is entirely beside the point. The purpose of Callicott's subjectivist approach is to account for our moral attitudes toward natural entities, and his difficulty lies in the fact that his theory requires that those entities not simply be given moral consideration, but given moral consideration *specifically and precisely because we and they are co-members of a community in just the same sense that human beings alone are co-members of a community*. But this reasoning clearly just does not follow. In order for it to follow, saying that human beings are co-members of a community would have to be conceptually equivalent to, and would have to communicate nothing more than, the claim that human beings share a common evolutionary history. This, however, clearly does *not* exhaust our meaning when we talk about human communities. It seems frankly uncontroversial that human communities incorporate so much more, and exhibit so many additional properties than, biological communities. As Partridge points out, though science has discovered connections between ecosystems and human communities,

> the social sciences also point out significant dissimilarities between ecosystems and human communities of persons, with their complex

> systems of moral controls—e.g., reciprocating rights and duties, procedural and distributive justice, sanctions, moral sentiments, etc. To be fully "well-informed" is to be aware both of the similarities and the differences of these two "communities" (Partridge, 1996, 155).

Clearly, the logic of Callicott's argument, and so the logic on which his whole position rests, is flawed, making his bio-empathic ethic wholly non-compelling. Thus, even if we as environmental philosophers attribute value to non-humans, we cannot do so for Callicott's reasons without first setting aside the requirements of deductive logic.

My Criticism

Although these two distinct problems with Callicott's environmental ethic seem already quite profound, I believe there is a third, even more profound problem with it, one heretofore not found in the literature. In my opinion, the theory's tie to facts about evolutionary history is not only quite burdening and arguably quite stretching, but demonstrably misguided altogether. I believe that facts about shared DNA and shared evolutionary origins are not only problematic grounds for an environmental ethic, but in fact no good grounds at all. At the very most, I believe that Callicott's shared-history orientation can only compliment some other ethical grounding. My criticism proceeds by means of two simple and similar thought experiments. Let us examine them one at a time.

To begin with, we can all imagine, at least as a logical possibility, that evolutionary theory is false, and that mankind did not evolve from lower life forms on planet Earth. One could imagine, for instance, that, unbeknownst to us, human beings were planted on Earth by a supernatural entity bent on making it seem as though we evolved on it. Alternatively, we could imagine that human beings originated, either by an alternate sort of evolution or more extremely by some other unanticipated means entirely, elsewhere in the universe and then travelled to Earth. Nothing hangs on the likelihood of any of these things actually being true. All that is required is that we imagine, for argument's sake, that one of these turned out to be the case. What would happen to our convictions as environmentalists? Although they might be impacted, would they really, as Callicott's theory clearly implies, lose all of their grounding? Would we really suddenly have no non-anthropocentric, non-instrumental grounds for criticizing environmental destruction or mass-extinction? Would we suddenly deny intrinsic value to the bison, the butterfly, or the birch tree? Surely not. In fact, I believe that we as environmentalists would be just as compelled as before to think that the Earth's ecosystem has either intrinsic or inherent value, and *just as much* value. Even though the Earth's flora and fauna would no longer be our literal kin, this would not extinguish our belief that those flora and fauna would still have value. This conclusion, however, can make no sense on Callicott's account. His theory clearly makes our currently accepted evolutionary facts pivotal, so that a failure in those facts could spell nothing else but the destruction of a green environmental ethic. It therefore follows that Callicott's sentiments-based orientation cannot accurately capture our environmental convictions. Even if his approach can amplify our values, it certainly cannot ground them, and so we should reject Callicott's bio-empathic subjectivism.

The second thought experiment leads us to the same conclusion. This time we proceed not by excluding *ourselves* from the kinship relation, but by excluding certain newly encountered *individuals, species, or ecosystems* from that relation. Imagine, for argument's sake, that we encounter extraterrestrial life-forms, either intelligent or not, that share no evolutionary kinship with us at all. To make the point even stronger, we can optionally imagine extraterrestrials that have either no evolutionary histories at all, or else radically different kinds of histories, perhaps so different that we could not call them evolutionary. Would our lack of kinship prevent us from attributing value to the aliens? Could we really imagine, for instance, enslaving intelligent extraterrestrials, or else obliterating alien species, for sport or for profit, with clear moral consciences? As in the first thought-experiment, I believe we again see that the kinship relation simply is not pivotal in our attribution of non-anthropocentric intrinsic or inherent value. Alien individuals and species, even if they were in no way our kin, would still seem entitled to the same moral respect that DNA-based life seems to warrant. Clearly, we again see that it is not kinship that is relevant to moral standing but some other factor. If I am correct, then this thought experiment, just like the last, shows that Callicott's theory does not accurately capture the nature or scope of our ethical attitudes. Once more, we are given good reason to abandon Callicott's kinship-focused approach, and to seek another, more plausible environmental ethic. Callicott's bio-empathic subjectivism is therefore not only either problematically biologically determined or relativistic and unconvincingly stretching for the environmentalist who wants to extend moral standing to non-humans, but on the wrong fundamental track altogether.

Although this kinship-denouncing argument is as far as I am aware original, there seem some clear ways that a person might react to it in hopes of salvaging Callicott's position. In anticipation, I would like to comment on these ways. To begin with, one might argue that in both sets of cases Callicott's position is not really threatened because the kinship relation can be sufficiently broadened to accommodate the new situation. One might explain that though the co-evolver relation would not hold, a para-evolver relation still might, where "para" is meant to signify a similarity rather than a causal connection. Still more broadly, one might expand the kinship relation to include all co-inhabitants of the universe simply as co-inhabitants, thereby encompassing even the most extreme, most non-similar, examples mentioned under the kinship umbrella. This solution, however, seems fairly unattractive. To begin with, it threatens to make the concept of kinship so thin that it would be nearly meaningless. Certainly, the various life forms in the examples would be made kin, but the making would become quite uninteresting and quite a poor foundation for a environmental ethic. Arguably, without non-kin to contrast against, "kin" threatens to become a vacuous term. Certainly, such vacuousness would prove quite devastating to an environmentalist hoping to accomplish meaningful goals in our current environmental crisis. Second, this sort of tactic would seem obviously *ad hoc*, a way of stepping around a problem rather than addressing it. Certainly Callicott himself shows no sign of approving of this response. In his discussion of extraterrestrial life, he says specifically that a Leopoldian land ethic "simply has nothing to say about extraterrestrial life" (Callicott, 1989, 262). The kinship relation is meaningful and interesting specifically because its scope is limited to beings with a shared natural history, and so any modification of that term seems highly dubious.

Another way one might react to the two thought experiments is to deny their relevance to Callicott's philosophy. Callicott's own words, in fact, potentially fuel this reaction:

> the land ethic seems almost parochial in extent and even tribal in nature because it restricts itself to local—that is, terrestrial—beings, and rests their moral value on kinship and mutual dependency. The

> very failure of the land ethic to provide moral considerability for extraterrestrial life reveals at once its strength for Earth-oriented environmental ethics—*which is of course the only variety of environmental ethics with any genuine practical interest or application* (Callicott, 1989, 262).

This reaction, however, would be unsatisfactory for two reasons. First of all, the kinds of cases covered in the two thought experiments certainly *would* be of interest. Although no moralist would consider such cases practically interesting at this time, the possibility of such cases being realized has clear practical implications for any environmental philosophy. Second, and more importantly, this sort of reaction would seem to miss the point of the thought experiments entirely. This is because the experiments both chiefly deal not with our possible attitudes to various kinds of non-kin, but with our actual attitudes to our actual kin right now. My point is not that Callicott's theory cannot handle my imagined cases, but rather that its inability to handle the imagined cases shows that it actually does not accurately handle our present moral attitudes toward actual earthly living things. Even if none of the imagined cases are true, the experiments show that our current environmental ethics do not hinge on kinship relations as Callicott insists. Therefore, this reaction too seems unfruitful.

Two more ways of reacting are much more interesting. Rather than accommodate or dismiss the two thought experiments, one might choose instead to take them seriously, and to bite one of two bullets. In the first place, one might simply uphold Callicott's position in the face of the two thought experiments by simply limiting the position's scope to earthly kin alone. Callicott himself seems clearly prepared to do just this. In cases involving earthly, DNA-based beings, he upholds his Humean/Darwinian/Leopoldian position, but in cases involving extraterrestrials, he, perhaps surprisingly, is prepared to abandon this approach entirely and take up a reverence-for-life ethic in the spirit of Kenneth Goodpaster and Albert Schweitzer (Callicott, 1989, 262–68). This option, however, seems to concede too much. In my opinion, it amounts to an admission that Callicott's subjectivist framework is generally inadequate. As I have already explained, the issue is not about how to accommodate thus far only imagined situations but rather how to properly accommodate our current environmental situation and how to form an appropriate ethic for that situation, given that we react the way I believe we do to the two thought experiments. If we are prepared to adopt a reverence-for-life ethic in cases where our communitarian ethic stumbles, then a very natural and very good question to ask is why we are not adopting a reverence-for-life ethic exclusively. In my opinion, this reaction is an admission of at best clear inferiority and at worst theoretical defeat, and I can see it as nothing but an admission of the inadequacy of Callicott's original position.

There is, however, a second bullet to bite. One might, as a Callicott supporter, maintain Callicott's environmental perspective, accept the thought experiments as relevant and potentially dangerous, and simply deny that those experiments do in fact pose any threat by denying that we would in fact grant moral standing in any of the cases mentioned. One might simply refuse moral standing to any living thing that turned out to be non-kin, be it a DNA-based earthly organism that we until now have mistakenly considered our evolutionary kin, or be it the alien organism that clearly has no kinship tie with us. In my mind, this is the strongest, most consistent way to react to my argument against Callicott's position, and although I do not feel any pull toward it, it seems to me a reaction that I simply cannot give a clear argument against. For those who might find it compelling, however, I have a few points to make. First of all, the history of the environmental movement, though difficult to generalize about, seems to definitely support rejecting this reaction to the thought experiments. As Eugene Hargrove explains, the historical growth of the environmental movement was stimulated not by discoveries in evolutionary science but rather by innovations in geology and biological classification that predated broad acceptance of Darwinian principles. Clearly human beings, at least historically, have been prepared to extend value to beings without there first being some sort of identified kinship relation. Second, our current efforts to discover and even make contact with extraterrestrials clearly belies any claim that we would not extend moral standing to such beings simply because they have no evolutionary connection with us. Third, and most poignant, such an attitude would itself seem unjustifiably chauvinistic. Bluntly put, it would seem extremely bigoted to exclude living things from moral consideration purely on the basis of their having causally distinct or radically dissimilar origins. I realize that my point here cannot help but take the form of begging the question (as, I am sure, is the case with any claim made on this issue), but it seems to me that this is an extraordinarily easy and compelling question to beg. All I can ask is that we imagine, in all seriousness, morally dismissing a life form, not for who or what it is, but for *where or in what manner it originates*. In my mind, this would be simple and unacceptable bigotry, and so though I accept this response as open, I cannot see it as either potentially popular or at all palatable.

A Final Remark

Clearly, Callicott's communitarian subjectivism cannot successfully ground a general environmental ethic. In the end, the theory seems either biologically determined or else hopelessly relativistic, undeniably fallacious, and unjustifiably heavy in its emphasis on the kinship relation in the first place. This does not mean, however, that we should entirely dismiss it. As I have mentioned, even though Callicott's outlook cannot satisfactorily ground an environmental philosophy, it could still quite feasibly serve to amplify or compliment our environmental values. My only claim is that Callicott's approach, as it stands, is unsatisfactory. Whether we should pursue an alternative monistic meta-ethical grounding for our non-anthropocentric moral theory or instead abandon the search for a monistic grounding altogether remains an open question.

References

Callicott, J. 1989. *In Defense of the Land Ethic*. Albany: SUNY Press, 1989.

———1994. "Moral Monism in Environmental Ethics." *Journal of Philosophical Research* 19: 31–48.

———1984. "Non-anthropocentric Value Theory and Environmental Ethics." *American Philosophical Quarterly* 21: 48–57.

———1990. "The Case against Moral Pluralism." *Environmental Ethics* 12: 99–124.

———1992a. "Rolston on Intrinsic Value: A Deconstruction." *Environmental Ethics* 14: 129–43.

———1992b. "Can a Theory of Moral Sentiments Support a Genuinely Normative Environmental Ethic?" Inquiry 35: 183–98.

Fieser, J. 1993. "Callicott and the Metaphysical basis of Ecocentric Morality." *Environmental Ethics* 15: 171–84.

Fox, W. 1985. "A Postscript on Deep Ecology and Intrinsic Value." *The Trumpeter* 2/ 4 : 19–31.

———1990. *Toward a Transpersonal Ecology*. Boston: Shambala Publications.

Hume, D. 1957. *An Inquiry Concerning the Principles of Morals*. New York: Liberal Arts Press.

Partridge, E. 1996. "Ecological Morality and Nonmoral Sentiments." *Environmental Ethics* 18: 149–61.

Rolston, H. 1988. *Environmental Ethics: Duties to and Values in Nature*. Philadelphia: Temple University Press.

Regan, R. 1981. "The Nature and Possibility of an Environmental Ethic." *Environmental Ethics* 3: 42–54.

Stone, C. 1987. *Earth and Other Ethics: The Case for Moral Pluralism*. New York: Harper and Row.

Chapter 14

The Implications of the Use and Abuse of Darwinian Ideology for Ethics

Anoop K. Gupta, University of Ottawa

Darwinist theory could challenge a universal ethics by leading us to understand the good in terms of survival alone. I argue, however, that there are at least two ways of making the engagement between Darwinism and ethics fruitful (even in the domain of animal rights).

In section 1, I consider the biological politics present in the *The Descent of Man*, and in section 2, the cultural-ethical concerns; in section 3, I utilize M. Harris' appropriation of the Darwinian theory as a case study to illuminate the ethical problems I iterate in section 4. Finally, in section 5, I argue that if one does not want to limit the scope of Darwinist theory to the biological, a universal ethics can be possible if (1) the theory is conceived as a description and not justification for an ethics or (2) there is optimism about a consistency between ethics and our survivalist desires (in which case ethics is naturalized).

1. The Politics of the Theory

The first danger arises when the scope of Darwinist ideology is applied only within the realm of the clearly biological. One could say that the theory stipulates that the survival of certain traits are merely consequent to natural selection, and hence the environment, which leads to viewing those who do not survive as inferior (which indeed, in some sense they are). Darwin writes: "There is reason to believe that vaccination has preserved thousands, who from weak constitution would formerly succumbed to small-pox. Thus the weak members of civilized society propagate their kind ... this must be highly injurious to the race of mankind ..." (D 138–39). Again he says:

> Both sexes ought to refrain from marriage if they are in any marked degree inferior in body or mind.... When the principles of breeding and inheritance are better understood, we shall not hear ignorant members of our legislature rejecting with scorn a plan for ascertaining whether or not consanguineous marriages are injurious to man (D 641).

The political element is overt, as Darwin speaks of the legislature, and hence the law makers. The suggestion is both utilitarian and totalitarian in style. Society should, by force, regulate mating, such that it benefits the species as a whole.

Since Darwin's ultimate value, so it could be said, is survival of a species, any hindrance to that end cannot help but be looked upon with scorn. Moreover, he envisions nature, the process of natural selection in other words, as leading to progress.

We did not, so he says, fall from some golden age; rather, it is to that height we are ascending. Being caught up in this eighteenth-century preoccupation with progress not only exposes some of Darwin's value commitments, but what is devalued. For example, progress suggests moving from a "lowly" place to a highest plateau. In fact, we are told of man, "With his god-like intellect which has penetrated into the movements and constitution of the solar system—with all these exalted powers—Man still bears in his bodily frame the indelible stamp of his lowly origin" (D 643). Our superiority, says Darwin, was not God given, but something that has been the result of an arduous process-evolution.

Aboriginal cultures become the example, for Darwin, of the "lowly condition" from which we came. Before civilization, he tells us, there was more instinct and less reason (D 47). Indeed, one gets the feeling that Darwin is telling a certain story about these "wild men" (D 46). What is interesting is not that the natives represent a necessarily physically inferior state—although Darwin may have surmised as much. Rather, they have a different culture, which Darwin characterizes with the a host of adjectives: wild, barbarious, distrustful, merciless, and so on.

Natives have a different behaviour from our own. They have practices that are inferior. The proof, of course, is that our practices will supersede and survive, while theirs will linger only to die. Ethnocide is not so much a moral term as a description, one could say, for Darwin, of the natural selection of behaviours: Their culture will die, and our (European-modern) culture will persist. Darwin takes their behaviour to be "lower," which can only mean that it is not as efficacious in aiding in survival as ours.

Darwin's theory could be said to diverge into two theories. First, we have the theory of biological natural selection; second, we have the theory of cultural natural selection. Although both theories have in common that the explanation of the phenomenon in question is in terms of ability to survive, there are important differences. Biological natural selection is rooted in genetic traits that aid in the survival of a species, while cultural natural selection explains the persistence of socially learned behaviours that aid in the survival of the group—not necessarily an entire species—who exercise those very practices.

The theory of biological natural selection prompts Darwin to propose certain ethical practices that we may find morally repugnant (e.g., forced sterilization). The problem is that "good" is being defined in terms of what is beneficial for the survival of the species. Yet one could agree with the theory as an explanation of a given phenomenon—how it is that there are in fact different species—without being committed to any one ethic. Biological natural selection does not logically entail one adopt behaviours that aids in survival, if those practices are not necessary, i.e., rooted in one's genetic constitution. Thus, the biological aspect of the theory need not pose problems for a universal ethics.

Our worries begin when we consider expanding Darwinian ideology to account for behaviour. So, it is the expansion to behaviour that should occupy us here. The next question concerns what sorts of behaviour can Darwinist theory propose to account for?

2. What Counts as a Trait?

Some behaviour, it would seem, does fall very easily under Darwin's theory. A cry of an animal upon seeing danger to warn its mates, seems to be such a case. Other behaviours, however, seems suspect, as it may merely represent the idiosyncrasies of any one culture. For example, we often see things that we deem "beautiful." Darwin even naturalizes our aesthetic sense. We see X as beautiful, generally speaking, because of the structure of our brain.

The basic idea could be said to be twofold. First, aesthetic senses either attracts one—a mate, for example—or repels an enemy—as with the odour of some animals. Second, the idea of attraction or repulsion figures in a greater end: survival. For instance, those animals that can successfully attract a mate have a greater chance of carrying on their genes. Those animals that can avoid danger, as perceived though their senses, have a greater chance of survival also.

Darwin seems to suggest that behaviour is, to use Kropotikin's phrase, "a factor in evolution." Darwin, like Kropotikin, sees co-operation as aiding in survival (although this is little remarked upon). Darwin writes:

> He manifestly owes this immense superiority to his intellectual faculties, to his social habits, which lead him to aid and defend his fellows, and to his corporeal structure.... Through his powers of intellect, articulate language has been evolved; and on this his wonderful advancement has mainly depended (D 49).

Darwin not only views co-operation and man's social nature, in general, as a sign of his superiority within the creation, but credits these very modes of behaviour to man's advancement. Following Darwin's thesis one could say certain behaviours persist because they aid in survival.

In fact, Darwin does seem to expand what could count as a character trait beyond the overtly physical. So a trait need not just apply to "bigger teeth" and "faster legs," for example, but also behaviours. He writes:

> An advancement in the standard of morality will certainly give an immense advantage to one tribe over another ... a high degree of spirit, patriotism, fidelity, obedience, courage, and sympathy, were always ready to aid one another, and to sacrifice themselves for the common good, would be victorious over most other tribes; and this would be

> natural selection ... morality is one important element in their success (D 137).

Darwin uses "morality" to indicate a type of behaviour, especially of an other-regarding nature. Moreover, he considers this moral behaviour as a factor in the survival of the human species.

It is, no doubt, an immense expansion of the scope of Darwinist theory to include behaviour. But how exactly does natural selection play a role in the persistence of any one behaviour? It is not that some physical-genetic trait is being carried on from generation to generation. Rather, we are speaking of the persistence of certain practices, such as morality. So, for example, if tribe X discovered it could catch more fish after a rain storm, and this practice was carried on from generation to generation, one would be saying that such behaviour was the result of a behavioral natural selection that erased a former practice: i.e., fishing before a rainstorm, let us say. We have to be clear, however, to distinguish biological natural selection, from its behavioral counterpart. While the biologically grounded characteristics lead to necessary traits in any one generation, behaviour is far more open to change at any one time, at least in principle. If a birds behaviour of building a nest is grounded in genetics, this practice is more resistant to change than if it was a learned behaviour—then it could be taught otherwise.

Darwin's story could be portrayed thus: (1) natural selection allows for the persistence of a certain physical trait, sympathy (D 635), allowing for, (2) the social instinct, which in turn serves as the foundation for, (3) a moral sense. So, even though morals (a certain class of behaviours and beliefs) are learned, they are so only because of a biological inclination that predisposes one towards them.

To the extent that learned behaviour depends upon holding certain attitudes or beliefs, they too are acquired in a way that renders them arbitrary. For example, Darwin considers different attitudes regarding skin colour, women, and so on. The essential point is the same. There are, in different groups, various values and accompanying behaviours. The question is, do these values-cum-behaviours aid in survival? Darwin seems to think so: For example, he attributes the success of English colonists to their "daring and persistent energy" (D 147). For Darwin, a trait could be as broad as behaviour in general, understood in terms of, let us say, statistical trends in a group.

3. A Case Study: Harris's Darwinist Approach to Cultures

M. Harris claims that when we examine a culture we notice there are certain beliefs and practices. But, these can be explained. That is to say, Harris can explain why culture X does and thinks Y. The reason is because those beliefs and practices aid in survival (AM 129). There are economic reasons at the base. As he says, he seeks "causal explanations" for lifestyles (C viii). Although cultures are "wrapped" in myths and legends, they conceal the "naked truth," which requires removing "this oppressive burden" (C 5).

The reason for any one cultural practice, according to Harris, cannot be traced to the individual's consciousness (C 62). In fact, even the society as a whole need not be aware of the "real" reasons it maintains X, Y, and Z (DS 14). So, for example, one could think a certain society are cremating their dead as part of their religion, yet, Harris may uncover the "real reason" is the lack of land for burial. Harris wants to uncover the pragmatic-survivalist motivations for any one cultural-ideological practice. He considers his approach to be a type of cultural materialism (DS 2).

Harris' claim is basically this: "In culture, as in nature, systems that are the product of selective forces frequently fail to survive, not because they are defective or irrational, but because they encounter other systems that are better adapted and more powerful" (C 173). Certain lifestyles or patterns of behaviour arise or decline as the result of their ability to aid in survival of the group. Harris says he can explain, by considering an economic state of affairs, the interest in religion in the 1960s in America (AM 145); the behaviour of war as an ecologically adaptive lifestyle (C 67); and the practice of population controls (C 69), (both the views and practices concerning abortion, infanticide, and homosexuality, for example) (AM 89).

Harris tells us, where education and machinery is introduced, for instance, and there is no need of children to work the land, people have less children (DS 177). Again, a practice—that of having X number of children—is eliminated to aid in survival.

The point can be reiterated: the values and practices of any one society can by explained by uncovering their survivalist motivations; the persistence of certain values and behaviours, moreover, are the result of a behavioral natural selection. But what happens to ethics if we follow this Darwinist line of thinking?

4. Negative Consequences For Ethics Upon Adopting a Darwinist Ideology of Culture

Adopting a materialistic reductionist account of the "good," however, raises the problem of determinism. Even if cultural natural selection allowed for some freedom—i.e., dissent from one's group—it still raises a perhaps more dangerous concern, relativism.

Assuming that certain lifestyles persist as a result of a cultural natural selection (where this is the sole explanation), seems to offer a naturalistic justification for ethnocide. For instance, if all cultures were to be wiped out and replaced by American popular, consumer culture, this would not raise a moral issue because it would simply be the way of nature: one cultural practice would have replaced another, just as one species survives and another does not. In fact, there would be no such thing as ethics. Any set of so-called "ethical" beliefs and/or practices would merely reflect a certain strategy for survival. There is nothing that is right or wrong. Even warfare could be viewed as merely a strategy to survive, (in order to maintain population levels and so on)—as indeed it was by Harris.

The destruction of cultures comes to be viewed as a natural process. There would be no appeal to what ought to be the case beyond what is the case—because "ought" is co-extensive with what cultural practices are pragmatically efficacious, which in turn is defined by what behaviours are in use, i.e., those that persist. Transposing a juxtaposed formulation of the materialist notion that "those practices that aid in survival are deemed good" into a moral maxim such that "the good is that which aids in survival" is lethal for ethics. In a nutshell, if one equates morality with practices that persist, one loses the basis upon which to criticize behaviour that is in vogue but perhaps immoral. One loses the ability in fact to appeal to any standard of morality beyond the conventions of the day.

There does not seem that there is anything that Darwin could say if it so happened that what we normally think of as amorality aided in the survival of a group. In cases where the ethical is opposed to survival, Darwinist theory justifies, what we generally take to be amorality: What is "right" is what aids in the survival of the group. In fact, any set of cultural practices that survive would be "alright" (e.g., warfare, infanticide, sacred animals, voting, academics etc.) simply by virtue of having persisted.

On the worrisome front, some anthropologists, like Harris, I have suggested—picking up on Darwin's positivistic idea—that "lifestyle" (i.e., behaviour, cultural practices and so on) are prey to a type of natural selection rendering ethical universality null an void. Those practices that aid in the survival of a group persist, and those that do not are abandoned; there is not goodness beyond survival.

5. Solutions: Positive Consequences for Ethics

(a) The first strategy for handling the problem of ethical relativism is to limit the scope of the theory. The materialist-Darwinist approach goes too far if it is to claim that it offers the sole explanation for a cultural practice, because, for one reason, as we have seen, it renders ethics null and void. For example, the reason let us say, according to Harris, Hindus do not eat cows is because it is economically efficacious to exploit them in other ways (e.g., milk, physical power, etc.). Yet in order to maintain a universal ethics, one must admit not only that there is some free will, but that any one cultural practice's claim to rightness or wrongness transcends the simple criterion of having persisted.

One way to maintain a universal ethics would be to conceive of the explanations for cultural practices as the result of several factors without privileging any one. This would mean, phenomenon X is consequent to certain economic pressures, religious-ethical beliefs, tradition (which included the intervention of free agents) and so on, without privileging any one type of explanation. Having largely relegated Darwinist theory to account for only biological traits (in any complete way), we can criticize cultural practices because we are not limited to pointing out they persisted and therefore they have some moral standing on those grounds alone. Rightness and wrongness is not just a matter of survival of the group. According to this strategy, the justificatory criterion for what counts as good is not linked to survival (and may very well conflict with it). Crudely put, Darwinist theory just does not apply to behaviour (at least not in any way that threatens a universal ethics).

There are yet another way of handling the worry about naturalizing ethnocide and relativism; these strategies does not require delimiting the scope of the theory to the biological.

(b) According to the second strategy, survival would be neither a necessary or sufficient condition of what counts as ethical, but it would just be a happy coincidence that all such behaviour aided in staying alive. Darwinism could offer a naturalized description of a common sense morality. It would merely explain how we ended up with the ethics we have, but it would not justify that code of behaviour.

(c) According to the third strategy, survival (of the group) would be a necessary condition in assessing if an action was good or bad. Survival would function as a clue to goodness, since the two things are co-dependent. We only have to accept the verdict that the extension of Darwin's thesis to behaviour, beliefs, lifestyles—and hence cultures—threatens ethics if one assumes that the ethical is opposed to pragmatic ends such as survival.

It could be that the good, the ethical, are in fact those types of behaviour that do aid in survival. If there was a coherence between the ethical and survival, Darwinist ideology could be naturalized without harm to a universal ethics. Darwinist theory could be the very justification of an ethics, in fact.

(d) The expansion of the theory to cover behaviour (as we saw in the case study), however, raises a problem for even the possibility of a universal ethics. Rightness could be rendered relative when equated with strategies that aid in the survival of the group because they can change. "Rightness" or "good" then become morally vacuous; the very definition of these terms becomes relative and devoid of universality. In a nutshell, what is good today (i.e., aids in survival at this time) may be bad tomorrow (i.e., not aid in survival in the future).

One strategy is to delimit the scope of the theory, accept that Darwinist type explanations for behaviours may be insightful, yet deny that they could be privileged as the sole explanations without the spectre of justifying the ethic of "might is right" for the collective actions of groups. A Darwinian explanation can fully cover the transmission of biological traits without offense to a universal ethics; but it cannot do so for the migration of cultural characteristics because it seems to render the standard of rightness relative.

One should only base an ethics on a survivalist criterion, I have argued, if (1) being worried about relativism, we adopt the following stance: Darwinist theory serves not as a justification for an ethics but a description of an ethical standard we already assume or (2) being optimistic about a consistency between ethical practices and our survivalist desires, we adopt the strategy to naturalize ethics. In the case of (1) Darwinist theory merely serves as a description of how we got the ethics we have; but survival does not figure as either a sufficient nor necessary condition for what counts as good. In the case of (2) where Darwinist theory justifies an ethic, survival becomes a necessary condition for judging X as good or bad.

If there is one thing learned in philosophy in the second half of the twentieth century, is that foundational epistemology does not work. It was, admittedly, an old lesson. Nonetheless, since ultimate justification for truth candidates (regardless of what domain of inquiry), is a non-starter, one has an impetus to utilize theories like Darwin's to justify things already believed in (just because they happen to work well with the daily business of living).

For instance, even the animal rights movement, as Peter Singer had envisioned it, rests on an argument about consistency. If we believe in human rights for such-and-such reasons, it would logically follow, Singer argued, that we should be committed to animal rights. He was correct. But what Singer's argument also shows is that even he had to start with some assumptions. If one denies that one should be concerned about the interests of sentient beings, or that there even exists a world, there is not much one can do. All the failures to offer final foundations for knowledge claims can be stored away in the same warehouse.

Epistemology is largely an attempt to rationalize what we already believe; however, because of its reflective nature epistemology can also exert influence upon our practices. Getting clear about what our values and assumptions are, and being consistent with what follows from them is an important task for philosophers. Systematizing our knowledge theoretically discloses that our values stand as the base of our epistemic outlook, which in turn are derived from our life experiences—that is where the spade turns. Yet when our values increasingly take into account the interests of the planet (perhaps the universe) as well as other animals, we should not hesitate to utilize theories like those of Darwin to tell a foundational story—after all, it may end up being true (that is, as true as anything gets).

Abbreviations

Darwin
D–*Descent of Man*

Harris
C–*Cows, Pigs, Wars, and Witches*
AM–*America Now*
DS–*Death, Sex, and Fertility*
M–*Minorities in the New World*

References

Darwin, C. 1909. *The Descent of Man and Selection in Relation to Sex*. Ohio: Werner.

Harris, M. and C. Wagley. 1958. *Minorities in the New World: Six Case Studies* NY: Columbian University Press.

———1974. *Cows, Pigs, Wars, and Witches: The Riddles of Culture*. NY: Random House.

———1977. *Cannibals and Kings: The Origins of Culture*. NY: Random House.

———1980. *Cultural Materialism: The Struggle for a Science of Culture*. NY: Vintage.

———1981. *America Now: The Anthropology of Changing Culture*. NY: Simon and Schuster.

Harris, M. and E. B. Ross. 1987. *Death, Sex and Fertility: Population Regulation in Pre-industrial and Developing Societies*. NY: Columbia University Press.

Singer, P. 1975. *Animal Liberation*. NY: NY Review of Books.

Chapter 15

God, Svend, Euthiphro and the Enlightenment Project

Calvin Hayes, Brock University

Characters: Socrates, Aquinas, Hume, Nietzsche and Svend Robinson.

This Dialogue is set in Purgatory and involves four Dead White European Males and a still living Canadian politician. Prior to this dialogue however Mr. Robinson was struck by lightning on the way to the Supreme Court of Canada:

Socrates: So Svend I understand that you met a premature and tragic end on the way to a courthouse. What were you intending to do?

Svend: I was planning on prosecuting the Canadian constitution for its excessive piety.

Socrates: Surely you mean Impiety, the trumped up charge they nailed me on?

Svend: No I mean Piety. It is written in the preamble of the Canadian charter of rights and freedoms that "Whereas Canada is founded upon principles that recognize the supremacy of God and the rule of law...."

Socrates: And you disagree with that?

Svend: Of course, I am a secular humanist who thinks that this marginalizes non-religious and anti-religious people as well as non-theistic religious people like Buddhists, Taoists, Sikhs and Confucians for example.

Socrates: Well you will probably want to meet two of my colleagues with whom I have frequently discussed these issues, although you may have to enlighten me on the Canadian Charter of Rights and Freedoms.

Svend: Actually you should be able to appreciate my point since the religious fundamentalists of your day prosecuted you for impiety. Ever since my under graduate days when I did a course in Greek philosophy I always admired the three major arguments in your dialogue "Euthyphro." Are these your two colleagues approaching now? O my God! one of them looks like a medieval monk and the other like an 19th century mad man!!

Both are lost in intense dialogue so do not notice Socrates and Svend until they bump into them.

Socrates: Svend, I would like you to meet Monsieur Aquinas and Herr Nietzsche.

Svend: I can't honestly say I am pleased and cannot understand the point I am not a philosopher but a pragmatic politician committed to protecting the marginalized, promoting social justice and a secular humanist perspective in Canadian society. Why would I want to meet a medieval monk and a modern fascist philosopher?

Aquinas: So you are the one who wants to eliminate God from the Canadian Constitution?

Nietzsche: I congratulate you for that. Here's to you Mr. Robinson. But all this rhetorical BS regarding equality, social justice and the marginalized just shows you have not emancipated your self from the worst aspects of the typical Christian slave ethic, an ethic invented by and for wimps, not for really macho men.

Socrates interrupts to explain both the ground rules and how Purgatory is now completely wired to the Net thank to Bill Gates. This is why all four characters are so well informed on developments since their lifetime.

Svend: Of course that capitalist pig Gates, I should have known. He even wants to extend his monopoly to the after life?

Aquinas: A TV evangelist apparently told him that, while he can't take his money with him he can send it on ahead.

Socrates asks Svend to explain what he referred to earlier concerning the three main arguments in The Euthyphro.

Svend: First you argued (or asked the question) "Is an act one of piety because it is willed by the gods or do they will it because it is pious?" Second, the gods continually contradict each other. The same is true of the One God of theism. Not only do Jews, Christians and Muslims disagree with each other but within each there are numerous disagreements. The third point may be in the *Republic*: (I don't remember) but it is the argument that conduct regarded as atrocious if done by humans is attributed to the gods. The same again is true of the Old Testament which commands genocide, promotes the subjection of women as well as cruel and unusual punishments.

Socrates asks the Saint to comment on this.

Aquinas: I will comment on the second one about the contradictory interpretations of theistic ethics. This leads to the major advantage of Roman Catholic Church *viz.* that it is the infallible interpreter of God's will.

Nietzsche: Well in the words of my favorite philosopher Zarathustra,

> No people could live without evaluating; but if it wishes to maintain itself it must not evaluate as its neighbour evaluates.
>
> Much that seemed good to one people seemed shame and disgrace to another: thus I found. I found much that was called evil in one place was in another decked with purple honours.
>
> Truly, men have given themselves all their good and evil. They did not take it, they did not find it, it did not descend to them as a voice from heaven.

Aquinas: But this of course is just what creates the great quandary of modern moral philosophy as one of my most distinguished followers, Alasdair MacIntyre argues regarding the Enlightenment project. Actually your great contemporary Dostoevsky realized this as he put it, "If God does not exist, then anything is permitted."

Nietzsche: Exactly, if God does not exist we can, we *must* create our own values uninhibited by the scruples of both traditional Christian slave morality and of its secular counter parts who have failed to see this, especially those arch typical philosophical wimps Kant and Mill. They are just so many sophistical attempts to recreate traditional ethics on pseudo-rational foundations.

Aquinas: Let me then mention two problems if you surrender the traditional Virtue approach to ethics: 1. You flounder on two areas much discussed in 20th century philosophy the meta-ethical problem of foundations and the more practical problem of motivation. I have been reading lately on my web site about the Prisoners' Dilemma and it reminds me so much of Plato's Gyges' Ring problem and various temptations to cheat.

Socrates intervenes here to comment and redirect the discussion.

Socrates: Let me apply my dialectical skills that so annoyed the Athenians to Herr Nietzsche's argument that I will label Argument Z There are four key premises: The first is factual, i.e., that people differ and have differed over moral judgments. The second, is that there are no objective values given either by God, or nature or whatever. You however appear to argue enthymematically i.e., you omit crucial logical and epistemological premises e.g., that there is a logical gap between is and ought or facts and values and that moral judgments are empirically and rationally inaccessible as well. I have labelled this Argument Z, out of honour for Zarathustra.

Nietzsche: Well I don't see how you can deny the factual premise given the immense differences between societal values both diachronically and synchronically. Just to stick to theistic religions, whereas the ancient Hebrews and modern Muslims accept polygamy, Christians and modern Jews believe marriage should be monotonous.

Aquinas: Yes and No. I will not for these purposes deny the claim but refer to C. S. Lewis' *The Abolition of Man*, which argues that a common set of principles under gird several of the world's major religions and cultures. But I will concede that difference over specific examples not general principles is widespread.

Nietzsche: This shows that what humans have done is project their own values on to the gods. This is the significance of my well-known "God is Dead" thesis.

Aquinas: That is quite a logical leap Herr Nietzsche.

Nietzsche: But the other premises, the logical and epistemological were filled in by my contemporary and compatriot, Max Weber.

Aquinas: The epistemological premise rests on a version of positivism or radical empiricism that has been thoroughly refuted in 20th century epistemology and philosophy of science.

Socrates: As for the so-called is-ought, fact value distinction, no one has shown that a *reductio ad absurdum* argument in ethics is not possible.

Aquinas: Again, as MacIntyre has argued, rejection of Virtue ethics has led to the modern equivalent of the Biblical tower of Babel i.e., modern moral philosophy. There are all these numerous, various isms: intuitionism, subjectivism, emotivism, presciptivism, utilitarianism, Cultural Relativism etc. As, once again MacIntyre argues so well, this leads to the problems of incommensurability of values both inter and intra-personal conflicts.

Nietzsche: I am tired of this philosophical goobledgook. Moral philosophy is for wimps. I am leaving to check out the new Zarathustra homepage- I understand it is filled with wonderful advice.

Socrates: Herr Nietzsche you are an excellent illustration of my thesis on how misology, the hatred of reason, leads to misanthropy. Any one who despises syllogism, dialectic and concern with accurate definitions is bound to ...

Svend rudely interrupts.

Svend: I am also tired of all this philosophical goobledgook, fascist propaganda by Hitler's favorite philospher and typical scholastic nit-picking. What do you argue about down here today? How many angels can dance on the head of super computer chip? I am leaving too.

Aquinas: You obviously never did a course on medieval history or philosophy. Although maybe those later fools like Occam and Duns Scotus argued about angels on the pin of a needle but in my day we sure didn't.

Nietzsche and Svend then depart to engage in a furious debate about equality, Superman, the will to power and the correct implications of the idea that man creates his own values.

Socrates: Well Monsieur Aquinas that leaves just the two of us as in Euthyphro. Do you care to continue the dialogue?

Aquinas: Well actually I was hoping to continue it with this fellow David Hume, whom I see approaching now. As you may know neither of us (myself and Hume) will escape from here unless and until we persuade the other of the truth of our position. We have on numerous occasions discussed the reasonableness of belief in God. Despite his being here Hume retains his notorious scepticism. He keeps saying that just because it has been hot here for over two centuries is no reason to believe that it will still be hot tomorrow. Further survival after death, as he continues to point out does NOT logically imply immortality. You should appreciate Hume since his scepticism is not dissimilar to your "I know that I do not know." However what I would prefer is to discuss a topic the two of us have never discussed i.e., the foundations of morality.

Hume arrives, meets Socates. for first time who says,

Socrates: Mr. A wishes to discuss the foundations of morality with you.

Hume: Well I think I would prefer that to useless speculations on metaphysics and epistemology. As you may recall, Mr. Aquinas, it was works such as yours on metaphysics and scholastic divinity that I wished to commit to the flames, albeit not their authors.

Socrates: I too preferred to bring philosophy down from the clouds and cease useless speculations on the nature of the universe, its ultimate furniture and underlying substances and causes. I thought we should be concerned with virtue, justice, piety, courage, love, beauty, pleasure and other such topics of more relevance to human life.

Aquinas: Let me begin by raising with you the same problems I confronted Nietzsche with and trust that your cool, calm voice of reason will respond unlike N's typical hysterical rhetoric.

I wish to distinguish between the problems of rational foundations and motivation, i.e., the is-ought and the ought-is problems: the former out of honour I will label the Humean problem the latter I will label the Machiavellian problem. It cannot be expressed better than in Machiavelli's own words:

> There is such a gap between how one lives and how one ought to live that anyone who abandons what is done for what ought to be done learns his ruin rather than his preservation ...

Notice that these will be difficult questions to answer, as Aristotle realized, without delving into metaphysics and theology. A theory of virtue supplemented by Christian revelation seems to me the only way out of our quandary.

Hume: Let me raise two similar problems for your position both of which grow out of Socrates' dialogue. First however let me state my main premise: Reason is and ought to be the slave of the passions. Unlike Mr. Nietzsche we do not invent but discover our values but unlike Socrates and yourself we do not discover them outside of ourselves either in the arbitrary will of the divinity or in some strange theory of natural law but in our moral sense. When it comes to motivation I don't think that theism has the huge advantage it claims—the thought of an after life is too remote. My basic point is that reason anyway cannot motivate. This is one of the problems I have with modern moral philosophy or in fact any moral philosophy in the tradition of Socrates and Kant as well. I don't understand why modern moral philosophy does not take seriously the ideas mooted by myself and developed by my good friend Adam Smith regarding the moral sense. The moral sense theory solves both of the two problems without either the metaphysical baggage of natural law, virtue theories and platonism or the even more grotesque theological baggage of traditional theism.

Socrates: Let me point out that the type of moral reasoning I represented has had some interesting developments not only since my heyday but that of Mr. Hume. What I attempted to do, i.e., reduce my opponents to contradictions, is a technique used both by a slightly junior contemporary of David's (Kant) and by the modern US philosopher, Alan Gewirth. Both employ what is now termed a *reductio ad absurdum* to show that if you deny their views this leads to contradiction. (just as Euclid proved there is no highest prime number).

Aquinas: My sainted follower MacIntyre has written powerful refutations of both these claims and in addition I don't see how their hyperrationalism can cope with the motivation problems. As more moderate rationalists in the Christian tradition, Descartes and Leibnitz have pointed out, self-interest and morality can only really coincide in a theistic perspective where there are no true Prisoners' Dilemma or Gyges' Ring situations. As Bishop Berkeley pointed out "God is always about in the quad to observe us."

Hume: My own critique of Kant, (of whom I don't remember hearing in my day), is that he totally fails to recognize the impotence of reason. These rationalist philosophers are merely trying to provide a philosophical Viagara but it won't work. Even if, (a big IF) Reason is able to justify, it cannot motivate. This fellow Gewirth keeps talking about the pain of contradiction if you reject his theory of rights but by god, if he were here, he would know how mild the pain of contradiction is!! Who is this coming our way now?

Socrates: It is our friend Svend. How was your dialogue with Nietzsche?

Svend: That guy is impossible! He is a crude combination of Hitler, Ayn Rand and that fascist biologist Richard Dawkins. He told me that the trouble with Canada is that it is the product of 3 losing traditions: The French, the Scottish and the United Empire Loyalists. This is why we are all such wimps. Now who is this person? He looks suspiciously like a typical 18th Century aristocratic snob. Am I going to meet all the politically incorrect DWEMs my first day here?

Aquinas: Don't be so rude Svend. Mr. Hume was the member of a marginalized group in his own day the Scottish, one of those three losing traditions Nietzsche mentioned.

Hume: In fact as I understand it your country was largely founded by my fellow Scots.

Svend: So that is what is wrong with it? if you were such a marginalized person why did you find it necessary to insult women and Afro-Americans in your day? You were an elitist snob and friend of that great capitalist apologist, Adam Smith. You may be hero to other secular humanists but your views are reactionary rot to me.

Hume: Must you have recourse to invective and declamation? You are starting to remind of that fool Rousseau.

Socrates: If I may interrupt and return the discussion to the path of reason and virtue I would be curious to have Svend comment on the interesting situation I understand exists in his country. Is it presently ruled, amazingly enough, by both a philosopher Queen and her philosopher husband?

Svend of course corrects this misunderstanding but does approve of the Governor General since she is both an Asian and a woman.

Socrates: I understand she is from Rosedale, Toronto. Are there quite a number of marginalized people living there?

Aquinas: I understand her husband wrote a book called *Voltaire's Bastards.*

Hume: Is that the same Voltaire who was my contemporary? And do you mean Voltaire the bastard? He was almost as big a fool as Rousseau and almost as much of a disaster since both of them lead the gullible French down the primrose path to a blood thirsty revolution

Socrates: I understand that book has something to do with the tyranny of Reason. I do not understand that. How can it be reason rather than unreason and misology that leads to tyranny?

Aquinas: It is giving up the truth of the Roman Catholic Church and Aristotelian virtue that leads to the tragedies of tyranny, despotism and disastrous revolutions. Surely this is what we have learned from 20th Century history.

Svend rudely interrupts:

Svend: This is reactionary claptrap. I'm leaving again and am going to write up a charter of rights and liberties for my fellow citizens here, and then present the petition with signatures to whoever is in charge.

Svend departs (to the left of course). Everyone else is laughing because Svend has failed to realize that Purgatory is a pure Hobbesian state of nature, with no one ultimately in charge.

Hume: OK now that this dam politician has gone for good let's get back to serious philosophical discussion. While I do not understand why anyone would associate the tyranny of Reason with Voltaire (who was a mere literary figure not a serious philosopher not much better than Rousseau), I do understand why Reason is seen as tyrannical when it tries to do too much. I understand that Kant, as much as anyone, realized that this was what I was saying and then tried to say something similar in that barbaric language of his. But he confined his points to epistemology and metaphysics. He should have also realized that they apply to the foundation of morality as well instead of all this tortuous stuff about the categorical imperative etc.

Socrates: At the risk of sounding immodest, contrary to my reputation for humility, I must point out that my original challenge in the Euthyphro has still not been met, nor have we finished with Argument Z.

Aquinas: OK let's focus on the other two premise, the logical and epistemological in the Z-argument. Let us examine the other two premises needed to fill the gap.

Hume: Happy to provide them i.e., the is-ought logical point and the positivist epistemic point i.e., knowledge is genuine if and only if it is logically provable or empirically verifiable. I understand Nietzsche tried to give credit for this to his compatriot Max Weber.

Socrates: But no one in the Hume-Weber tradition (such as Moore or Hare as well as numerous social scientists) even attempted to (let alone succeeded) in rebutting my logical point about the use of *reductio ad aburdum* as a way of overcoming the so-called is-ought gap.

Aquinas: And I want to repeat the point made earlier to Herr Nietzsche regarding the 20th century's devastating critique of positivist theses by Karl Popper especially. In addition there have been crude non sequiturs made by simplistic "logical" positivists such as Ayer. He concluded from the alleged unverifiability of morality that ethics was basically emotivist. But it is just as logical to conclude (as Hare did) that it is prescriptivist.

Hume: Well whatever it is, I need to reaffirm my point regarding the weakness of motivation argument as well as dubious ethics of God (or the gods) rewarding and/or punishing virtue and/or vice. I understand that even the present Pope has given up the dogma of hellfire.

Aquinas: I must reiterate my claims that both justice and motivation require the traditional Christian solution. Both a modern Hobbsean social contract and moral sense motivations are too weak.

Socrates: Since we are all starting to repeat ourselves and are running out of time perhaps I should bring the dialogue to a close. Besides it is time for the worst part of being in this place.

Aquinas: The daily torture?

Hume: No, sensitivity training!

All depart to weeping, wailing and gnashing of teeth.

Chapter 16

The Glory—Vainglory Interplay in the Two Ethics—the Two Spiritualities—the Two Sciences

David Goicoechea, Brock University

The Windhover
I caught this morning morning's minion, King-
dom of daylight's dauphin, dapple-down-drawn Falcon, in
His riding
Of the rolling level underneath him steady air, and striding
High there, how he rung upon the rein of a wimpling wing
In his ecstasy! Then off, off forth on swing,
As a skate's heel sweeps smooth on a bow-bend: the hurl and
Gliding
Rebuffed the big wind. My heart in hiding
Stirred for a bird,-the achieve of, the mastery of the thing!

Brute beauty and valour and act, oh, air, pride, plume, here
Buckle! And the fire that breaks from thee then, a billion
Times told lovelier, more dangerous, O my chevalier!

No wonder of it: sheer plod makes plough down sillion

> Shine, and blue-bleak embers, ah my dear,
> Fall, gall themselves, and gash gold-vermillion (Hopkins, 1967, 69).

We know of Kant's wonderful saying:

> Two things fill the mind with ever new
> and increasing admiration and awe,
> the oftener and more steadly we reflect
> on them: the starry heavens above me
> and the moral law within me (Kant, 1956, 166).

If glory is a manifestation of the unmanifest even in its unmanifestness is not this saying of the sage glorious in itself? Does not this living word continue to fill the mind with a new and more awesome vitality as it ponders itself within us over the years? Is it not the very interplay between the natural and the moral that gives it a tension and a mystery? Are there two laws here that hint of a lawgiver in himself behind the appearance of the laws? Is there a natural law and a moral law? Or, is the moral law only a natural law? Or, are there two moral laws—one which is natural and one which is counter-natural? And if the second has to do with the ever new in the sense of a radical newness can it even be a law? Is not this saying of Kant a glorious phenomenon which prompts us to ponder afresh the wonder of some mysterious noumenon?

If glory is the visibility of the invisible even in its invisibility is not this song of the poet a thing of glory itself? Do not the first eight lines of this fourteen line sonnet take the shape of a flying falcon in his kestral glide? Does not the song give as much joy from itself in its figure, form and content as it takes from the bird? Is there not already in the interplay of the title and the subtitle the tension and mystery of the visible and the invisible? Is the glory of Christ our Lord visible in the Windhover? Is the grain of wheat that falls to the ground and dies somehow visible in the buckling of the falcon when in the midst of his outstretched dappled glide he pumps his wings? Is the noumenon not right within the phenomenon in some near sacramental way for Hopkins in a way that it is not for Kant?

To further ponder these perplexities of glory let us go for a moment to Kierkegaard. Whereas Kant is brought to reverence by the twofold glory of the stars above and the moral law within Kierkegaard builds his philosophy around four stages of glory: the aesthetic which is like the basement of our house, the ethical which is like the first floor, the mystically religious which is like the second floor and the prophetic religious which lives on all floors of the house at once (Kierkegaard, 1980, 43). With Kierkegaard we can go: outward to aesthetic glory in the stars and nature, inward to the glory of the moral, upward in the glory of the mystical ascent and backward to everything in its incarnational existential glory. Let us first look inward and reflect upon the glory of the moral.

Two Ethics

What is it that fills us with admiration and awe as we reflect on the moral law? Every culture cultivates its formulation of morality. The history of Greek thinking is a story of the refinement of the law of justice. So is the story of the Hebrew Bible. The ancients and medievals developed varieties of natural law morality. The moderns worked out the utilitarian calculus and the categorical imperative. In our existential-postmodern times the exploration of morality goes on. Deleuze sees Spinoza as the modernizer of Stoic morality (Deleuze, 1993, 35–42). There are the matters of fact of all that happens to us, but we can emotionally interpret them so as to be in bondage or in bliss. There are three elemental emotions and getting them just right is the key to the happy life. They are joy, sorrow and desire. The positive network of feelings is derived from joy. The negative network is derived from sorrow. Desire moves both. We desire to continue in the empowerment of the positive. We should desire to discontinue the disempowerment of the negative. We can be either negative or affirmative in our feelings toward existence. Negativity disempowers us and affirmation empowers us. But our affirmations can be passive or active. To become active with the adequate ideas of reason and intuition is to become further empowered with courage, endurance and generosity. If our affirmation arises from only a passivity borne of imagination then even it can result in a self-centeredness that results in disempowerment, discouragement and fickleness. The moral law of Spinoza is the universal moral law of the golden rule. If I really love and empower myself then I will love and empower others for we are all parts or modes of an intersubjective whole.

Deleuze reads Nietzsche as continuing the Spinozistic vision. Our will to power in the *conatus* of its desire can go in the servile direction of resentment or the noble direction of *amor fati*. Resentment is an attitude of reaction or passivity and negativity. I suffer and feel impotent or disempowered to do anything about it. I can brood and interpret the world negatively. But if joyfully I focus on joy I can desire the same life of joy even with all of its sorrow over and over again.

Deleuze himself like so many of the postmodernists refines the morality of joy-sorrow-desire by revising the concept of desire. Desire from Socrates to Sartre was interpreted as a want or a need or a lack. But desire can be seen also as productive and creative and not merely as needy and lacking. Deleuze interprets all of our suffering from schizophrenia to alcoholism to being lonely or mortally wounded in terms of this interplay of the two kinds of desire. My embodied being is composed of many desiring machines that need-want-lack. They can torture me. But within me there is also the body without organs that can become more glorious even as the desiring machines and organs are frustrated and break down. If we understand our desires as actively and affirmatively productive then we can valorize our afflictions and see them as gloriously militant ways of even working against totalitarianism. If desire becomes productive we need not feel our depression only with depression; we might also feel it with joy. We might feel its repetition not only as mechanical but also as being pregnant with a new future. Its repetition might begin to reveal wondrous differences. Taking joy in and valorizing the differences can be the best strategy against totalitarianism which only makes the differences servile.

Levinas is especially instructive concerning our present day meditation on morality. In his 1961 book, *Totality and Infinity*, he described morality as responsibility from, to and for the other. I do develop as an ego through enjoyment. I am not primarily a thinking thing or a willing thing, but an enjoying thing. However, responsibility does not have to do primarily with my own self-realization. Responsibility and ethics begin when I am called by the suffering other. If the cry of the widow, orphan or alien is heard by me and I respond with a "here I am" then I am not in the realm of self-realization or even of enlightened egoism. To welcome the other is to curtail my freedom for the sake of the other. Levinas still sees this in terms of joy-sorrow-desire. My desire for infinity, as a metaphysical desire instead of a psychological need, is the horizon for my welcoming of the other. If I have developed through enjoyment into a mature ego then I will be able to respond to the sorrow of the other. In desire for the infinite which calls to me from the face of the other, I will be able to welcome and serve him or her as would the good Samaritan.

But Derrida pointed out to Levinas that there was still too much violence in his metaphysics. Welcoming the other out of affirmative and active desire is still self-seeking and even vainglorious. It gives the primacy to an autonomy that is not responsible to heteronomy. The ethics of the golden rule and of the good Samaritan is based on that kind of affirmation and activity which Deleuze clarified. But, that kind of desire can unwittingly be self-seeking and thus violent. In response to Derrida, Levinas developed the philosophy of *Otherwise Than Being* in which he moved from the morality of the good Samaritan to that of the Suffering Servant. When I am persecuted by the other and made his or her hostage, I can let my very suffering become redemptive for the persecutor. This is what Jesus did. When he was dying on the cross the Roman soldier beheld him and said: "Truly this man is the son of God." This according to Levinas has to do with the glory of the moral act. Being good for the good of the other especially my enemy who is persecuting me is glorious. It lets the Good become manifest even as it was for the Roman soldier. Now Levinas described morality not in terms of joy-sorrow-desire, but in terms of joy-sorrow-glory (Levinas, 1981, 144–52). When my sorrow is used for the joy even of my persecutor then the glory of the Good is witnessed to and prophetically others can be called by that Goodness.

This does fit in with the thought of Kant. In his book, "Religion Within the Limits of Reason Alone," Kant did a phenomenology of radical evil and showed how even when we are trying to do good we can still do evil. We need grace and something beyond the limits of reason if there is to be an affirmative religion that can bring good out of radical evil. By being totally passive as the hostage is passive the vainglory of self-seeking can be eliminated. When the hostage suffers evil gracefully, morality can be awesome. The unmanifest Good is made manifest for a moment even for the persecutor when the hostage passively suffers the negative as a prophetic witness for the good of the persecutor.

The good act especially when it is self-sacrificial has the power of a special glory. In the very moment of buckling when Christ our Lord dies like a grain of wheat there is already glory. You do not have to wait to see the new wheat in order to witness the glory. There was glory before the resurrection even in the glorious death. The buckling of the windhover is glorious in itself. But to further understand this, Kierkegaard's distinction between the two kinds of spirituality is helpful.

Two Spiritualities

Kierkegaard's distinction between two kinds of religion and thus two kinds of ethics can be understood if we consider the interplay of the two loves in his book, *The Works of Love.* Affection, friendship, eros may be glorious. Familial love is all important in its nurturing of the child and of each other. The security it gives can let friendship become a noble standing side by side in which we appreciate values together. It can let lovers stand face to face enraptured by each other in an enthusiasm that energizes them. But love for my family, my friends, my beloved if it becomes absolute will self-destruct. If I put my child, my friend or my beloved on the throne in my heart then I have a preferential love that is really a self love. Glorifying my beloved is really a self-glorification. It is an egoism for two. Self-glorification always proves vainglorious. So according to Kierkegaard there are collisions between the aesthetic and ethical dimensions of our love. These collisions can let the religious dimensions of love be revealed to us.

If I absolutely love the relative then I will fall into various forms of despair. I must dethrone my preferential loves so that I absolutely love the absolute or absolutely love God as love. That is, I must come to love God with my whole heart, mind and soul. But that is only religiousness A or mystical love. If I am infinitely resigned to the limits of any finite love then I can become enlightened and unified. But living only on the superb second floor is still despair according to Kierkegaard. Faith for him after absolutely loving the absolute is to come back and to relatively love the relative. Faith for Abraham was not only giving Isaac up, but also believing that he would get Isaac back.

So for Kierkegaard there are two kinds of spirituality and two kinds of glory. After giving up all for the absolute and loving the absolute absolutely we need to come back and love our neighbour as ourself. Glory for Kierkegaard begins as it does for Levinas in the suffering servant's surrender which lets the Good be revealed. It begins for Kierkegaard with the gift of the incarnation that was there even before the buckling of death. But then once we have been freed from the trap of vainglory all our loves should become glorious. All things sweet-sour, adazzle-dim can become glorious.

Spirituality for Kierkegaard and Hopkins is similar. It has to do with what Kierkegaard calls the dethroning and Hopkins the buckling. That is the mystical process of purgation or catharsis which allows for illumination and unification. The young Hopkins was a nature poet like Keats. But then he went through his long, nine-year, poetic abstinence. He gave up writing poetry so that he could live the poetry of "*Adoro te devote*" of "I devoutly adore you." He sought to absolutely love the absolute. But then when he was a Jesuit his superior asked him to write a poem to celebrate the lives of five Franciscan nuns who drowned in shipwreck. Now his poetry had a new dimension and he was very different from Keats. With his heart on the love that is divine there in the second floor of his house he could re-relate to the first floor and the basement. From his new perspective of absolutely loving the absolute he could now relatively love the relative. A result is this poem, "The Windhover," which is about the buckling with its new glory. After the dethroning and buckling there can be a repetition of affection-friendship-eros that lets each in its newly ordered way display a glory that is no longer in vain. Once he loved the God that is love he had a standard so as to avoid the love that is not God. Once he no longer secretly loved himself absolutely so as to seek self-glory all things could be loved in their glory. Once he no longer put himself on the pedestal by putting his lover on the pedestal he could be beyond vanity. Then when true love came on to the pedestal as love of the Good each singular being could be loved as good and glorious.

The Two Sciences

There is a similar difference of spiritual context for ancient and modern science. The ethics-spirituality-science connection was there from the beginning of philosophy with the Presocratics. Anaximander already thought in terms of order-principle-necessity-justice. Cosmos was cosmetic and not chaotic. Thus Aristotle could understand science as based on the principle of causality. Something can not come from nothing. Whatever is has always been at least in the potentiality of its matter and form. In simplest terms, as Plotinus would show, movement within the universe takes place according to an emanation of what is potential to what is actual. There will never be more in the oak than there is in the acorn.

But in the Middle Ages, with Scotus and Ockham, this changed. God had always been thought of as conforming to order and justice. God had to act in a certain way because it was perfect and he was perfect. However, by thinking more deeply about creation as different from emanation, Ockham saw God as omnipotent and outside any form of necessity (Boehner, 1958, 308). God does not have to do something because it is just. Something is just because God wills it to be just. This thinking brought about the transition from the closed universe of emanation to the open universe of creation. Before, necessity was the great assumption making the science of ordered things possible. Now, freedom and newness become another assumption making modern science possible.

Hume first clearly worked this out by showing the limitations of causality and the reality of belief and custom. Science in our time, built on the model of modern physics, is based on uniformity and does not claim certainty or necessity. Its method is Humean and not Aristotelian. Hume accounted for the inductive thinking that was implied by the new worldview of Scotus and Ockham. The Franciscan influence was especially strong in the British Isles on religion-poetry-science-morality.

This second science fits in with the second ethics and the second religion insofar as each springs from a concept of creativity. Levinas and Derrida have as their chief philosophical point to make this clear. Consider Levinas. Creativity for him must be qualitatively different from emanation. According to emanation, the oak is contained in the acorn in seed-like form. When the acorn's potentiality is actualized there is the oak (Derrida 1984, 174). But the passivity of creativity must be more passive than that of matter or of potentiality (Derrida, 1991, 233). If something comes simply out of my own potentiality it cannot be creative. But if it is called from me by the other then it can be new and unpredictable. Creativity must include the concept of a radically new future and that implies a radical alterity. In the asymmetrical act of the hostage suffering for the persecutor there is a passivity that can let there be creativity. The persecutor as other calls forth an act from the hostage that the hostage could never perform by himself. This is the mystery of prophetic ethics in which I am called to suffer for the mighty and serve the lowly.

It is this prophetic, asymmetrical ethics of the suffering servant that Kierkegaard calls religiousness B. It comes back from the second floor and lets the symmetrical ethics of the Golden Rule and the good Samaritan operate without despair. Religiousness B has the creative dimension of the suffering servant which religiousness A lacked. The second kind of ethics and the second kind of religion are two perspectives of the same reality.

The second kind of science is connected with their radical creativity. Hume and Kierkegaard are very similar in seeing the limits of objective or causal reasoning within a universe that has as much possibility or creativity as necessity or emanation. They could each treat mathematical deduction as Kierkegaard treated the proofs for God's existence. Kierkegaard says that in letting them go there is a creative leap. Once you believe in belief with Hume then you can believe in the realm of unpredictable possibilities such as the incarnation. Then you will let go of arguments based on necessity. They cannot absolutely reveal the new absolute, the God-man, but they can still relatively reveal the relative in the realm of hypothesis. Once you believe in the realm of the expanding universe with Scotus-Hume-Kierkegaard-Levinas you can still value uniformities within contingency. In fact, becoming things can reveal the hidden, creating God. Buckling things can reveal the buckling divinity once the buckling divinity reveals the glory of buckling.

From Vainglory to Glory

And so, if we reflect upon the moral law within with Kant, as did Kierkegaard and Levinas, we see that it is glorious. In the creative vocation it bequeaths us it is even more than a law. The moral call in the asymmetry of the suffering servant makes the unmanifest Good manifest right through the paradox of the happy fault. Perhaps a falling star can be the most awe inspiring of all. After all, as Hopkins sang, they are "flake doves sent floating forth at a farmyard scare." We live in a fragile universe of Heraclitean fire where everything buckles. The problem of evil and innocent suffering is often seen as an objection against God and as the strongest reason for atheism. But that only applies against the God of necessity and not the buckling God-man of contingency. But once you believe in the buckling God-man and then the buckling windhover and then the falling and galling of the blue bleak embers, then Ah, my dear, you can see the glory of the happy fault. It is the scare of the fault line that is the mysterium tremendum. And when humans are graced so as to grace others when even their own star is falling then, truly, the Good can be manifest. The falling star that is flaked off like a spark from flint can be a flake dove. When the hostage like Simone Weil does not desire glory, but lets the Good be her standard, then her very buckling can let the flake dove "over our bent world brood with warm breast and with, ah, bright wings" (Hopkins, 1967). Nietzsche laid down the challenge to our postmodern age when we can no longer live within the limits of reason alone.

Once upon a time, in some out of the way corner of that universe, which is dispersed into numberless twinkling solar systems, there was a star upon which clever beasts invented knowing. That was the most arrogant and meandacious minute of "world history," but nevertheless it was only a minute. After nature had drawn a few breaths, the star cooled and congealed, and the clever beasts had to die (Neitzsche, 1979, 79).

It is the glory of science to let us see these numberless twinkling solar systems and to let us see that our star will fizzle and fall. It is the glory of morality to let us see that in the world of the happy fault our loss of glory can be our loss of vanity. It is the glory of spirituality to let us believe that our falling star can be a flake dove. Once we trust that cosmic buckling, which trust can come when the good witness gracefully to the good, then with Hopkins our souls will sing the glory of the ten thousand things. For "Christ plays in ten thousand places, lovely in limbs and lovely in eyes, not his, giving glory to the Father through the features of men's faces." The more we gracefully buckle the more we will sing with Hopkins:

> I kiss my hand
> To the stars, lovely-asunder
> Starlight, wafting him out of it; and
> Glow, glory in thunder;
> Kiss my hand to the dappled-with-damson west:
> Since, tho' he is under the world's splendour and wonder,
> His mystery must be instressed, stressed;
> For I greet him the days I meet him, and bless when I understand (Hopkins 1967).

With Ecclesiastes, we might behold even the stars and feel "vanity of vanities all is vanity." But then with Second Isaiah we might see the moral wonder of innocent suffering redeeming evil. It is our challenge to cultivate that wonder of the Good that it might be under the culture of science and the culture of spirituality—letting them manifest together the unmanifest even in its unmanifestness.

References

Boehner, P. 1958. *Collected Articles on Ockham*. New York: The Franciscan Institute.

Deleuze, G. 1993. *Difference and Repetition*. Trans. Paul Patton. New York: Columbia University Press.

Derrida, J. 1984. *Glas*. Trans. J. Leavey Jr. and R. Richard. Lincoln: University of Nebraska Press.

———1991. "Che cos' e la Poesia?" In *A Derrida Reader: Between the Blinds*. Ed. Peggy Kamuf. New York: Columbia University Press.

Goicoechea, D. and M. Zlomislic. 1997. *The Resurrection in Derrida's Glorious "Glas."* St. Catharines: Thought House Publishing Group.

Hopkins, G.M. 1967. *The Poems of Gerard Manley Hopkins*. Ed. W. H. Gardner and N. H. MacKenzie. London: Oxford University Press, 1967.

Kant, I. 1956. *Critique of Practical Reason*. Trans. Lewis White Beck. New York: The Bobbs-Merrill Company.

Kierkegaard, S. 1980. *The Sickness Unto Death*. Trans. Howard and Edna Hong. Princeton: Princeton University Press.

———1995. *The Works of Love*. Ed. and trans. Howard and Edna Hong. Princeton: Princeton University Press.

Levinas, E. 1979. *Totality and Infinity: An Essay on Exteriority*. Trans. Alphonso Lingis. The Hague, Martinus Nijhoff.

———1981. *Otherwise than Being or Beyond Essence*. Trans. Alphonso Lingis. The Hague, Martinus Nijhoff.

Neitzsche, F. 1979. *Philosophy and Truth: Selections from Nietzsche's Notebooks of the Early 1870s*. Ed. and trans. Daniel Breazeale. Atlantic Highlands: Humanities Press.

Chapter 17

The Extended Mind: Understanding Language and Thought in Terms of Complexity and Chaos Theory

Robert K. Logan, University of Toronto

Introduction

Ideas from dynamic systems theory will be used to address a number of fascinating questions related to the origin of language and thought and the dynamic relationship that exists between them. This paper builds from the results of *The Fifth Language* (Logan, 1995) in which the nature and evolution of language is examined using ideas from chaos theory, informatics, linguistics, and McLuhan's approach to media studies. To this mix I will now add ideas and evidence from cognitive science, evolutionary psychology, and archeology of early hominids to develop a dynamic systems model of the brain, the mind, language, and cognition which, I believe, sheds light on the mind body problem. I also hope to develop insights into how chaotics and complexity theory helps us to understand two features of evolution namely vestiges and punctuated evolution or the so called "missing links." Finally, I use this dynamic systems model of the mind to understand the connections between technology, commerce, artistic expression, narrative and science to generate what I have playfully called the Grand Unification Theory of Human Thought.

The Fifth Language and the Evolution of Language

In *The Fifth Language* I have propose that a language is both a system of communication and an information processing tool. I proceed by suggesting that speech, writing, math, science and computing form an evolutionary chain of languages. I consider each of these activities as a separate language because each allows us to think differently, create new ideas and develop new forms of expression. Another consideration is that each of these five forms of language possesses its own unique semantics and syntax and hence, qualifies as a language in itself according to criteria set by classical linguistics (Logan, 1995).

But why an evolutionary chain? In the book I postulate that a new language evolves in response to some form of information overload or chaos that arises when the informatic capacity of the previous set of languages is unable to cope with some new level of complexity. The new language represents a bifurcation to a new level of order that was not possible with the previous set of languages. The new language vestigially retains features of the previous languages from which it springs but adds new elements specifically to deal with the information overload and chaos to which it is responding.

Mathematics and writing arose at exactly the same point in time around 3000 BC. They were part of a notational system to record commercial transactions to deal with the information overload brought about by the rapid increase in the administration and trade of agricultural commodities in the city states of Sumer. Writing and mathematics, the second and third languages after speech, immediately gave rise to the world's first formal schools to teach the new skills associated with these two languages. Schools required teachers who conducted scholarship and specialized study which in turn generated a new information overload.

The fourth language, science, emerged approximately 1000 years later. It represents an organized form of knowledge which brought a new level of order to the information overload created by writing and math. Computing, the fifth language, developed out of the need to cope with the information overload created by science just fifty years ago. The model of the evolution of language developed in *The Fifth Language* gives rise to two questions:

- How did the first language, speech, from which the other languages evolved arise in the first place?
- Will the process continue with the evolution of a sixth language and, if yes, what will that language be?

I first turn to the origin of speech and discuss the possibility of a sixth language later in the paper.

Bifurcations and The Origin of Speech

Starting from the basic premise of *The Fifth Language* we should anticipate that the origin of speech was a response to the chaos associated with some form of information overload. Hominid thought processes as inherited from our earliest ancestors was purely perceptual.

In the course of their evolution hominids acquired new skills, such as tool making, which increased the complexity of their lives. At first this complexity could be handled through additional percepts, but at some point the complexity became too great. The hominid mind could no longer cope with the richness of life solely on the basis of its perceptual sensorium. Perception alone did not provide sufficient abstraction to deal with the increased complexity of life. In the information overload and chaos that ensued a new abstract level of order emerged in the form of concepts and conceptual thinking. This idea can be expressed in a slightly different way making use of Ashby notion of requisite variety.

When the complexity of hominid life became so great that perception alone could not provide enough requisite variety to model the challenges of day to day life a new level of order emerged based on concepts.

What, we may ask, was the mechanism that allowed this transition to take place? Given that language is both a form of communication and an information processing system I have come to the conclusion that the emergence of speech represented the actual transition from percept based thought to concept based thought. The words of spoken language, as we shall see, are the actual medium or mechanism by which concepts are expressed or represented. We must be very careful at this juncture to make sure that we do not formulate the relationship of language and conceptual thought as a linear, causal one. Language did not give rise to concepts nor did concepts give rise to language, rather human speech and conceptualization emerged at exactly the same point in time. Language and conceptual thought are dynamically linked parts of a dynamic cognitive system, the extended mind which provides an environment for their mutual development.

We are still left with the question, however: what were the developments in hominid evolution that gave rise to the complexity, the information overload, and, hence, the chaos that led to the transition or the bifurcation from perception to conception and the emergence of speech? It was not a single development or breakthrough which triggered this event but rather the cumulative effect of a number of developments among which I would include the use of tools, the control of fire, the larger social settings that the use of fire engendered, the co-ordinated large scale hunting that resulted from the larger living groups and the emergence of non-verbal mimetic communication.

Percepts no longer had the richness with which to represent and model hominid experience once these elements of stone age hunting and gathering society were in place. It was in this climate that speech emerged and the transition or bifurcation from perceptual thinking to conceptual thinking occurred. The initial concepts were, in fact, the very first words of spoken language which served as metaphors and strange attractors uniting many perceptual experiences in terms of a single word and, hence, a single concept. All of one's experiences and perceptions of water were captured with a single word, i.e., "water," which also represented a simple concept. Spoken language and abstract conceptual thinking emerged together at exactly the same point of time as a bifurcation from the concrete percept based thinking of pre-lingual hominids. This transition was the defining moment for the emergence of the fully human species Homo sapiens sapiens.

Chaos and Darwinian Evolution

The way in which a new level of order suddenly arises in chaos theory provides a possible explanation for the missing links in Darwinian evolution. The so called missing evolutionary links do not exist.

Evolution is not the infinitely slow, continuous process Darwin imagined. Evolution is punctuated by rapid discontinuous transitions, which in my opinion, result from the sudden emergence of a strange attractor as a biological system passes through a patch of turbulence and settles into a new form of stability. The creation of a new species through bifurcation also provides a simple explanation of the retention of vestigial features of the earlier forms in the evolutionary line.

Ontology recapitulates phylogeny as the system moves through all of the state of stability through which it once passed. Languages, like species, also retain vestigial features of earlier forms of linguistic expression.

Three Proto-Languages: Tool Making, Social Intelligence and Mimesis

The transition from percept based thinking to concept based thinking represented a major discontinuity in human thought. The development of the skills required for speech and conceptualization stretched over a long period of time encompassing millions of years and a number of stages in hominid evolution including Australopithecus, Homo habilis, Homo erectus, archaic Homo sapiens and ending finally with Homo sapiens sapiens or humans. Merlin Donald has identified this transition as the period of Mimetic Culture:

> I propose a category of archaic but distinctly human culture that mediated the transition from ape to human. This mediating, or intervening, layer of hominid culture is called mimetic (Donald, 1991).

It is during this period that hominids developed the set of survival skills associated with tool making and use, the control of fire, the building of shelters, co-operative social structures, large scale coordinated hunting, and mimetic communication. These major breakthroughs in hominid cognition represent three distinct percept based proto-languages:

1. manual praxic articulation (or tool making and use),
2. social/emotional intelligence or the language of social interaction,
3. pre-verbal communication which entails the use of hand signals, mime, gesture and prosodic vocalization.

The reason I suggest that these breakthroughs in hominid cognitive development can be understood as three non-verbal percept based proto-languages is that they each represented a primitive form of communication and information processing, the two basic functions that define a language. These proto-languages were the cognitive laboratory in which the skills of generativity, representation and communication developed and, hence, were the source of the cognitive framework for speech.

The information processing elements of the three proto-languages is quite obvious but their communication dimensions may not be as apparent. Merlin Donald who identifies these three proto-languages as mimetic skills has described the way in which they function as a system of communication and skills transmission:

> Mimetic skills or mimesis rests on the ability to produce conscious self-initiated representational acts that are intentional but not linguistic.... Although mimesis may not have originated as a means of communication, and might have originated in a different use of reproductive memory, such as toolmaking, mimetic acts by their nature are usually public and inherently possess the potential to communicate. Mimetic skill results in the sharing of knowledge, without every member of a group having to reinvent that knowledge (Donald, 1991, 168, 172–73).

Mimetic skills created social skills because of their capacity for communication. They led to forms of social control and co-ordination, coordinated hunting, knowledge sharing and the creation of a social culture and identity. The mimetic games of children modeling adult behavior provide a living contemporary example of these skills in action. Much of the training of children especially in hunting and gathering societies is mimetic as is much of contemporary apprenticeship training. The period of child rearing increased as hominids evolved and developed more skills which needed to be learned by the young.

Further justification for regarding the mimetic skill set identified by Donald as proto-languages is that each one possesses its own unique primitive form of semantics and syntax. The semantics of manual praxis or tool making and tool use are the various components that go into making of the tool, i.e., the materials and the procedures needed to create the tool. The tools themselves become semantical elements in the proto-language of tool use. The syntax of tool making and use is the order in which the procedures for making and using the tools are carried out. If the correct order is not adhered to then the task to be completed will not be accomplished.

We have seen that the emergence of a new language is always associated with some form of information overload. We can identify the chaos or information overload that led to the emergence of the proto-language of tool making and use. It was the flood of extra information that the earliest hominids had to deal with in order to survive as bipeds in the savanna where the protection of swinging in the trees was no longer available. Tools were created to deal with the new challenges of living at ground level where there were far more dangers than in the tree tops.

Tool making led to the control of fire through the construction of baskets that allowed fire to be transferred from one site to another. The control of fire led to new and more complex social structures as nuclear families banded together to take advantage of the many features that fire offered such as warmth, protection from marauding beasts and cooking, which increased the number of plants that could be made palatable. In the larger social structures that resulted from this development a new form of information overload developed because of the increased complexities of social interactions. In this environemnt a new language of social interactions emerged with its semantics of social transactions which included greetings, grooming, mating, food sharing, and other forms of co-operation appropriate for clan living. The syntax of the social intelligence was the proper ordering of these transactions in such a way as to promote social harmony and avoid interpersonal conflict. Being able to create social harmony and cooperation and avoid conflict had significant survival value and hence contributed to the evolution of hominid culture.

The overload of interacting with many people and carrying out more sophisticated activities led to the need for better communications to better co-ordinate social transactions and co-operative activities such as large scale hunting. From the chaos of this complexity emerged the proto language of mimetic communications. The semantics of mimetic communication, the third proto-language, consisted of the following elements: the variety of tones of non-verbal vocalization, facial gestures, hand signals and miming actions. The syntax of this form of communication is the ordering and co-ordination of these elements.

Combining a gesture and a vocal tone would have a different meaning than the same tone followed by the gesture after some delay or the gesture followed by the tone. As the syntactical complexity of mimetic communication grew and became more sophisticated it set the stage for the next development in hominid communication, namely, verbal language in the form of speech which vestigially incorporated the elements of mimetic communication. It is not the literal meaning of words alone which convey the message of spoken language but the tone of the words, the way they are inflected, as well as the facial gestures and hand motions which accompany the spoken words.

Imbedded in the syntax of each of the three proto-languages there is a generative grammar which allows:

1. different ways of articulating tools and manual praxis to carry out a variety of new tasks as new challenges arise;
2. the creation of new forms of co-ordination and social cohesion to meet the infinite variety of challenges life presents including the navigation through different forms of social conflict, the variety of which is endless;
3. the expression of a large number and shades of feelings through mimetic communication.

Starting with the manufacture and use of tools hominids began to develop the capability of generativity essential for verbal language. Employing the correct syntax of the proto-languages, i.e., doing things in the proper order, evolved into the generative grammar of verbal language. This model supports Chomsky's theory that human's possess a generative grammar that makes the rapid acquisition of speech by young children possible. It also provides an alternative explanation to his notion that the generative grammar is somehow magically hard wired into the human brain.

The work of Merlin Donald reveals that the generative grammar for spoken language evolved slowly over hundreds of thousands of years through tool making, social interactions and mimetic communications, i.e., through the use of the three percept based proto-languages that I have just identified.

From Proto-Language to Prototype: The Origins of Technology, Commerce and the Fine Arts

The three percept based, pre-verbal proto-languages represent more than just the transition to spoken language and abstract conceptual thought. Transformed by spoken language and the abstract thought that followed in its wake, they also served as the prototypes of three fundamental activities of modern humans, namely technology which emerged from toolmaking, commerce which emerged from social intelligence and the fine arts which emerged from mimetic communications. "There is a vestigial mimetic culture embedded within our modern culture and a mimetic mind embedded within the overall architecture of the modern human mind" (Donald, 1991, 162).

Manual Praxis: From Tool Making to High Tech

The generative tool-making skills that early hominids developed before the advent of speech is very much a part of the repertoire of modern humans as is evidenced by the activity of today's craftsmen who work almost entirely with their hands and have little or no need of spoken language. Generative manual praxis laid the foundation for the creation of human technology. With the advent of the verbal languages of speech, writing, math, science and computing, however, technology has evolved into progressively more sophisticated forms of high tech which are hybrids combining percept based manual praxis with concepts derived from the verbal languages. Vestiges of pure manual praxis remain in certain forms of traditional technology such as the ox cart used in rural India whose design emerged over a long period of time from percept based trial and error. A scientific analysis of these carts revealed that they had achieved an optimum design long before the principles of analytic science based engineering had ever been developed. These examples illustrate the importance and power of percept based reasoning and thinking which is a vestigial cognitive structure derived millions of years ago and still an essential part of the modern human mind.

Commerce as a Form Social and Emotional Intelligence

Another example of a percept based, vestigial cognitive structure which is still very much part of human intelligence is social or emotional intelligence. The social intelligence that early hominids developed found one of its first applications in large scale co-ordinated hunting and eventually found its way into other forms of human commerce.

Social/emotional intelligence is the basic building block of all forms of commerce. What is commerce afterall? It is nothing more than the activities that a group engages in co-operatively to acquire the necessities of life and which works to the advantage of the group as a whole ensuring its survival. Commercial transactions are entered into voluntarily by all the players involved because it benefits each one of them. Any other transaction in which only one party benefits is not commerce but some form of theft, plunder, enslavement or exploitation.

My definition of commerce does not necessarily involve money and should not be confused with economics. Economics is a form of commerce which evolved as a hybrid system with the introduction of the highly analytic concept of money. Commerce does not depend of money but is a system of co-operation for the gathering, production and distribution of goods and services essential to survival. Commerce entails trade whose roots can be traced back to the earliest forms of social organization when the task specialization first emerged. The co-operation of individuals who perform specialized tasks for the good of the community laid the foundations of trade and commerce. This form of trade and commerce did not, however, entail a notion of a market which requires the concept of value to operate. Before speech and conceptualization there was no way of computing the value of the goods and services that were exchanged. No one counted or kept score. Those societies where individuals were generous had a better chance of survival than those whose members were selfish.

Before the advent of speech the commerce of hominids was a purely percept based activity based on hunting and gathering. With the arrival of speech and conceptual thinking and the passage of many thousands of years, hunting and gathering was transformed in to a more sedentary form of commerce based on animal husbandry and/or agriculture. The emergence of the industrial form of commerce can be traced to three developments that took place in Europe towards the end of the Middle Ages, namely the evolution of agriculture into the manor system in which agricultural products were transformed in a systematic way to commodities, the rise of a market system for the distribution of these agricultural products and commodities, and the transformation of technology into a systematic form of engineering through the rise of the science of mechanics. The industrial system combined new forms of social intelligence with the abstract conceptual skills of engineering, science and mathematics.

The Information Age economy—another hybrid system—arose from the development of the computing which gave rise to new forms of social intelligence. We are on the threshold of a still newer form of commerce known as the knowledge economy which will be quite different than the Information Age economy. The Knowledge Era will require much more co-operation and sharing than was the case in the Industrial Era or the Information Age—both of which were based on the hoarding of proprietary knowledge.

The Fine Arts and Fine Motor Skills

The roots of the fine arts can be traced to percept based, mimetic communication whose basic elements were prosody (the tones of vocalization), facial gesture, hand signals and mime. The very first art forms were all non-verbal and grew out of mimetic communication, the third proto-language. They include music, painting, sculpture and dance—all of which were part of ritual. The first forms of painting were body and face painting and the first forms of sculpture were masks and costumes which can be seen as attempts to enhance and intensify facial gesture and mime. With the advent of spoken language new hybrid forms of the arts emerged which combined mimetic communication with words to produce modern (post-verbal) art forms such as poetry which include both words and prosody, songs which combine words and music and theater which combines words with mime and dance.

Spoken language gave rise to a number of concept based cultural forms such as story telling or narrative, writing, mathematics, science and computing. Speech also transformed a number of earlier forms of percept based activities to generate new hybrid forms of human culture including science based technology; agricultural, industrial and computer based forms of commerce and the fine arts. Our model for human cognition combines the three percept based proto-languages of manual praxis, social intelligence and mimetic communication with concept and language based skills associated with speech, writing, math, science and computing. The Grand Unification Theory that emerges from this approach provides a common link for activities that are often treated as quite independent of each other, namely, commerce, technology, the fine arts and science.

Origin and Evolution of the Extended Mind

By combining ideas on the nature and function of language, the concept of bifurcation from chaos theory and Merlin Donald's notions of evolutionary psychology insights into the role that language plays in human thought have emerged. Armed with this understanding I would like to tackle the age old question of the relationship of the human mind to the brain. For some psychologists this is a non-problem as they believe that the brain and the mind are synonymous, and simply two different words to describe the same phenomena—one derived from biology, the other from philosophy. For others there is a difference. Some define the mind as the seat of consciousness, thought, feeling and will. Those processes of which we are not conscious, such as the regulation of our vital organs, the reception of sense data, reflex actions and motor control, on the other hand, are not activities of our mind but functions of our brain.

I believe that there is no objective way to resolve these two different points of view but that a useful distinction can be made between the mind and the brain based on our dynamic systems model of language as the bifurcation from concrete percept based thought to abstract concept based thought. I have, therefore, postulated that the mind came into being with the advent of verbal language and hence conceptual thought. Verbal language extended the effectiveness of the human brain and created the mind. Language is a tool and all tools, according to McLuhan, are extensions of the body that allow us to use our bodies more efficiently.

I believe that language is a tool which extended the brain and made it more effective, thus creating the mind. The human mind is the verbal extension of the brain, a bifurcation of the brain which vestigially retains the perceptual features of the brain while at the same time making abstract concept based thought possible. It also represents the final bifurcation of hominids from the archaic form of Homo sapiens into the full fledged human species Homo sapiens sapiens. Humans are, therefore, the only species to ever have experienced mind.

This is not to deny that our ancestors, the earlier forms of hominids, experienced thought and consciousness. Their thought patterns, however, were purely percept based and their brains functioned as percept processing engines operating without the benefit of the abstract concepts which only words can create and language can process.

In summary, the emergence of language represents three simultaneous bifurcations:

1. the bifurcation from percept to concept
2. the bifurcation from brain to mind
3. the bifurcation from archaic Homo sapiens to full fledged human beings, Homo sapiens sapiens.

This hypothesis or model provides a possible explanation of the fate of Neanderthals who had a slightly larger brain than Homo sapiens sapiens but who, it seems, did not use spoken language and were less intelligent than humans. Neanderthals who survived for over one hundred thousand years were dominated by their human rivals and disappeared in Europe after only 10,000 years of cohabitation. Obviously the mind, which combines the features of both the percept engine which is the brain and the concept generator of verbal language, is a more powerful instrument of reasoning than the brain alone. Once language emerged the size of the brain alone was no longer the sole determining factor in intelligence as had been the case of the evolution of the hominid brain.

As the brain of hominids increased in size and complexity certain biological limits were reached. The head of an infant could only become so big and pass through the hips of a woman if humans were also to retain their capacity for mobility, an important factor for survival. One evolutionary strategy for packing more reasoning power into the small space of the head was the development of convolutions of the brain; another the gender differentiation of the male and female anatomy and the specialization of gender tasks. The females had broader hips for bearing large-headed babies and tended to spend more time attending to the tasks associated with the hearth while the males remained narrow hipped and roamed about as the hunters and defenders of the family from marauders. The gender specialization of task, a vestigial holdover dating back to Homo erectus, has survived into our own times. Happily it is slowly disappearing thanks to the feminist revolution and will hopefully fully disappear in the new knowledge based economy presently emerging with the new digital media.

After all the physical mechanisms for increasing human intelligence had been exhausted nature conspired through chaos theory to increase hominid intelligence with a software rather than a hardware stratagem. The software was verbal language from which emerged the human mind and conceptualization. Words encode basic concepts and hence allow for the more efficient processing of information and knowledge.

Conceptualization allowed for the creation of more words and new metaphors to achieve still higher levels of conceptualization and language sophistication. Concepts and words formed a dynamic systems bootstrap creating the conditions for their mutual and dynamic development. A possible metaphor for the role language plays in enhancing brain function is the disk doubler or zip drive in a micro computer (the artificial brain) which permits a more compact storage and processing of data and information.

Towards A Grand Unification Theory of Human Thought and Activities

We have proposed a Grand Unification Theory to explain the full gamut of human activities including technology, commerce, the fine arts, narrative, math, science and computing. The mind in our model is basically a system in which the vestigially retained percept system of thinking interacts dynamically with the abstract analytic forms of reasoning associated with the verbal languages. We therefore need to understand these two different cognitive styles and they way they interact with each other. The problem is that most studies seem to focus on one or the other rather than examining the two together. Hopefully the metaphor of language that we have used to link these two forms of thought will provide some insights into their dynamics.

As an extension of this approach we also need to examine the relationship between technology, cognition and evolution, and address the question of whether a new technology or language creates new cognitive structures and, hence, an evolution of the mind. Tool making generated a major shift in thinking that laid the foundation for spoken language and a number of other developments, hence, it should come as no surprise that new technologies and languages create new cognitive structures. With the emergence of a number of new digital media such as the Internet, virtual reality and expert systems we have a perfect laboratory to study this question. This is an area worthy of the joint efforts of cognitive psychologists, linguists and dynamic systems theorists.

I would like to propose that we can build a Grand Unification Theory of human thought and activities based on a dynamic systems model of the human mind, its percept based proto-languages and its concept based verbal languages. The evolutionary model of the development of the brain and the emergence of the human mind suggests that technology, commerce, fine arts, literature, mathematics and science form a dynamic system that needs to be studied holistically by making use of the ideas and tools of a number of disciplines integrated by a dynamics systems approach.

Digital Reality: The Sixth Language and Beyond

In this paper I have extended the ideas of *The Fifth Language* backward in time to understand the origin of speech and the human mind. Now I would like to run the clock forward and examine what new languages might be emerging with the new computer based digital media. Because of the title I chose for my book I am frequently asked what the sixth language will be. I have therefore given a lot of thought to this question in the past two years and believe that the Internet and the World Wide Web represent the sixth language in the evolutionary chain of verbal languages that I have already identified. The Net is transforming learning and commerce and accelerating the evolution or bifurcation of the Information Age into the Knowledge Era. The Net has its own unique semantics of Web sites, Web pages, Internets, Intranets and Extranets and it has its own unique syntax which is hypertext and hyperlinks. Every medium has its message and the message of the Internet and the World Wide Web is five fold. They are:

1. two way communication;
2. ease of access of information;
3. continuous learning;
4. alignment and integration; and
5. community.

These five features are driving the emergence of the Knowledge Era which in turn is reinforcing and accelerating the use of this medium.

Going even further out on a limb, I suspect that there are two other languages taking shape within the framework of the new digital media and that virtual reality (VR) and expert systems likely represent the seventh and eighth languages respectively in this chain of verbal languages. The evolution of these new languages, their trajectories and their impacts from a psychological, developmental and educational perspective are worthy of study and will be a source of new dramatic new developments in the months and years to come.

References

Donald, M. 1991. *Origins of the Modern Mind: Three Stages in the Evolution of Culture and Cognition*. Cambridge, MA: Harvard University Press.

McLuhan, M. 1964. *Understanding Media*. New York: McGraw Hill Signet Edition.

Logan, R. K. 1986. *The Fifth Language*. Toronto: Stoddart Publishing.

———2000. *The Sixth Language*. Toronto: Stoddart Publishing.

Chapter 18

The Call of Science: Theological Reflections on the Ethics of Vocation

Edmund Bertschinger, MIT

Introduction

During the twentieth century, the standard greeting of introduction changed from "How do you do?" to "Hi, how are you, and what do you do for a living?" Work has come increasingly to dominate our lives not only from economic need but also from a spiritual and moral perspective. If we are what we do, ought we not then to ask ourselves, *how* do we do? Do we *do*, that is, do we pursue our work, with love? If so, love for whom, or what? What are the ethics of vocation? How do we choose what we do?

As a teacher, I am frequently asked for advice by students who wish to know what it is like to pursue a career in science, what the job prospects are, and whether the student is capable of success. Usually I advise students to follow their hearts more than their minds. "Do what you love." From love flows enthusiasm, passion, drive, and perseverance, all qualities that contribute to success in a demanding vocation. Of course one also needs particular talents, but love usually turns elsewhere if the talents are insufficient. If love exceeds talent, the result is no less satisfactory: an amateur, who does something purely out of love.

Rarely do ethical questions of vocation come up between my students and myself. However, they arose in my own student days, and they have returned in mid-life as I contemplate more broadly my own calling in life. As we will see, love—the foundation of Christian ethics—plays a significant role in the ethics of vocation.

The word vocation comes for the Latin *vocare*, "to call." Its usage originates in the biblical calling of God to Abraham, Isaac, and Jacob, and to the New Testament calling of disciples by Christ. Originally a term restricted to a strictly religious station in life, vocation has become secularized to mean occupation. The subject of vocation has a strong place in theology. However, its consideration in secular philosophy and ethics appears to be more limited. In my own brief study of ethics, I have not seen the question of vocation raised outside of the context of Christian normative ethics. While my essay here is grounded in the Protestant worldview, I suspect that the ethics of vocation is of broader philosophical and practical interest. It may also cast light on the dialogue between religion and science.

In his Gifford lectures on Natural Theology published in 1934, William Temple wrote,

> ... [W]e have seen sufficient ground for the conviction common to all great religious traditions, that the whole universe, the whole process of the world, is grounded in the Will of creative Deity, so that this divine Will is at once the source of world-order, and also the determinant for every finite mind of its special place within that order and of the appropriate contribution of each such mind to the life of the whole. If this be true, *the solution of the outstanding problems of Ethics is to be sought in terms neither of Utilitarianism however ideal, nor of Intuitionism, but of Vocation* (Temple, 1934, 406–7, italics in the original).

Temple did not mean that a theory of ethics must be founded on vocation. Instead, he was concerned with the ethical practice. In his view, "the chief practical problem of ethics is solved not by volition but by conversion, so the chief theoretical problems are solved not by reference to a Categorical Imperative but by reference to Vocation" (Temple, 1934, 407).

This is exaggeration; a society in which conversion replaces volition would be either utopian or totalitarian. However, Temple emphasizes the link between ethics and vocation, and this will be the central theme of my essay.

A second theme is the dialectic between love for God and love for others as the foundation for Christian ethics. In the Gospel of Matthew, Jesus reduces the Ten Commandments to two: "You shall love the Lord your God with all your heart, and with all your soul, and with all your mind. This is the greatest and first commandment. And a second is like it: You shall love your neighbor as yourself. On these two commandments hang all the law and the prophets" (Matt 22:37–40).

In this essay, I will first review the history of ethical theory relating to vocation in the context of Christianity. I will then focus on the ethics of vocation in Puritan thought and the role of theology and ethics in fostering the development of Enlightenment science. I will conclude with some personal reflections on the relationship between science, ethics, and religion.

Ethics and Vocation Through the Reformation

In the ethics of Socrates and Plato, the improvement of the soul by contemplation of virtue was the ultimate goal toward which all men should strive. These ideas, and their implications for vocation, were incorporated into Christian thought by Augustine, who devotes much space in *The City of God* to a discussion of Greek philosophy. In the Augustinian synthesis of Christ and Plato, the classical triad of virtues—truth, beauty, and goodness—become part of the Christian ethic.

In his book *Fact, Value, and God*, Arthur F. Holmes writes that, for Augustine, "God is truth, as well as beauty and good. The love of truth, beauty, and goodness, then, all draw the soul toward God." The classical triad of virtues becomes an expression of God and of love. "Love for God … is the inclusive, unifying, virtue that brings life into proper balance and harmony. The other virtues are functions of love" (Holmes, 1995, 53).

Here we see the emphasis on the first commandment, love for God. In Augustinian thought, love for God subsumes all other virtues. In his *Basic Christian Ethics*, Paul Ramsey emphasizes Augustine's views with a quotation from *On the Trinity*:

> Neither let that further question disturb us, how much of love we ought to spend upon our brother, and how much upon God: incomparably more upon God than upon ourselves, but upon our brother as much as upon ourselves; and we love ourselves so much the more, the more we love God (Ramsey, 1950, 119–20).

Augustine's view of love provides a strong vocational ethic for clergy, teachers, and, perhaps, scientists. In *The City of God,* he writes,

> But as this divine Master inculcates two precepts—the love of God and the love of our neighbor—and as in these precepts a man finds three things he has to love—God, himself, and his neighbor—and that he who loves God loves himself thereby, it follows that he must endeavor to get his neighbor to love God, since he is ordered to love his neighbor as himself (Augustine, 1950, Book XIX, ch. XIV).

Plato's student and successor Aristotle expanded the contemplation of virtue into a systematic contemplation of God, Nature, and humanity. His writings formed the basis of Western science until the Enlightenment some two thousand years later. They had a profound impact on theology and ethics. Incorporated into Christianity by Thomas Aquinas, Aristotle's hierarchy of being formed the medieval hierarchy of stations in relation to God. Contemplation of God became the highest occupation.

The Reformation shifted the emphasis from God-love to Other-love. In place of the classical triad of truth, beauty, and goodness, Protestants placed self-sacrificing love, agape, at the crux of moral virtues. Ramsey writes, "*Whose* good? Is the main, perhaps the only, concern of Christian ethics ..." (Ramsey, 1950, 114). With a shift in the focus of one's love comes a shift in vocational ethics.

Ramsey squarely faces the relative standing of the two commandments of love (for God, for others) in a section entitled, "Is love for God part of the meaning of Christian love?" He writes,

> Standing as they are, these two formulations of the love commandment threaten to divide Christian loyalty if ever there is a difference, let alone contrast, between love for God and love for neighbor. If Christian love itself is divided into two sorts of love or love for two different objects, disunity in obligation results, and frequently Christians have spoken of religious duties due to God different from ethical values

> owed to man. Christian ethics thus imitates Don Quixote dashing off at once in at least two directions (Ramsey, 1950, 116–17).

Protestant theology resolves this question in favor of love for others. Christ's sacrifice on the cross was the focus of Luther's theology. Luther broke with the Catholic Church in his doctrine of justification by grace through faith. Because of Christ's love for others, the Protestant is no longer required to pursue good works in order to achieve salvation. However, good works follow naturally from gratitude for Christ's redemption. Moreover, the Christian has the moral obligation (and Christ's Great Commission) to seek the salvation of others, and to love his neighbor through works of good.

According to Luther, the church was no longer needed to mediate between the sinner and God for salvation, with profound consequences for vocation as well as theology. In the Catholic Church of Luther's time, "calling" or vocation referred to the ascetic life of monks, nuns, and priests, who withdrew from the world in order to gain justification for themselves and those who remained working in the world without a holy calling. Luther squarely rejected this distinction. He resigned his own monastic orders and he taught that all vocations rank the same with God.

An online study guide for a freshman honors seminar at Augsburg College summarizes Luther's doctrine of vocation:

> If we are saved by grace through faith and not works, then the world becomes an entirely different place. It is no longer the realm where we try to placate a demanding God. Moreover, "vocations" are not limited to a special class of Christians who by the supposed holiness of their lives have placed themselves closer to their Creator. Instead the world is now the network of relationships where Christians become instruments or vessels of the love that God has bestowed upon them. Thus all Christians have callings or vocations whereby they live out their lives in the world (http://honors.org/Courses/101/FaithReason.html).

In Reformation thought, love for others becomes the purpose of vocation. The ethics of vocation is based on loving one's neighbor as oneself. The focus is on worldly needs, not contemplation of God. However, this does not eliminate the place of reason:

> Vocation properly locates the role of reason in the Christian faith. Reason cannot be used to comprehend a God who would die on a cross. As Paul says, this is foolishness to the world. However, once one has come to faith, reason must be used in service of neighbor and culture. The worlds of science, literature, arts and commerce are the proper realms of reason (http://honors.org/Courses/101/FaithReason.html).

In this discussion we see how vocation follows ethics. Returning to my question at the beginning, we *do* what we value. What we love, and how we love, are the foundation of the ethics of vocation.

Luther's doctrine of stations was expanded into a practical philosophy of vocation by John Calvin. As in the Protestant doctrine of salvation, the new thinking was based on the New Testament writings of St. Paul, who advised the Christians in Corinth, "Let each of you lead the life that the Lord has assigned, to which God called you" (1 Cor 7:17). In his *Institutes of the Christian Religion*, Calvin wrote,

> … The Lord commands every one of us, in all the actions of life to regard his vocation.… He has appointed to all their particular duties in different spheres of life.… Every individual's line of life … is, as it were, a post assigned him by the Lord, that he may not wander about in uncertainty all his days (Ramsey, 1950, 154).

This passage illustrates two essential features of Calvinism. First, God has predetermined everyone's position in life; it is up to each individual to determine God's calling. This reflects the doctrine of predestination present in Calvinistic theology. Second, vocation is raised to the level of a command to industrious work for everyone, no matter how high or low the position. Indeed, because good works follow from Christ's redemption, Calvinists felt driven to perform good works to show themselves that they were predestined to be saved!

Puritanism and the Rise of Science

Imported into England, Calvinism became Puritanism, where it imbued what has come to be known as "the Puritan work ethic." Transported from England to North America, the Puritan way of life contributed to the rapid development of the New World. It also fostered the development of empirical science, and therefore to the Enlightenment era, according to a widely-accepted thesis advocated by historian of science Robert Merton. This leads our discussion from the ethics of vocation in general, to the ethics of a scientific vocation, or a calling in science.

In the book *Technology and Society in Seventeenth Century England*, derived from his doctoral dissertation, Robert Merton summarizes his thesis as follows:

> Puritan sentiments and beliefs prompting rational, tireless industry were such as to aid economic success. The same considerations apply equally to the close connection between Puritanism and science: the religious movement partially "adapted" itself to the growing prestige of science but it initially involved deep-seated sentiments which inspired its followers to a profound and consistent interest in the pursuit of science (Cohen, 1990, 113–14).

Prior to the Reformation, the manual labor implicit in empirical science and technology had lesser standing than philosophical contemplation. However, with the theology of Calvin and the ethos of Puritanism, thinkers could now reach into the world and thereby serve both aspects of Christian love: Glorification of God and service to mankind. Merton quotes the physicist and chemist Robert Boyle, one of the founders of the first important scientific organization, the Royal Society:

> … it will be no venture to suppose that at least in the Creating of the Sublunary World, and the more conspicuous Stars, two of God's principal ends were, the Manifestation of His own Glory, and the Good of Men (Cohen, 1990, 115).

Boyle goes on to articulate the view of natural theology, that science can provide a fuller account of God:

> … the knowledge of the Works of God proportions our Admiration of them, they participating and disclosing so much of the inexhausted Perfections of their Author, that the further we contemplate them, the more Footsteps and Impressions we discover to the Perfections of their Creator; and our utmost Science can but give us a juster veneration of his Omniscience (Cohen, 1990, 127).

Love of God has become love of Creation, and the first commandment becomes a directive to study Nature.

The Calvinistic incentive to demonstrate one's salvation through good works also played a role in the Puritan advancement of science, as Merton notes:

> Puritanism itself had imputed a threefold utility to science. Natural philosophy was instrumental first, in establishing practical proofs of the scientist's state of grace; second, in enlarging control of nature and third, in glorifying God. Science was enlisted in the service of individual, society, and deity.... [T]he "glorification of God" thus came to be, in Puritan hands, the "fructification of science" (Cohen, 1990, 116–17).
>
> The efforts of Sprat, Wilkins, Boyle or Ray to justify their interest in science do not represent simply opportunistic obsequiousness, but rather an earnest attempt to justify the ways of science to God. The Reformation had transferred the burden of individual salvation from the Church to the individual, and it is this "overwhelming and crushing sense of the responsibility for his own soul" which accounts in part for both the acute longing for religious justification and the intense pursuit of one's calling. If science were not demonstrably a "lawful" and desirable calling, it dare not claim the attention of those who felt themselves "ever in the Great Taskmaster's eye." It is to this intensity of feeling that such apologias were due (Cohen, 1990, 127).

The Puritan conception became so powerful, of course, that science and its derivative, technology, eventually displaced theology from her chair as Queen. However, once a religious justification was no longer necessary, science became for many a complete worldview, naturalism. Once fact became severed from value, the ethical basis for science as a vocation was threatened. Is there any longer a place for love in the ethos of science?

Reflection on the Ethics of Science

In posing the metaphorical question of love, ethics, and science, I can only provide a personal answer based on my own spiritual beliefs, which are rooted in Lutheranism. I believe there are several ways in which science has an obligation to maintain its ethical basis.

First, it is a fallacy to say that scientists should deal only with facts and not values. While I reject the extreme relativism of postmodern critiques, it is clear that societal and ethical values affect the course of science, in physics and astrophysics as well as in biology. (Nuclear energy and space exploration are two obvious examples.) As a Christian, I would go further to argue that scientists are obligated to consider more than purely materialist values. Luther wrote that each of us has several callings, not just the calling to our work. A scientist's calling can be to God just as much as a theologian's is. Scientists are often reticent to speak of their spiritual or religious beliefs, thinking that they have no station to do so. Theology makes no such claim.

Second, scientists are in a unique position to advance the appreciation of nature and thereby increase the value placed on it in the hearts and minds of our neighbors. Boyle's remarks quoted above remain, in my view, as valid as ever. Science can affect more than just the knowledge leg of the classical triad of truth, beauty, and goodness. Like art, it establishes connections between the virtues.

Perhaps the integration of science and religion as individual callings can be elaborated into a broader ethical integration of religion and science in dialogue. Immanuel Kant's tombstone is engraved with the words from his *Critique of Practical Reason*, "Two things fill the mind with ever new and increasing admiration and awe, the oftener and more steadily they are reflected on: the starry heavens above me and the moral law within me." Although Kant rejected the classical arguments for the proof of God, he advanced an ethical argument based on moral and natural law. Natural law is written in the heavens and in our hearts. Following Kant, by using our hearts as well as our minds, perhaps we can discern our callings to God and mankind.

References

Augsburg College, "A Reader's Guide to the Commission's Dialogue on Faith and Reason." (Honors 101 freshman seminar, online at http://honors.org/Courses/101/FaithReason.html).

Augustine, St. 1950. *City of God*. New York: Modern Library.

Cohen, B. ed. 1990. *Puritanism and the Rise of Modern Science: The Merton Thesis*. New Jersey: Rutgers University Press.

Holmes, A. 1997. *Fact, Value, and God*. Grand Rapids: Eerdmans.

Ramsey, P. 1950. *Basic Christian Ethics*. New York: Scribner.

Temple, W. 1934. *Nature, Man and God*. London: MacMillan.